Crime and Justice in American Society

Edited and with an Introduction by

Jack D. Douglas

THE BOBBS-MERRILL COMPANY, INC.

Indianapolis   New York

Contents

Preface

The American system of criminal justice faces a grave crisis. It does not prevent crime. It shapes crime. It does not change criminals into noncriminals. It makes them more criminal. It does not administer justice. It negotiates bargains.

Equal adjudication in terms of a morality and beliefs shared alike by the victims, the judges, and the perpetrators of crime is the basis of justice. In our system there is no equality and the administered morality is not shared by the judges and the accused.

Deterrence is the practical justification for the entire system. The system does not deter.

Those who have most loudly proclaimed the crisis are its administrators. They have cried incessantly that crime is increasing at a terrifying rate. They have cried for longer sentences, harsher prison conditions, and more death penalties to end the distressing frequency with which the punished return for more punishment. They have cried for an end to the "excessive" legal rights of the accused and the "excessive" civil rights of the public in order that we might achieve greater "justice" in a "free society."

They deplore the supposed failures of the system—more crime, high recidivism, the presumed need to restrict civil rights —only to argue that the system must be made bigger and bigger by providing it with more and more money and power. Their cries, of course, are not intended to produce any searching analysis of what part they themselves might be playing in the failure of this system. But in view of the fact that their forces have grown enormously in size, wealth, and power over many decades, the argument that more of the same will produce less of the same is manifestly suspect. The truth is that more of the same for the system has led to more of the same in crime.

These are harsh indictments and many Americans are not yet ready to see their validity. Perhaps they are stated too baldly.

Certainly there are exceptions, and qualifications are always necessary. But I believe their general truth, however disturbing, is unassailable and easily established. What will not be easy to establish, however, is a just and workable alternative to our present inadequate system of criminal justice. Nonetheless, we will never find this just and workable alternative unless we begin the creative and painful search for it.

This volume is intended to be a beginning in that search. It is not the first step, for it will be apparent to the reader that many steps have already been taken. It could not possibly be the last, for our steps have yet to be set upon the sure path to success. But it is a beginning of the more systematic search that we hope will lead in time to a fundamental reconstruction of our understandings of crime and of our ways of giving each man his just due.

The search has been unrestrained by any considerations of political "practicality," for nothing could be more shortsighted, or impractical in the long run, than proposals based on the assumption that today's practicalities will be tomorrow's. In a world undergoing the most radical technological and social changes man has yet experienced, the one thing we can be sure of is that what is practical today will not be so tomorrow, that what was practical many decades ago is no longer practical. Our search and our attempts at reconstruction must be directed at the future, not at the past or the present. What happened in the past and what is happening now are clearly "impractical." We must search for ways that we hope will be more practical, even by the unknown standards of the future. We must worry about truth and justice now, and then create the practical means to achieve them. Anything less must surely be deemed unworthy by free men in a free society.

Introduction

Most Americans now see crime as one of our most important social problems. In fact, in recent years the fear of "crime in the streets" has spread so rapidly and become so pervasive that we have good reason to believe that millions of people have been seized by a sense of hysteria over crime. The mass media have reported a "rising tide" of criminality in most of our major cities and increasing numbers of people report they are afraid to go out into the city streets at night. Millions have bought guns to protect themselves from what they strongly believe to be a growing menace of violent attack in the streets and in their own homes.

For years this sense of hysteria has been fanned by the emotional outcries of impending doom coming from those with a vested interest in having crime rates rise—the police and other official agents of control. J. Edgar Hoover has become a veritable Cassandra of national doom, issuing ululations of agony and outrage on schedule every year as the latest F.B.I. figures show the inevitable increases. We have been told again and again that this inevitable rise in the rates of "dangerous crimes" is absolute "proof" of the rising "crime menace," and that the "decay of our national moral fiber" will lead to the "destruction of our society" if we don't take the "necessary steps"—that is, give the police more money and stop the spread of "civil rights."

For several decades Democratic and Republican administrations alike have resisted most of these emotional pressures. Perhaps they have done so as much out of a desire to duck the political issues involved as out of hope to avoid the budgetary difficulties that would attend efforts to really do anything about crime. Regardless of the reason, the overall result has been the maintenance of our American civil rights. Indeed, as the Supreme Court became more and more concerned with protecting individual rights in an age of massive organizations and expanding governmental powers, the period from the 1940's through the 1960's saw a steady and accelerating growth in the legal protections of our civil rights.

The growing hysteria over the crime problem, however, has recently threatened to reverse all this. The Johnson administration tried to manage the problem in what it saw as a rational manner; it appointed a presidential crime commission of well-known officials, famous academics, and prestigious laymen from many parts of our society and entrusted them with providing a general and specific review of the many aspects of crime, law enforcement, and justice in our society. The President's Commission on Law Enforcement and the Administration of Justice was also charged with making specific recommendations for improvements in our methods of dealing with the problems found. Beginning with the publication in 1967 of its general report, *The Challenge of Crime in a Free Society,* and continuing with the publication of its special task force reports, the crime commission produced the most massive report on crime, law enforcement, and justice in America that has ever been made.

But the commission's attempt to manage the problems related to crime and justice failed. The evidence and arguments of the report did not stem the hysteria over crime. Rather than the report overcoming the hysteria, within two years the hysteria had overcome the report. By 1970 the report had been shelved by the public and by most government officials.

The long siege of the ghetto riots of the 1960's was probably the turning point in national feelings about the problem of crime. The violence and the burnings had a profound effect on the attitudes and beliefs of a large part of the American public. Some saw the flames and the gunfire as symbols of outrage and appeals for help from one of America's poorest minorities. Yet the ensuing years have made it apparent that many more saw them as symbols of "lawlessness" and "criminality." They were the signal to begin arming and to pass increasingly repressive legislation. The subsequent rise of black militant organizations and of the white militant groups on college campuses, each calling for revolution in the mass media and each brandishing its fists, guns, and bombs, fed the fears of violence, anarchy, and crime.

The tide now began to run strongly against the protection of civil rights. A new administration, elected partly in answer to its call to arms against the "liberal courts" and all "forces of crime," proposed an unending series of repressive measures. No-knock laws, conspiracy and anti-riot laws with vague criteria, laws allowing detention without right to bail, and laws allowing enforced examinations, even of urine, without prior arrest were strongly urged on the nation as "necessary" to preserve us from the depredations of the criminals and the revolutionaries. The Nixon administration fought desperately to have judges on the Supreme Court who were thought to be reliable "strict constructionists" and who could, presumably, be counted on not to allow the further "insidious" spread of civil liberties. The police and federal agents of control carried out what many public figures saw as an illegal nationwide campaign against militant organizations, and a national commission charged the police of the nation's second largest city with rioting against antiwar demonstrators.

Not since the fear of anarchists half a century ago had the nation been seized with such a fear of lawlessness and revolution. And, while there was some relaxation in official action against such increasingly middle-class actions as abortion and marijuana use, agents of control had not been so systematically involved in the violation of civil rights since the infamous Palmer raids following the First World War.

Many of those who participated directly or indirectly in the research and writing of the President's crime commission report had great hope that their efforts would result in new approaches to understanding and dealing with crime, law enforcement, and justice in America. They realized that the ancient ideas about crime and deterrence, which lay behind our present institutions and practices, had been hopelessly outmoded by the vast changes that have swept our society and the world in the last hundred years. These were knowledgeable and rational men. They knew that much of our criminal and judicial practices had become a fanciful hodgepodge with little rhyme or reason to them, the result of makeshift attempts to cope with rapidly changing problems in terms of ancient ideas and with very limited funds. As members and staff of the commission said with great hope at the beginning of their report, they intended to propose revolutionary changes to meet the truly revolutionary changes that had taken place in the world (the italics are mine):

> The report makes more than 200 specific recommendations—concrete steps the Commission believes can lead to *a safer and more just society*. These recommendations call for a greatly increased effort on the part of the Federal Government, the States, the counties, the cities, civic organizations, religious institutions, business groups, and individual citizens. They call for *basic changes in the operations* of police, schools, prosecutors, employment agencies, defenders, social workers, prisons, housing authorities, and probation and parole officers.
>
> But the recommendations are more than just a list of new procedures, new tactics, and new techniques. They are a *call for a revolution in the way America thinks about crime.*[1]

From the standpoint of practicality, of its capacity to actually influence the directions to be taken in the short run, *The Challenge of Crime in a Free Society* was a failure. It was a failure for essentially three reasons, the first being that it was a highly liberal document urging generally liberal and vastly expensive measures on an increasingly conservative public—a public that was about to elect a far more conservative administration than the one that had appointed the commission. But it was a failure also in that it did not provide any radically creative understandings of crime and justice in our society and, worse, in that it did not offer alternatives to our present practices that would work. Rather than calling for a "revolution in the way America thinks about crime," the commission simply tried to provide an official aegis for the same tired, old liberal ideas about crime and justice—at vastly greater cost.

The liberal "corrective," rather than "revolutionary," nature

[1] President's Commission on Law Enforcement and Administration of Justice, *The Challenge of Crime in a Free Society* (Washington, D.C.: United States Government Printing Office, 1967), p. v.

of the report is seen most clearly in its basic commitment to the fundamentals of all current ideas and practices concerning crime, law enforcement, and justice. Most important, the report never seriously examines the possibility of changing any basic aspect of our present laws and legal institutions for contending with the problems of crime and justice.

This commitment to the status quo is obvious from the very beginning of the commission's report in its implicit acceptance of the official definition of "crime." Instead of asking itself what should be legally defined as "crimes" in our society today, the commission in its report takes it for granted that those activities should be crimes that are now legally defined as crimes. It is this acceptance of the ancient meanings of "crime" that led the commission to concentrate almost all its attention, both in its vast research and in its hundreds of pages of reports, on such activities as "drug abuse," "juvenile delinquency," and "organized crime."

While social scientists and criminologists have become more and more convinced that the "potential crimes" (or those crimes that could be charged against individuals if there were adequately enforceable laws and adequate funds to do the enforcing) of businessmen, professionals, and white-collar workers result in the loss of far more money by the public than all the crimes of lower-class thieves or vandals, they are discussed on only about three pages of the almost 300-page report (pp. 46–48). At the same time Ralph Nader and many other social critics were demanding that corporations be held responsible for deaths due to unsafe automobiles or polluted air and water, the report was neglecting to consider these forms of potential crimes in the modern world of technology and giant corporations.

Again, while millions of the young and their adult supporters were crying out that a thorough review and overhaul of the drug laws must be made, the report was failing to give any realistic consideration at all to such demands. At a time when literally hundreds of thousands of college students, and several million citizens in general, were liable to arrest and imprisonment for smoking marijuana, a "weed" that had never been shown to be dangerous when smoked in the amounts normally used, the crime commission report contented itself with proposing that legislative bodies "weigh carefully" the implications of such laws:

> At the heart of some of the predicaments in which the criminal law finds itself has been too ready acceptance of the notion that the way to deal with any kind of reprehensible conduct is to make it criminal. There has been widespread scholarly debate in recent years on the extent to which conduct that does not produce demonstrable harm to others, but is generally considered abhorrent or immoral, should be made criminal. Some argue that lowering the criminal bars against such behavior might be understood as a license to engage in it. Others maintain that the limited tool of the criminal law will work better against the most dangerous and threatening kinds of crime if it is confined to the kinds of crime it can deal with most effectively. Beyond recognizing that criminality and immorality are not identical, the Commission has not found itself in a position to resolve this issue. However, it does urge the public and legislatures, when code reform is being considered, to weigh carefully the kinds of behavior that should be defined as criminal.[2]

Only in the case of "drunkenness" did the commission propose "de-criminalizing" any presently illegal activities; and it seems to have proposed this largely to free the police from an unhappy task.

The commitment of crime commission members to official orthodoxies is further evident in their commitment to the use of ideas and information provided by the criminal-justice officials themselves. Thus, they present us with the paradox of trying to propose "revolutionary" reforms for a system of criminal justice that is to be understood and judged primarily in terms of the information provided by those who run the system and who benefit from its present operations. This is a situation comparable to trying a man for murder entirely on the basis of his own testimony about what happened.

This dedication to orthodox information about crime and justice is most apparent in the commission's treatment of the

[2]Ibid., pp. 126–127.

complex problem of organized crime. The special task force entrusted with understanding organized crime and proposing methods for dealing with it relied almost entirely on the information given it by the police involved in a deadly fight against organized crime. Moreover, the task force relied on this information in an almost totally uncritical fashion, so much so that it reproduced organizational charts that could well be the fantasy of some psychotic prisoner seeking public attention— and judicial consideration. The task force's picture of organized crime depicts it in the classic pose of the Mafia or the Cosa Nostra. The Mafia is described as some highly organized, powerful, immensely successful, national conspiracy. And this is done in spite of the almost total lack of hard evidence of any such giant organization and in spite of the internecine "mob wars" that intermittently pop up in the homelands of the Mafia. A critical analysis of the evidence presented by the F.B.I. to support its ideas about the omnipresent Mafia gives us ample reason to doubt that there is any such mammoth criminal organization with tentacles reaching across the nation and around the world. On the contrary, the evidence indicates that there are many small, would-be organizations—"syndicates" —that have great conflicts with each other and interrelationships more like those between hostile nations than those at the board meetings of G.M. Some of the evidence and reasoning supporting this conclusion go back at least to Daniel Bell's brilliant analyses of "The Myth of Crime Waves" and of organized crime in the 1940's and 1950's. But Murray Kempton has also recently presented an excellent argument showing how poor the Mafia in New Jersey, supposedly the homeland of the whole conspiracy, appears to be from the official F.B.I. transcript of telephone conversations between one "chieftain" and a lesser member of his "family":

It is clearly not an environment productive of millionaires. Any given DeCavalcante soldier can hardly sit in his presence without giving way to confessions of indigence:

Frank Cocchiaro told DeCavalcante that he has money problems, as he gives his wife $50 a week, pays $125 a month rent in N.J. and $115 rent per month for his wife . . .

In December, 1964, DeCavalcante and Frank Majuri, his under-boss, meet to arbitrate a protocol dispute between Joe Riggi and Joe Sferra, two *capiregime*. "Sam, I came to you yesterday," Riggi says, "because I felt that, as an *amico nos* and a *caporegima,* I'm not getting the respect I should from Joe Sferra." Sferra's *regime* was the Elizabeth Hod Carriers local; his affront was in not relieving Riggi's father from carrying brick and finding him a lighter assignment . . .

Still there are overtones in DeCavalcante's long courtship of the Gambino Family which raise doubts even about *its* majesty. His control over the Elizabeth hod carriers union was mainly useful to DeCavalcante for providing jobs for unemployed soldiers; and Carlo Gambino seems to have felt more gratitude at having its courtesies extended to his Family than comports with one's image of a great prince of unlimited resources.[3]

The glaring and fundamental inadequacies of the crime commission report were the initial stimulus for this book. The other contributors and I believed quite strongly that its misconceptions about crime and justice in our society, and the often misguided and uncreative proposals that flowed from such misconceptions, should not go unchallenged. Certainly none of us found ourselves in disagreement with the entire report. Parts of that gargantuan work are very good, especially some of the original research work done by the many social scientists involved: even this work, however, was seriously hampered by the severe time constraints placed on the project out of political considerations, such as beating the presidential election deadline. For example, had there not been such time contraints, the generally good analysis of court procedures might have been improved with proper attention given to issues raised here in the essay by Lindsey Churchill. No matter how good parts of the commission's work might be, we all nevertheless shared certain fundamental disagreements with it which we believed must be communicated to the public. We believed, further, that many of our viewpoints must be incorporated into our national

[3]Murray Kempton, "Crime Does Not Pay," *New York Review of Books* (September 11, 1969), p. 5.

policies if we are ever to solve the changing problems of crime and justice in American society.

It will be obvious to all readers that our impetus has carried us far beyond this initial stimulus. Our criticisms of the crime commission report appear at many important points in this book, but taken as a whole they make up only one of its many major themes. Our main focus has been on a creative and over-all reevaluation of ideas and proposals on crime, law enforcement, and justice in our society. We have gone into some specific issues in considerable detail, but only when this seemed necessary to clarify a general argument bearing on fundamental issues. We have been constrained by space and other considerations to exclude certain subjects. For instance, those used to thinking about crime and justice in more conventional terms might find it surprising to find no essay on juvenile delinquency. While we have dealt with the major aspects of "delinquency" in many parts of our essays, this did not seem to be an important exclusion because the distinction between the minor and adult felons is a legal distinction with few consequences other than the elimination of most of the juvenile's legal rights—something we have dealt with. Wherever possible, we have avoided getting too deeply into detailed considerations because what is needed most of all at this stage is a reappraisal of the fundamental issues. Only when we have found the right starting points can we hope to arrive at the right answers to specific questions, but once we do start from the right point, it should be no great problem to work out the details.

The volume as a whole is integrated primarily in two ways. It is integrated first in terms of its subject matter—crime, the law, and the American system of criminal justice. It is integrated as well in terms of its major themes. One of the principle themes that runs through the work, and one that is progressively developed, is that the public outcry over "crime in the streets" is a form of hysteria which distorts realities and which, consequently, must not become the basis for any national policies pertaining to the fundamental issues of crime and justice in our society. In my own essay I have begun by arguing that this great public concern with crime is largely the result of a growing fear of the poor, especially of the black poor in the large northern cities, and that it is comparable to the nineteenth-century European fear of the urban poor, a fear that led to beliefs that "dangerous classes" committed more crime than "respectable classes." The essay by Abraham Blumberg on "Criminal Justice in America" starts with a brief treatment of the inevitability of crime in any society and an argument that the degree of crime in our own day is probably less than that of many societies at other times. In his chapter on "Crime and Its Impact in an Affluent Society" Leroy Gould has shown that even the official statistics of the F.B.I., the *Uniform Crime Reports,* do not support any belief in a rampaging rise in violent crimes. But, more important, his essay also shows that such statistical reports must not be taken as valid evidence of the amount of crime.

The second important theme that is advanced by these essays is that laws, law enforcement, crime, and justice are largely determined by political decisions. The existence of laws and, therefore, "crime," must be seen as the result of political decisions. If there were no groups trying to control the activities of other groups, and capable of exercising sufficient power to try to enforce their wills upon those other groups through the legislative processes, there would be no laws making some activities "crimes" and there could, consequently, be no "criminals." In "Crime and Justice in American Society" I have argued that criminal laws are specifically enacted by the middle and upper classes to place the poorer classes under the more direct control of the police, while the middle and upper classes pass only civil laws to control violations within their own ranks. In his essay on "The Social Reality of Crime" Richard Quinney has developed a general theoretical treatment of the ways in which power and political decisions are important in determining whether there will be criminal laws and what they will be like. Blumberg has also shown how politics and power play major roles in determining how "justice" is administered in our courts. In his essay on the police Peter Manning has described how law-enforcement strategies are devised to give the police the appearance of solving the manifold problems they face in carrying out a troublesome, contradictory public mandate.

A third common theme in our essays is the belief that present laws, law-enforcement procedures, judicial practices, and methods of punishing those found guilty of crime are based on a number of assumptions that are no longer true, if they ever were. We also believe that the legal practices resulting from these assumptions are creating a greater and deeper sense of injustice among those subjected to them and that this sense of injustice, especially when combined with the criminal attitudes and knowledge learned as a result of imprisonment, only produces more crime. The two most damaging of these false assumptions are (1) that crime is an individual action emanating from some "evil" part of a "criminal self" or "criminal mind" and (2) that our present criminal laws represent a set of absolute morals that should be enforced against all. We have argued throughout these essays that we must now view crime and each criminal act as largely the result of social processes commonly involving serious disagreements over values between those violating laws and those enforcing them. Because of these disagreements over values, legal proceedings frequently produce a great sense of injustice—rather than that sense of contrition which those who assume there is only one set of absolute, God-given laws seem to expect of the "guilty." While these arguments are found in almost all the essays, they are especially important in understanding the effects of efforts to legislate morality, as analyzed by Troy Duster in connection with "Drugs and Drug Control" and the almost total failure of attempts to rehabilitate "criminals," as analyzed by Leroy Gould and Zvi Namenwirth in their essay on "Contrary Objectives: Crime Control and the Rehabilitation of Criminals."

The authors of this book also share many ideas on how Americans must go about reconstructing the foundations of their laws and legal procedures in order to increase the safety of their person and their property while at the same time increasing the sense of social justice and the degree of social order. It is particularly noteworthy in this respect that none of the essays argues that we must have any kind of socio-economic reordering of our society to produce these results. Whereas the crime commission report continually insisted we must end slum living and every other form of social ill before we can solve our worst problems connected with crime and injustice, these essays have little to say about the social reorganization of priorities and resources. I suspect most of us are in favor of more equitable social policies in one form or another, yet it has been our implicit assumption that the critical, basic problems with our laws and legal practices are causing our most severe problems of crime and injustice. The presidential commission's choice of placing the blame for these problems on social imbalances became a way of absolving legislators and legal authorities from responsibility for their own failures to create and administer practicable and just laws and legal procedures. We do not absolve them. We hold them to be most culpable, collectively and personally, for our most urgent problems of crime and injustice. They will continue to be so as long as they continue to administer and support the present system of unworkable and unjust laws and legal procedures. No amount of rhetoric, mystification, denial, or blame-gaming can change this fact.

It should be apparent to all readers that our placement of responsibility on legislators and legal authorities is in no way inspired by personal feelings or ideological commitments. There are times when our arguments are made with strength, and even fervor, for we are deeply involved in our common national fate and we believe the changes we advocate are vital to our common American and human interests. But we have not approached our task with any political axes to grind or any commitments to narrow interest groups in our society. Indeed, such subjects never arose among us and are not discussed in these essays. Rather, our commitment has been to getting at truths backed by all available facts and following our reasoning to what seem sensible conclusions. Only in this way can we hope to find solutions to our deep-rooted problems of crime and injustice.

If legislators, legal authorities, and much of the general public will join in this undertaking, we can surely resolve the worst aspects of these problems. Yet, while we must not allow our sympathies for the criminal underdogs to cloud our thinking about crime, we must not launch any great crusades against "evil." As long as there are laws and men, there will be violations and injustices. A burning zeal to eradicate all the infamies in our society will only create more violations and greater injustices. We must have fundamental changes in our laws and legal procedures. But we must seek them through community commitment and democratic methods. We must not seek them through the angry and bloody conflicts that in recent years have only compounded our problems and made their solution more and more difficult by convincing all too many Americans that tyranny is not too great a price to pay for tranquillity.

PART I

Crime and Justice in American Society

Crime and Justice
in American Society

JACK D. DOUGLAS

Felon is as bad a word as you can give to man or thing.

MAITLAND

There are times when the members of Western societies become deeply concerned with problems of crime, social order,
and justice in their everyday lives. In the early part of the nineteenth century, most of them were troubled about what they
believed to be a veritable mania for immorality and criminality
and what some believed to be a sign of impending social chaos
and destruction. The middle classes were particularly fearful
that the new classes—the industrial workers and the industrial
poor—were increasingly devoting themselves to lives of crime
and depravity. Urban riots by the industrial poor[1] and the growing revolutionary political movements convinced many that
these were indeed "dangerous classes." Much of the early
work of the fledgling social sciences, therefore, was devoted
to trying to determine whether these classes were in fact more
dangerous than any others.[2]

Partly inspired by this anxiety of the average man, but
also arising out of other, more philosophical concerns, intellectuals undertook a thorough reconsideration of the causes
of crime, the relations between legal institutions and crime,

[1]See the discussion of nineteenth-century urban riots by Allan Silver, "A
Demand for Order in Civil Society," in *The Police: Six Sociological Essays,* ed.
David J. Bordua (New York: John Wiley & Sons, 1967).
[2]See Louis Chevalier, *Classes laborieuses et classes dangereuse à Paris
pendant la première moitié du XIXème siècle* (Paris: Plon, 1958).

3

and the nature of justice. Out of these reconsiderations developed the positivistic conceptions of crime and the theory of deterrence. These ideas became the cornerstones of the new—or greatly changed—legal institutions that still form much of the structure within which we deal with crime and justice today.

Members of American society, as we have seen so clearly in recent presidential elections, are now just as deeply concerned about questions of crime, social order, and justice. This concern is also largely inspired by the rise of new classes of the poor concentrated in urban areas, by urban riots, and by the expansion of revolutionary movements. And, just as in the nineteenth century, we have all the anguished predictions of chaos and destruction resulting from "rising crime waves."

And once again it is the intellectuals, as well as all educated men in America, to whom it has become obvious that the situation calls for fundamental reconsiderations of crime and justice in our society, with the goal of producing fundamental changes in the ways in which we deal with crime, maintain order, and provide justice. But there is one vital difference. While the nineteenth-century reformers were by no means presented with a clean social slate, opposition to their proposals was relatively unorganized; today, the forces of opposition to reform are as well entrenched as they are powerful.

Though centuries of fears, hatreds, and traditional ideas about criminals supported the old ways of handling crime and justice, the populations of Western nations were not generally united in support of the long-established practices. As a result, organized opposition to the new programs and practices was neither massive nor effective. On the contrary, the organized efforts were mainly on the side of the reformers. One major reform was the creation of official control organizations, such as police departments. Moreover, civil-service careers were established in other governmental bureaus dedicated to making control more effective. The objective of all these innovations was less crime, more social order, and more justice.

The situation we face today is in no way analogous. As has happened so often before, the organizations created to carry through basic reforms in one era have become the bulwark of reaction in the next. The official organizations of control, created in part to bring the objective knowledge of experts or professionals to bear on crime and justice, have developed and so institutionalized their own ideas about these matters that they now steadfastly resist any efforts by "outsiders" to change those ideas or the practices associated with them. What is more, officials of these control organizations have become locked in a great and prolonged war with the people they see as "criminals"; to the official, as to the "criminal," this war often means life or death. Unlike the doctor who fights a dread but impersonal disease, the control agents fight a very personal war in a very personal arena with very personal consequences. They have become the captives of their situation.

In recent years, more and more of these officials have come to view their war as a lonely crusade that they must wage against foe and erstwhile friend alike. They believe that the justness of their war against crime and immorality is not understood by the public, and certainly not by their critics. They have become increasingly isolated and alienated from critics who would revise the system of crime control in the United States to make it more efficient and just. In many instances, particularly in the case of police officials, control agents have made it plain that they consider justice to be secondary to, or even a by-product of, their attempts to maintain social order. Furthermore, most of them see no necessity whatsoever to change current ideas and practices; rather, they have adamantly and moralistically insisted that any faults within the system of criminal justice are to be found in the "criminals" and the "potential criminals." Only more support and more power for our official organizations can, in their opinion, solve our problems of crime, order, and justice.

This resistance to change will be very difficult to overcome or overrule. For one thing, those in a holy war are rarely in a mood for self-criticism or objective evaluations of the foe. For another, the size of our official organizations of control has grown so rapidly in the last hundred years that today there are

few spheres of our everyday lives that are not surveyed by
agents of some official organization of control—police, F.B.I.,
S.E.C., C.I.A., F.C.C., I.R.S., F.A.A., I.C.C., zoning boards, draft
boards, school psychologists, welfare investigators, court
psychiatrists. With almost total public acquiescence, our society has become an *officially controlled society.* In an only
half-conscious attempt to restrict the freedoms of the few in
order to protect the freedoms of the many, political leaders,
inspired at times by the highest ideals of freedom and justice,
have created more and more official control agents. Competitive
zeal, the desire for self-enrichment, and the need to transform
themselves into "professional experts" in order to belittle their
critics and continue to control their own destinies have committed these officials to a policy of endless expansion of their
resources and power. Their counterattacks on critics have often
been extreme, including the devices of investigation, rousting,
and arrest. For many reasons the public has generally accepted
the self-proclaimed positions of these officials as experts and
has been unwilling to challenge them. The mantle of "expert" is
a powerful one in a technological society such as ours has become.[3] Unfortunately, it will not be easy to strip this mantle
from our control officials, or to convince the public to try anything rejected by these so-called "experts."

Still, real grounds for hope do exist that the fundamental
reexamination of our ideas and practices regarding crime,
social order, and justice will go on and that in time the reforms
needed will be carried out. An ever larger part of the public
has come to the conclusion that the problems related to crime
are basic and demand new approaches. The control officials,
as seen in the report of the President's Commission on Law
Enforcement and the Administration of Justice, have had little

---

[3] I have previously discussed the public's unwillingness to challenge self-
proclaimed "experts" in "Deviance and Order in a Pluralistic Society," in
Theoretical Sociology: Perspectives and Development, ed. Edward A. Tiryakian and John C. McKinney (New York: Appleton-Century-Crofts, 1970); I
have also discussed the "expert" in "Freedom and Tyranny in a Technological Society," in *Freedom and Tyranny: Social Problems in a Technological
Society,* ed. Jack D. Douglas (New York: Random House, 1970).

more to propose than ample infusions of tax money to increase the scope and influence of their old organizations, modified slightly by new techniques and programs. The massive cost in taxes to implement these schemes should make the public wary of traveling further along that route, thereby raising the possibility that the public will yet become more open to new ideas concerning the nature of control organizations. Hopes that needed reforms will someday be instituted also arise from the fact that a few of the most important control officials are themselves beginning to have some serious doubts about basic aspects of our system of control and justice.

The growing problems help to assure us that changes will be made. The essential question is whether they will lead to less crime, more social order, and greater justice or whether the "expert" control organizations will be allowed—or ordered—to try to repress crime and increase order by methods that are becoming more and more unjust and tyrannical.

THE PROBLEMATIC MEANINGS
OF LAW AND CRIME

In many ways it would appear obvious that a "crime" can be defined simply as the violation of a law. Since, however, it is equally obvious that infractions of most laws in our society are not called "crimes" by anyone, but, rather, "violations," "misdemeanors," or nothing at all, this initial definition of "crime" must be amended to cover only those violations that constitute "felonies." As students of law and society are always disconcerted to discover, however, felonies can generally be defined only as "serious crimes," which makes our amended definition circular. Moreover, there is no property possessed by all violations called "felonies" that could be used to provide their definition.[4] Even worse for those who seek a high degree of rational order in law and law enforcement, there is no general property possessed by all of those "things" called "laws."

[4]For a general analysis of definitions of crime, see W. L. Marshall and W. L. Clark, *A Treatise on the Law of Crimes* (Chicago: Callaghan, 1952).

There have been innumerable discussions of the definitions and meanings of law. But the idea that laws are officially enacted proscriptions against or prescriptions for action, involving the imposition of a specified negative sanction for noncompliance, probably comes closest to describing what most people consider "laws" today, even though there are, to be sure, exceptions to this description in common-law nations.

Much more order exists in the laws and precedents of our common-law tradition today than in the seventeenth century when Francis Bacon sought to discover some order in the multifarious local laws of England by collecting them and comparing their common elements and principles. But the difference is one of degree, not of kind. Contrary to the common-sense assumption of rationality in our legal traditions, fostered by those who wished to glorify them, these traditions are very complex and cannot be rationalized. In general, they have been devised primarily to deal with pressing practical problems rather than in accordance with the demands of rational system building. So complex are these traditions, and I emphasize their pluralism, that one of the more important branches of American law is concerned with the problem of deciding which laws of which governing body have jurisdiction in a given political locality. Many important legal decisions are reversed on the ground that the governing body that passed the violated law did not have the jurisdiction to do so.

The so-called "system" of legal appeals, which is actually no system at all, and the checks and balances between the segments of our pluralistic government and courts add further to the problematic meanings of laws in our society. So problematic are these meanings that only the fact of a legal decision can make the concrete meaning of a law definite and clear to members of our society,[5] even to the so-called "experts"; in other words, only the official decision that a law is legal or illegal in a specific case can make it legal or illegal. Furthermore, appeals and changes of court decisions, including re-

[5]For discussions of the concrete meanings of law, see Morris Cohen, *Reason and Law* (New York: Collier Books, 1961), and Paul A. Freund, *On Law and Justice* (Cambridge: Harvard University Press, 1968).

versals by the United States Supreme Court of earlier Supreme Court decisions, mean that what is clearly legal today may be clearly illegal tomorrow. At the extremes, we find that confessed and convicted murderers can be declared not guilty (non-murderers) and set free; and teen-agers who intermittently smoke the nonnarcotic cigarette, marijuana, can be jailed for possession (or for being in the presence of those in possession) of narcotics.

All degrees of problems are, of course, encountered in the meanings of laws. For some laws, Americans share reasonably common ideas and would probably be able to agree in many instances on a proper interpretation, at least as long as they were not personally involved as litigants. Yet this in no way means that a particular action could be generally agreed upon as a violation or, given agreement that it is a violation, that the individual charged is guilty or, given agreement that he is guilty, that the consequences of his act are now clear. On the contrary, decisions on these matters are even more problematic.

The commission of a crime, of a violation, usually involves consideration not only of the observable events but of the mental states (*mens rea*) of those involved as well. In most cases the observable events are as potentially ascribable to an "accident" or a "mistake" as they are to a "crime." It is only some implicit or explicit assumption about the mental state of the actor that allows one to appropriately impute the category of "crime" to his actions. While members of our society take many aspects of this mental state into consideration in deciding whether an act or an event constitutes a crime, the crucial factors are knowledge and intention, and knowledge itself is primarily important only insofar as it contributes to deciding the intentions of the actor. Intention is the crucial factor in deciding whether the event constitutes a crime or something else.

For members of Western societies, intention is fundamentally problematic both in the abstract and in specific situations. That is, there is no clear and distinct, unidimensional, and universally agreed upon social definition of "intention"; as a result, members of our society find it fundamentally problematic to decide whether an action was intended or not, and if it was what the consequences or objectives of that action were supposed to have been.

Since the imputation of the category of "crime" is dependent upon the prior imputation of intention, we can see that the decision as to whether an act constitutes a crime is inherently problematic. And this, as we know, has provoked an intolerable situation. It would probably be intolerable in any society, since definite decisions and actions are demanded, but it has been especially intolerable in ours. The moral absolutism of the Christian tradition, which has been especially strong in the United States, demands absolute answers to questions of right and wrong and certainly to questions of crime.[6] Various devices have been created to bridge the chasm between this absolutist criterion and the essential uncertainties involved in "knowing" the unseen realm of an individual's spirit and mind. In our legal traditions, the chasm has been bridged in two important ways. The first is through adversary proceedings, by which opposing sides try to convince a jury or judge of their position, even if they don't believe in it. These proceedings assume that the nature of intention is fundamentally problematic and that the question of guilt can be resolved by verbal combat and appeal to higher authority—God, for example, or voters in a democratic society—so that the resulting truth can stand for the absolute truth. The second way in which this chasm is bridged is through the use of many common-sense and legal forms of *objectivation* to establish intention or make it "observable." That is, certain observable actions and relations are accepted as the standard bases for assuming intention (or nonintention); in other words, these observable actions or relations have come to represent intention so that one can then proceed *as if* he had objective knowledge of intention.[7] For example, the time between an event denoting that a person might do something and the actual fulfillment of the deed can

[6] I have enlarged upon this point in "The Impact of the Social Sciences," in *The Impact of Sociology,* ed. Jack D. Douglas (New York: Appleton-Century-Crofts, 1970).

[7] See the analysis of objectivation in Peter L. Berger and Thomas Luckmann, *The Social Construction of Reality* (Garden City, N.Y.: Doubleday, 1966).

be used as an indication of forethought or planning, both in turn indicative of intention. Certainly statements of intention ("Someday I'll kill you") followed by acts that fulfill the expressed purpose (murder of the person threatened) are presumptive evidence of intention. Theodore Dreiser's *An American Tragedy,* however, is a classic example of the recognition that no matter how much presumptive evidence or objective evidence there may be for intention, it may still all be wrong. In the ultimate analysis, intention remains necessarily problematic. In recent years psychiatrists, presumed to be scientists with objective (absolute) knowledge of mental states, have been used increasingly as "expert" witnesses to establish or prove intention. Yet the "scientific objectivity" of this testimony is invariably completely undermined by the frequency with which psychiatrists, testifying at the same trial, take opposite positions concerning intention or even knowledge of right and wrong.

PROBLEMS OF RATIONALITY AND JUSTICE

No matter how diligently legal authorities may seek to objectify intention in order to establish the absolute truth about it, they are doomed to failure. Intention remains problematic. Accordingly, the different sides in legal disputes will inevitably have grounds for sincere disagreement over "guilt," even if the other grounds for disagreement, to be discussed shortly, were to be eliminated. With guilt disputable because intention is problematic, there will, then, always be an irreducible sense of injustice in our society whenever the judgers and those to be judged converge. And this sense of injustice means that a necessary absurdity is involved in our ancient conceptions of guilt and innocence.

This sense of injustice has, to be sure, always been with us. On the whole, it has not been intolerable to most members of our society; certainly it has fired few revolutions. It should not be assumed, however, that this absurdity will not fire future revolutions against our institutions of law and justice. Such a possibility is, in fact, real.

Western societies have for centuries usually been very

tolerant of such basic absurdities. But, as Lecky and Weber realized so clearly in the nineteenth century, the basic trend in Western societies for several hundred years has been toward an ever greater rationalization of life. While intellectuals and even scientists in the twentieth century have muted some of the excesses of the nineteenth-century faith in rationality, the scientific and technological revolution has spread the new beliefs in rationality among more and more people. It is especially among the educated young that this demand for rationality has grown so rapidly, simply because more of them are being educated as scientists and technologists. They also are the ones who are coming into greater conflict with what they see as the irrationalities of our laws and legal procedures.

In a technological society, authority comes to be based increasingly on rational—and empirical—calculations. Power founded on traditionalism ("It's always been that way") and legalism ("It's the law") is seen more and more frequently as illegitimate. The result: as our society becomes more technological, more attacks will be launched against all forms of power not deemed rational.[8] The more irrational our laws and legal institutions appear to new generations, the more our laws and legal institutions will be attacked.

What we are now faced with, therefore, is an urgent, serious need to reconsider the foundations of law and legal institutions in our society, especially those pertaining to morality and crime. The criminal law and the laws concerned with "legislating morality" in which there are no victims'—laws, for example, dealing with marijuana or abortion—are still founded for the most part upon a traditional conception of morality. This conception, which Lon Fuller has very aptly called the "morality of duty,"[10] was based on the Christian assump-

[8] I have discussed these changes in *Youth in Turmoil* (Washington, D.C.: United States Government Printing Office, 1970).

[9] See Troy Duster, "Drugs and Drug Control," in this volume, and Edwin M. Schur, *Crimes Without Victims* (Englewood Cliffs, N.J.: Prentice-Hall, 1965).

[10] Lon L. Fuller, *The Morality of Law* (New Haven: Yale University Press, 1964).

tion that morality is absolute—that is, that morality is necessary, unproblematic, immutable, and externally imposed on man by the nature of God. The nineteenth-century reforms led to the superposition of the rational (utilitarian) theory of deterrence upon these traditional assumptions, without eliminating them. In some ways the reforms merely provided a rhetoric of rationality, a modern "rationale," for the ancient forms that remained. It is precisely these still existent traditional forms of moral absolutism, combined with a sense or feeling of injustice on the part of those convicted under such laws, that are increasingly unacceptable in our technological society. The nature of morality itself is changing. Morality is being rationalized, and this basic change is leading toward an insistence on rational authority. Morality is being changed from absolute principles to more rationally and empirically determined guidelines for actions that have consequences for others; it is being changed, that is, into a *social ethics.* Rather than being absolute, ethical rules are now being seen as rational (and tentative) attempts to regulate the lives of individuals only insofar as this is necessary to protect the interests of other individuals in the society. The general objectives in terms of which these interests are determined are more and more often the least-common-denominator goals most members of any society today would accept—life, health, freedom, and prosperity.[11] This *new ethics* is not primarily concerned with the traditional problems of "guilt" and "innocence"; indeed, those who endorse this new ethics do not believe "guilt" and "innocence" in the ancient sense are even possible, since both presume far too much in the way of "free will" and "intention" than is possible in an age in which the social sciences have made cultural relativism and determinism a widely accepted assumption. Instead, the new ethics is concerned with the situational reasons for an act, only one of which is the individual's choice, and its consequences.

This situational theory of "responsibility" is in strong conflict with the moral absolutism of the criminal law. In some aspects of our law, especially those of admirality and equity,

[11]Douglas, "Deviance and Order in a Pluralistic Society."

judges have long had considerable flexibility in allocating "comparative fault" to the parties involved. This allows them to hold parties responsible in varying degrees and to award proportionate damages accordingly.[12] In criminal law, however, as in common law generally, there is extremely little formal flexibility in assigning guilt; the defendant is either innocent or guilty, no in-between, and the other, more social reasons for his actions are not assigned any degree of comparative fault. In an age in which men have moved, at least intuitively, toward a *situational ethics* that assumes individuals are only partially responsible for their actions and that their social situations are important causes of those actions, there can be no justice in laws or legal procedures that assume absolute responsibility by the defendant. While grave problems are certainly involved in deciding how much an individual is responsible for his actions, rarely is there a basis for assuming that he alone is responsible. Moreover, while it is true that prosecuting attorneys and judges do at times give consideration to these "extenuating circumstances" in their charges and sentences, the moral absolutism of the present laws and legal procedures leads nowhere but to a growing sense of injustice throughout our society. Only the extraction of morality from our criminal laws, only their demoralization—by introducing rational and flexible allocations of responsibility, or comparative fault, into our laws and legal procedures—can reverse this trend.

The insistence in this new situational ethics upon consideration of the consequences of an act as the determinant of whether it is an appropriate subject for legal consideration also demands a de-moralizing of our laws. According to this view, if an act has no consequences for others, then it is not in any way a subject for moral or ethical consideration. The new ethics takes a totally libertarian attitude toward all such socially inconsequential acts; only where adverse consequences for others are a possibility should "law" become the appropriate means—and only then as a last resort—of providing outside arbiters and controllers to find an accommodation.

[12]Freund, *On Law and Justice.*

Granted that it is a serious question whether a few abstract goals, such as health and prosperity, can replace social "morality" as the basis of laws and legal procedures without leading to social disorder, there is little reason to doubt that our laws and our legal institutions can be de-moralized to an immensely greater extent without causing any increase in social disorder. To reduce the sense of injustice by de-moralizing most of our laws would be to reduce disorder in our society and prevent many lifetime careers of crime.

Of course, some of our laws have already been progressively de-moralized and turned into devices of rational control and arbitration of conflicting interests. Very few of our modern laws, which are primarily those concerned with business activity, retain much of the absolutist "morality of duty." The criminal law, on the contrary, has retained most of the aspects of the absolutist morality, and those accused of crimes are still subject to all the ancient stigmatisms of the absolutist moral code.

For a number of reasons, our criminal laws have been largely excluded from this de-moralizing process, not only because of the dead weight of tradition but also because our criminal laws have become *class laws*. Most criminal laws are state or local laws passed by legislators who are almost entirely middle- or upper-class businessmen or professionals selected and elected by the middle-class party organizations and public. Members of these middle and upper classes and, above all, their legislators find purse-snatching, burglary, and gang fights more threatening—and morally damnable—than the carefully planned, fraudulent practices and conspiracies of businessmen who cheat them of many more billions of dollars each year than do lower-class thieves.

Because lower-class thievery sometimes involves the use of a weapon or force, it might appear at first glance that it is more dangerous to the public than the frauds of businessmen. There is, however, no good reason to think this is so. Evidence on improper auto repairs, the faulty construction of new automobiles, inadequate testing of new drugs (such as thalidomide), the prescribing of unnecessary drugs, and the performance of unnecessary operations indicate that the physical dangers from business fraud are probably much greater.

Even in instances in which business violations of the law are subject to criminal prosecution, they almost never are. Instead, they are treated as civil cases and the violators are subject to fines rather than to the stigmatization process of criminal charges, criminal prosecution, findings of guilt, and imprisonment. Antitrust violations are an excellent example of how discriminatory enforcement can be. As Sutherland long ago showed, virtually every major American corporation has been found guilty of violating antitrust laws since their enactment,[13] even though the laws deliberately make "proof" of such activity impossible in most cases. The antitrust laws permit the federal government to bring either civil or criminal charges against violators, yet no criminal charges had ever been made prior to those brought against the persons involved in the "incredible electrical conspiracy."[14] Since that particular case of fraud involved billions of dollars and was carefully planned by top executives of most of the major corporations producing electric circuit-breaking equipment, the government finally came to the conclusion that something extraordinary was demanded. At that, only a few of the many involved were sentenced to prison, and the sentences were extremely light. Teenagers who steal a car for joy-riding often receive far harsher penalties.

The conclusion to be drawn from the discriminatory enforcement of the law is inescapable: lower-class violations are still dealt with as crimes and their perpetrators are still subjected to all the severity of moral stigmatization simply *because* they are from the lower classes. Being lower-class or poor is itself a stigma in our society, and part of the social meaning of that stigma is that the poor have a tendency toward immorality, depravity, and crime. That is, individuals who are

---

[13]Edwin H. Sutherland, "Is 'White Collar Crime' Crime?" *American Sociological Review* 10 (1945), pp. 132–139.

[14]Richard Austin Smith, "The Incredible Electrical Conspiracy," *Fortune* (April 1961), pp. 132–180, and (May 1961), pp. 161–224.

lower-class or poor are thought by the middle classes to be more immoral and criminal *by nature,* or by some other necessity. It is this conception that has served as the foundation for all the biological, physicalistic, and racial theories of crime that have continually inspired fear in middle-class individuals. This fear, together with its beliefs, has led the middle classes to enact and maintain harshly moralistic laws and law-enforcement practices against the lower classes.

By the very nature, then, of both the legislative process and the laws enacted in our society, crimes are necessarily those actions committed primarily by lower-class individuals. Indeed, it can be safely predicted that whenever many middle-class people begin to commit a given form of crime, the laws will be changed to remove that activity from the category of "crime." Today, for example, abortion is already being redefined; the use of marijuana probably will be as well.

This social treatment of lower-class violations as "crimes," while middle-class violations are treated principally as civil cases, is probably not simply the result of some middle-class desire to punish those regarded as feared enemies. Blind fear and revenge may play their part in this process, but more tangible reasons are not difficult to find. Insofar as lower-class violations are defined as "crimes," they are subject to the direct surveillance and action of the police who are allowed to exercise wide discretion in the maintenance of "order." The criminal law, therefore, is a major device for giving the police greater direct power over the lower classes. If we remember that police organizations were established in the nineteenth century in order to control the urban poor, then it becomes clear that the maintenance of criminal laws, which are the primary laws whose enforcement is entrusted to the police, is an important device by which police can control the actions of the poor. Yet this enforcement process is carried out under the guise of "equal treatment," a tenet so crucial to the sense of justice in our society. Today no one has to make a policy decision that police action will be directed mainly at the urban poor; all one has to do is insist upon enforcement of the criminal laws by the police—and make certain that any changes in

the law do not place middle-class actions under the criminal
code, thereby making them also subject to police action. Where
enforcement action might possibly be directed toward the
middle class, for violations, for example, of the laws against
fraud, it is then merely necessary to maintain old criminal laws
in such a form that they are almost impossible to enforce. To
make doubly sure that prosecution is impossible, it is also
necessary for the middle class to provide almost no funds for
any police work concerned with the enforcement of such laws.
All state and local governments have done just this.

The continuance of the moralistic and stigmatizing criminal law for lower-class infractions, combined with the progressive de-moralizing of laws directed at middle-class activity,
has had several significant consequences. First, the growing
discrepancy between the legal treatment of the different classes
has produced a great sense of injustice among the urban poor.
While the urban poor have not been able to understand the
intricacies of these legal practices, neither have they been taken
in by official strategies intended to preserve a front of "justice." Instead, growing numbers of them have become *totally*
alienated from the police and other legal officials. They have
such a profound sense of injustice that they seem unable to
appreciate even those legal practices which serve to protect
them. It is this sense of injustice and this growing alienation
that have led to the increases in community attacks on the
police and other officials by the urban poor. One of the few
things common to all the urban riots of the 1960's was the expression of hatred for the police. In a very real sense, the urban
riots were police riots, for the nature of criminal law and legal
processes in our society has led to a permanent state of war
between the urban poor and legal officials, especially the often-
hated police. No amount of community-relations rhetoric or
community programs, such as those proposed in the President's
crime commission report, can end this deep sense of injustice
and this hatred so long as the police and other officials seek
to enforce criminal laws that are necessarily discriminatory by
means that are also necessarily discriminatory.

Secondly, insofar as a sense of injustice and hatred of legal officials are conducive to criminal actions, the continuance of the present criminal law system and legal procedures will lead to a continuance of crime. While the relationship between a sense of injustice and the persistence of crime is somewhat cloudy, it seems reasonable to presume that the deep feeling of being treated unjustly will contribute to further crime.

Thirdly, and even more importantly, the preservation of our moralistic criminal laws and legal procedures will continue to cause the moral stigmatization of many hundreds of thousands as "criminals," which in turn acts as a strong force toward causing these persons to embark upon or persevere in a criminal career. Many sociologists have come to believe that it is this stigmatization of individuals as "criminals" and, hence, outside the human community, that leads most persons convicted of crimes and punished for them to go on committing more crimes.

And, finally, the continuance of the moralistic criminal law will only lead to a greater feeling that our laws and legal procedures are illegitimate and unjust. This is true because of the expanding demand for rationality and because the acceleration of changes in our technological society will make it more and more difficult to judge and control patterns of criminal actions in terms of a relatively inflexible set of laws and legal procedures. A moralistic approach in a rapidly changing society will almost certainly prove ineffective.

What we Americans must do is reconstruct the social foundations of our laws and legal procedures, especially those currently termed "criminal" and directed chiefly at lower-class activities. These laws must be progressively rationalized and de-moralized in order to achieve a greater sense of justice. At the same time, laws designed to control the enormous amount of middle- and upper-class fraud must also be rationalized in order to make them enforceable. Only these measures will make our laws and legal processes just in the eyes of most members of our society.

De-moralizing our laws is, in one sense, essential to rationalizing them. As long as serious "moral" considerations (in the traditional sense of the term) exist, it will be necessary to make decisions about intention, which are not easy to rationalize. The rationalization of our laws and legal procedures will eliminate direct considerations of intention, yet these changes in the laws will have to be made in such a way that they are not arbitrary. What is demanded is an explicit and more systematic application of the ideas and rules concerning *adequate knowledge* of the consequences of one's actions, combined with a nonmoralistic, nonpunitive approach to social control. Once laws and legal institutions are no longer seen as an impossible attempt to decide ultimate questions of good and evil and are seen, instead, as a form of social engineering used in an attempt *only* to control individual behavior to that minimal degree necessary for the maximum progress of all toward generally shared goals, then our laws and legal institutions will not be as subject to impossible demands and will be much more subject to rational reconstruction.

It has already proved impossible for our official agents of control to administer and enforce our laws by the traditional standards of morality and justice. As Abraham Blumberg and others have argued so forcefully, the "justice" meted out in our society is in fact a *negotiated justice.* That is, for many different reasons, the vast majority of criminal cases in our society are handled *administratively;* relatively few are processed by the "ideal" means of a jury. Because of the immense practical problems involved, there is no significant possibility that we could institute legal procedures that would fit the "ideal." Moreover, the problems resulting from any attempt to determine "intentions" by using the jury system make it undesirable to institutionalize the jury system for any large portion of cases. Today the need to maintain the illusion of the "ideal," combined with the impossibility of doing it, serves only to corrupt the core of our legal procedures by causing officials to force defendants to plead guilty for a consideration upon threat of far more severe penalties. The result of seeking to maintain this illusion of "ideal justice" is further injustice. However regrettable we may find it, in order to produce greater justice we must abandon the illusory "ideal" of meting out justice by jury trial.

Instead of surreptitiously forcing guilty pleas for a consideration, while maintaining the front of "ideal justice," we must systematically perfect a publicly observable system of administrative justice in which defendants are not forced by threats to waive their legal rights. After we have de-moralized our laws and legal procedures, we must substitute clear, distinct, and generally agreed upon criteria for establishing reasonable knowledge of consequences so that there will be a minimum of arbitrariness in judicial decisions of guilt. We must then perfect institutions of nonpolitical, appointed jurists, comparable in form to the United States Supreme Court, who will serve as expert juries in deciding on guilt and sentencing. While there are some obvious dangers to individual liberties in such a legal procedure, few would deny that at the Supreme Court level this arrangement has led to greater protections of individual freedoms than juries of "peers" have normally insisted upon.[15] In addition, safeguards could be maintained, especially in the transition stages, by permitting jury trials on appeal. Even more importantly, by allowing every indigent defendant to hire his own lawyer, with government-supplied funds, instead of forcing him to rely upon court-appointed attorneys or public defenders, who are usually members of those secret teams engineering negotiated justice, individual rights will be far better protected than they are at present.[16]

By concentrating the available resources on the training and paying of such expert jurists, it will also be possible to solve one of the most basic problems of our present legal procedures: the grossly unequal sentencing of guilty individuals. Part of this unfairness can be attributed to the extreme variance in penalties from one state to another or to the fact that in ten

[15]A major problem with juries has been that those legally defined as "peers" for jury purposes have rarely actually been "peers" in criminal cases.

[16]We can learn from European experience with Roman law a great deal about more "rationalized" legal procedures. For comparisons in this respect, see Max Weber, "The Formal Qualities of Modern Law," in *Max Weber on Law in Economy and Society*, ed. Max Rheinstein, trans. Edward Shils and Rheinstein (Cambridge: Harvard University Press, 1954), pp. 301–321. It should be noted, however, that the present analysis of the relations between law and class is in direct conflict with Weber's emphasis on the determination of laws by the internal rationality of the law, as in "Formal Qualities," pp. 61–64.

states juries still decide on sentences. But nationalizing our systems of state laws, or simply standardizing them, will be necessary and sufficient to eliminate most of these problems. The flagrant inequalities produced by the frequently poor education and individual preferences of judges, however, can only be eliminated by making judges expert professionals, making them work as teams of jurists rather than individually, and using such devices as reeducation and judicial conferences on sentencing.[17]

OFFICIAL ORGANIZATIONS OF CONTROL, CRIME, AND JUSTICE

The traditional common-sense assumption of the middle classes, and one shared by the structural-functional theories in sociology, has been that laws and legal institutions are entirely a functional response to crime and that they tend to control crime. This one-directional view of crime is a total misconception of the present situation in American society. There is, in fact, a high degree of interdependency between crime, the laws, and the legal institutions: in numerous ways, each is both a cause of and a response to the others.[18] Moreover, crime and the official organizations of control are also substantially interdependent. Though official organizations of control were established largely as a response to crime, today they shape, cause, and perpetuate crimes by the nature of *their* responses to crime. In turn, crime has become in significant measure a response to the activities of the official control organizations. Just as we now have many iatrogenic diseases, or diseases caused by medical intervention intended to end other

[17]The President's Commission on Law Enforcement and Administration of Justice (hereafter cited as President's Commission), *The Challenge of Crime in a Free Society* (Washington, D.C.: United States Government Printing Office, 1967), p. 145.

[18]A strict interpretation of functional theory would, of course, lead one to see the interdependency between law, law enforcement, and crime, but the functionalists have almost never followed their own logic to consider the ways in which laws and law enforcement also cause crimes.

diseases, so do we have *iatrogenic social problems.* In the case of crime, the iatrogenic problems appear to be growing faster than the original problems.

Official organizations have become responsible for crimes in a number of ways. The most elementary way in which they have increasingly become the "causes"[19] of crime, and one so basic it was virtually overlooked until Howard Becker and others focused attention on it,[20] is by their ability to get new criminal laws passed or by their enforcement of old laws under new interpretations in order that behavior once considered either legal or merely a violation of civil law becomes a crime. In this way, law-abiding citizens can become criminals by an attenuated form of ex post facto criminalization of their behavioral patterns. The classic example of this transformation is narcotics addiction and the use of marijuana. At the beginning of this century, as Troy Duster carefully points out, both narcotics and marijuana were legally sold and used in the United States. The narcotics were used mostly by mothers, in the form of laudanum, to quiet crying babies, and by ailing adults. Largely as a result of the enterprising activities of the federal Bureau of Narcotics, new laws and strong enforcement procedures were instituted so that both the use and mere possession of narcotics and marijuana were successfully criminalized. From being the "harmless," though addictive, palliative of little old ladies and former medical patients, the narcotics were transformed in two or three decades into the most frightening form of drugs and their users were transformed into social outcasts. At the same time, the nonaddictive marijuana was transformed by official policy into a "narcotic" so that its users could be subjected to roughly the same kind of criminal treatment. Today the process is being repeated with LSD, mescaline, and other hallucinogens. Control officials are busily creating new

---

[19]In the strict (Aristotelian) philosophical sense, laws are first of all the "material causes" of crime in that they *are* the "material" substance or definition of crime. But I am also arguing here that laws have become "efficient causes" of crime by producing a sense of injustice.

[20]Howard S. Becker, *Outsiders: Studies in the Sociology of Deviance* (New York: The Free Press, 1963).

forms of "crime" and new "criminal" groups for the purpose of showing the public how urgently we need more police, more stringent laws, and more police power—which can then be used to create new "crimes" and new "criminal" groups.

The organizational properties of the official agencies of control and the career aspirations of their members have become the essential determinants of our criminal laws and legal processes, independently of any considerations of justice resulting from the operations of the agencies. This circumstance has evolved, as Skolnick has argued, because the police have been granted wide discretion in the methods they use to maintain order; they are relatively unrestrained by laws intended to restrain their actions to insure justice for the public.[21] It has also evolved because of the great hesitancy demonstrated by the courts to provide any clear and distinct answers to such basic questions as what constitutes "arrest," which would restrain the police by making it possible to apply clearly to their behavior the laws that do exist.[22] In addition, it has evolved because no effective agencies have been set up to control the control agents. Middle- and upper-class individuals can and do hire lawyers to sue the police for false arrest, which is bad for departmental public relations even if the suit rarely succeeds. The danger of prosecution for false arrest is another reason why police action is directed toward lower-class individuals, since they have neither the knowledge nor the money to sue anyone. And, finally, our control agencies have become the basic determinants of our criminal laws and processes because of their success in maintaining themselves as secret societies. No group in our society has more power than the police over the lives and freedom of millions of our citizens, and yet few groups have operated in greater secrecy. Furthermore, the police systematically use their own "investigative" powers to hide their own violations. For example, though there is definitely far less police brutality today than a few decades ago, it still exists in many forms; yet this brutality is almost impossible to

[21]Jerome Skolnick, *Justice Without Trial* (New York: John Wiley & Sons, 1966).

[22]See Claude R. Sowle, ed., *Police Power and Individual Freedom* (Chicago: Aldine, 1962), esp. pp. 9–36.

prove legally because the powers of the police include the legal right to isolate their investigations from all outside observation; when police do beat up suspects, they are able to do so out of sight and sound of any potential witnesses.

The organizational autonomy and power of the police have been greatly augmented by their growing success in laying claim to the status of being a professional group of "scientific experts." Like many groups, the police and other control agents have made more and more use of the professional rhetoric of science in an attempt to raise their prestige and legitimize their efforts to gain wider control over the ways in which they perform their jobs. They have placed greater emphasis on the many symbols of expertise, such as degrees in police science and criminology, that have such enormous prestige in our technological society.[23] They have employed these symbols in order to "prove" their professionalism and, thence, to legitimize their organizational autonomy. Their bitter campaigns against civilian review boards, for instance, are a consequence of this self-exaggeration. Unlike the traditional professions, however, the police are asking for—demanding—an organizational autonomy that really amounts to tyranny. Unlike the clients of doctors, lawyers, and other professionals, the potential "clients" of the police have no choice, and it would be casuistry to insist the police have the best interests of their potential clients at heart. Moreover, it must never be forgotten that every member of our society is a potential client of the police. What the police system is tending toward, then, is autonomy in surveying and controlling the lives of all of us to some degree and of many of us to an extreme degree. Such autonomy is the essence of tyranny. Even so, the police have been able to achieve ever greater autonomy, and their claims to professional expertise will no doubt allow them to gain even more.

The organizational autonomy of the police has been a major factor in allowing their individual and organizational considerations to displace considerations of justice—to determine the form of "justice" they administer. But organizational autonomy has not been the only factor. The unrealistic demands that the

[23]Douglas, "Freedom and Tyranny."

public makes on all officials in our society and the limited funds it is willing to devote to our legal organizations are basic forces causing compromises with the demands of justice.[24] The "good" administrators of the control organizations become those able to process the most clients, regardless of the compromising methods used, and those most willing to obey the commands of organizational expediency are advanced to head the organizations. The public's impractical demands provide the pressures and incentives for the compromises. What is more, the organizational autonomy of our enforcement and control agencies assures their "success"—and the secrecy and public rhetoric of justice that becloud the entire operation allow the public to hide from the consequences of its parsimony and unconcern. The result is a bureaucratic processing by, in Goffman's term, our "total institutions"[25] that dehumanizes their captive clients and determines "justice" on the basis of organizational requirements.

The ways in which this processing is done, its rationale, and its consequences have been analyzed by Matza in his study of juvenile courts. The juvenile court is essentially a court operating under civil procedures—hence, it is without the protections of due process in criminal procedures even though it administers not criminal laws involving restitution but criminal (moralistic) laws involving stigmatization, attempts to transform the evil self into a good self,[26] and punishment. The presumption has been that juvenile court judges would use the flexibility of civil procedures and sentencing to "protect" youngsters in order that the goals of justice would be better served. This presumption has been held despite the fact that juvenile court judges are merely administering criminal laws. As Matza points out, the situation has led to some serious questions: "Does the indulgence of the court in its sentencing outweigh the loss of

---

[24]I have outlined the reasons why official control organizations tend to become so total in Jack D. Douglas, *American Social Order* (New York: The Free Press, 1970).

[25]Erving Goffman, *Asylums* (Garden City, N.Y.: Anchor Books, 1962).

[26]David Matza, *Delinquency and Drift* (New York: John Wiley & Sons, 1964), pp. 72–73.

protection inherent in the relative absence of due process? And, is the 'protective care' or 'treatment' dispensed by the juvenile court a reality or mystification?"[27] Matza leaves little doubt that it is mainly a mystification—or rhetoric.

Matza first argues that the wide, or what he calls "rampant," discretion allowed by the principles of individualization that are meant to govern the juvenile court makes the judge a "kadi," or a judge who renders his decisions without reference to any reasons or principles. He then contends that

    . . . his traditional freedom is restricted by the peculiar bureaucratic setting in which it appears. His judgment and wisdom may reign but only precariously since he is simultaneously the manager of the court and must thus concern himself with public relations, internal harmony, efficient work flow and the rest. . . . The kadi's responses to the crosspressures obviously vary, but not as much as one might imagine. If we pay attention to what he actually does and not to the rhetoric by which he justifies his dispositions, some interesting and by no means unprecedented things seem to happen. A first order of business is to merely get through the day's work. The flow of juvenile cases is something to behold. Falling behind is consequential since there are other points on the juvenile assembly line, detention halls, for instance, that will suffer pile-ups. Cases must be handled routinely and efficiently or else there will be complaints to the management from other parts of the system. Much of the real work and real decision making is done behind the scenes where the recipient of justice cannot observe it. It is completely obscured from him. His court hearing is typically perfunctory, though occasionally a case is rather thoroughly explored.[28]

The organizational determination of the official actions, the compromising of the individual's sense of justice, and the attempt to reconcile by rhetoric the division between the individual's actual experience and his ideas of justice are found throughout legal institutions; but they are especially evident in police work. It is a basic assumption regarding all police work in American society that no more than a fraction of criminal

[27]Ibid., p. 73.
[28]Ibid., pp. 122–123.

offenses can be detected and, of these, no more than a fraction can be acted upon. The reasons for this discrepancy are because many problems are involved in detection and apprehension and because the number of police and other legal officials is always small in relation to the population. Consequently, regardless of the laws concerning police work, there are fundamental organizational reasons for a high degree of police discretion. Under these circumstances, the police feel forced to handle most cases informally and expeditiously at the lowest level, that of the patrolman. As a general practice, anything else involving more formal handling would cause a breakdown of the whole process. The local patrolman, relying almost entirely on his own ideas about crime and criminals, and receiving little guidance from either the formal laws or legal authorities,[29] must decide whom to charge and whom not to charge in such a way that he does not make too many arrests. Since his own career and the department's public relations are helped primarily by effective arrests, or arrests that bring convictions, it is little wonder that the patrolman's problem is resolved by arresting and charging those most likely to be convicted—or, to put it another way, those least likely to be able to defend themselves and least likely to cause a public ruckus by filing suit over such matters as false arrest and police brutality. Who, then, are the most likely candidates for arrest? The poor, of course. The organizational factor reinforces the criminal law's bias against the violations by the poor.

The assumption that police work cannot possibly detect or apprehend more than a small fraction of the potentially chargeable violations has also meant that the police must rely on a probabilistic method of deterrence with very low probabilities of actual detection and apprehension. Because the police have no possibility of detecting crimes and apprehending the perpetrators on anything like a one-to-one basis, they have devised methods they hope will maximize the probability of detection

[29]The police have little knowledge of the laws they are to enforce. Like other control officials, they must make use of "folk-laws," or common-sense conceptions of what the laws are and what they mean. I have discussed folk-laws in an unpublished report on my study of coroners, "The Official Classification of Suicide as a Cause of Death," for the National Institutes of Health.

and apprehension. From their standpoint, this "rational" strategy thus maximizes the risk of committing a crime and, thereby, maximizes the deterrent effect for any level of police forces. From the standpoint of the potential criminal, however, there is no evidence whatsoever that "rational" considerations on the part of the police lead to the same conclusions concerning the risks involved in crime; whatever the police disposition of forces, he views the objective and subjective probabilities of detection and apprehension as being extremely small. One side effect of this "rational" strategy, understandably enough, is to put the maximum effort into those forms of enforcement promising the greatest return and least risk to the police—enforcement against the poor. Indeed, since those successfully categorized as "criminals" almost always come from lower-class groups in which systematic surveillance, rousting, and arrests are common events, it is likely that the probability of false arrest (and possibly even false conviction) is greater than the probability of arrest for an action actually committed.

The overall consequence of this "rational" police strategy is that those who commit crimes do not give much "rational" consideration to the risks involved. Police action, therefore, does not serve to deter criminal action to anywhere near the degree that the middle class thinks it does. I do not mean to say that there is no sense of risk involved in violating the rules enforced by the police. There is. Indeed, considerable fear and excitement can be involved in committing crimes, precisely because of the—albeit small—risk of apprehension—or even of being shot by the police. The important point to remember, however, is that a sense of excitement or fear is engendered by these small risks—not a sense of dread of being caught and punished. The risks involved in most forms of crime, though probably not in the few "heinous crimes" such as murder, seem to be just enough to arouse great excitement; this excitement can itself become a positive motive for crime, particularly among the lower classes, who, according to Miller, place great stress on the value of excitement.[30] In fact, Werthman has found

[30]Walter Miller, "Lower Class Culture as a Generating Milieu of Gang Delinquency," *Journal of Social Issues* 14 (1958), pp. 5–19.

specific "games" in which lower-class boys pretend to steal only for the purpose of getting the police to chase them.[31] In these games, the excitement of the struggle against the police is the sole motive. Though excitement in most criminal acts is only one of several motives, the risk of police apprehension seems to serve more as an inducement for crime than as a deterrent, especially for the lower classes who are the prime target of police control.

The press of work on all governmental organizations in our society has mounted year after year. The demand for services, either for one's self or against others, has expanded as the proportion of social wealth available for any given unit of service has contracted, particularly in our core cities. Governmental officials, many of them trapped by the rigid career lines of the Civil Service and the declining opportunities of age, have been pressed ever harder. They have "solved" this problem of public pressure by building a network of total institutions to process their human products according to administrative needs—and with coarse disregard for individuals and *their* needs. As this solution has been found to work, it has in turn provided broader opportunities to process the same human product at less cost. And this success of total institutions has made them even more total. Computer technology, combined with a national data bank on all "criminals," now promises a wide extension in the totality of our control organizations: the entire life of a marked man will now become the object of surveillance and control; the single bit of information about his arrest could become the sole public meaning of his life.

As all too many lower-class members of our society see it, behind every grand symbol of justice lies the reality of injustice; beneath all the idealistic rhetoric about equal consideration of guilt and individual consideration of need lies the reality of our total institutions. The reality is mixed, one of both ideal justice and shabby injustice, but the middle-class citizen who

---

[31]Carl Werthman, "The Function of Social Definitions in the Development of Delinquent Careers," in President's Commission, *Task Force Report: Juvenile Delinquency and Youth Crime* (Washington D.C.: United States Government Printing Office, 1967), pp. 155–170.

supports his local police sees only the symbols, hears only the rhetoric, and is content never to attempt to penetrate the wall of secrecy. The lower-class man, who is not fully a citizen, either because his conviction as a felon has already stripped him of the essential rights of citizenship or because the standard operations of the legal powers have in fact stripped him of his constitutional rights, knows both the rhetoric and the reality. Because he does know both, he lives in a Kafkaesque world in which the implacable powers treat him as a nonhuman and in which his cries of outrage go unheard or elicit only contempt. After all, who can trust what a "criminal" says? At the least, he becomes a relentless foe of the legal powers, often precisely because he believes in our ideals of justice. At the extreme, he may develop total contempt or hatred for the ideals themselves and profound resentment against the legal powers and the entire society. He may even glorify what he himself feels to be evil. More normally, with his fellow outcasts and the sympathy of other lower-class people, he builds a *counterlegal subculture* intended, on the one hand, to demean the police and subvert their operations and, on the other, to provide some common protection and support for the self. This subculture is at its most virulent within prisons, where it is observable in the universal process known as "prisonization."[32] But it is also found on the outside where the marked men—"cons"—can count on little help other than what they give each other. Yet even the support and protection obtained from the counterlegal subculture is woefully inadequate, because most of its members still cling to the commonly accepted social ideals and are, consequently, ambivalent, and because the enemy is so powerful. However alone most members of society may be, and however many enemies they may have, the criminal and potential criminal are far more alone in their struggle with their enemy. The criminal can rely only on himself and, as a consequence, he develops a profound respect for physical courage and a tough exterior—"nerve." The criminal's heroes are men who stand

---

[32]The best treatments of "prisonization" are to be found in the essays in *The Prison*, ed. Donald R. Cressey (New York: Holt, Rinehart & Winston, 1961).

up for themselves unflinchingly, even against certain death. These figures, invariably more dreamlike than real, are completely alone. It is their real social situation that has stimulated the dreams and called forth the ideals of combat, yet it is a situation so foreign to middle-class experience that psychologists and sociologists have often called upon such mysterious forces as psychopathy and sociopathy[33] to explain criminality.

It is wrong simply to say that the lower-class man has a sense of injustice about his situation, as Matza and others have well argued. He does, indeed, have a sense of injustice. But to describe his true feelings in this manner is too pale, too civilized. It is more accurate to say that he has a profound fear and hatred for the legal powers. The middle-class individual who has never experienced this fear and hatred will find it difficult to understand the feelings that attend the "cop" as he patrols enemy territory. He comes with gun, club, blackjack, helmet, and boots. At times he comes with rifle, shotgun, and dog; and he comes in squads or platoons. It is an awesome sight calculated to create fear. And it does. However vast their bravado, few lower-class men have not felt fear—and the racing heart—at the approach of these foreign "troopers"; most know that they come not as friends to protect them, but to protect the property of others from them. They know that they themselves are the enemy for which this awesome arsenal is at the ready, for all of them are suspects and no lack of evidence can make it otherwise. By the same token, lower-class individuals find it hard to believe that the police often fear them, for the police, too, know they are hated and that unseen weapons might be turned against them at any time. No amount of community relations, goodwill, or rhetoric can eliminate these two armed camps. Only a greater force controlling both can possibly break the vicious circle of fear, distrust, and the increasing stockpiles of weapons and reverse the process so typical of suspicious nations. Only such a greater force can possibly reestablish trust and disarm the camps. Unlike the international scene, such

[33]See, for example, Lewis Yablonsky's use of "sociopathy" in *The Violent Gang* (New York: Macmillan, 1962).

a greater force exists in our society: the educated middle class does have the power to break the circle and reverse the process. Once it is aware of the problems and can see what actions are urgent, it may well accept the responsibility and bring about the fundamental changes needed.

THE FAILURE OF DETERRENCE, RATIONALIZING THE LAW, AND CONTROLLING THE POLICE

We have already seen the basic reasons why our laws, legal institutions, and legal processes have failed to deter crime and why, in fact, they shape and sometimes cause crime. They do so largely because the ancient stigmatization process involved in the criminal law and its administration creates a situation that forces the "criminal" into a pattern—if not a lifetime career —of crime. The social beliefs that "the criminal cannot be trusted" and that "once a criminal always a criminal" isolate the accused or the convicted from most noncriminal paths. Moreover, the permanent record system of the police, founded on the same premises, keeps him under such close surveillance that he is often rearrested and reconvicted for offenses that would not be detected in others. Regardless of his own desires, the accepted social connotations involved in the term "criminal" and the pervasive structure of police work push him back into crime. This occurs because the very nature of criminal law and the organizational methods of enforcing it are inherently discriminatory and destructive of all trust; both these character- istics create the sense of injustice in the lower classes. Further- more, even if the criminal law were not discriminatory toward the lower classes, its excessively moralistic (and problematic) nature would automatically prompt a sense of injustice in our society. Laws and law enforcement based on the assumption of a simple and homogeneous "morality of duty" can be en- forced with a sense of justice only in a simple and homogeneous society where members are in general agreement about that "morality of duty." American society, however, is a pluralistic society in which there is considerable disagreement about moral

matters. As a consequence, even if criminal laws were not discriminatory against class groups, they would almost certainly
be discriminatory against some other groups, producing the
same profound sense of injustice. In fact, we are witnessing
the development of this sense of injustice in college youth today
as authorities of one sort or another attempt to legislate their
morality through the criminal law; the result has been to make
the young more and more revolutionary.

Laws cannot be enforced effectively in a free society without a general conviction among the groups within the society
that both the laws and the processes of enforcement are ultimately just. If groups do not share this conviction of justice,
then laws can be enforced and "social order" maintained only
by the use of a degree of force which is necessarily tyrannical.
The social conditions of freedom and the conditions for police
surveillance and enforcement actions are, therefore, mutually
exclusive.

While most Americans seem not to have become aware of
it, perhaps because it has been a slow and steady process,
our society is becoming more and more tightly controlled. Official control organizations have greatly expanded in both number and size, and their methods of operation have become
constricting. The steady expansion of police power has caused
a steady expansion of the sense of injustice, a circumstance
that has caused less effective enforcement of the laws as
well as increased social disorder. The social disorders have
led to demands by the police and their class supporters
for even greater power, which, in turn, has succeeded in producing a greater sense of injustice. This spiraling relationship
between law-power, injustice, and violations will lead inevitably
toward police-state powers if we attempt to enforce social
order by the increased use of strategies seen as profoundly
unjust by the urban poor. The only way we can hope to create
a free society—and this obviously does necessitate the preservation of "law and order"—is by moving quickly and steadily
toward more just laws, methods of enforcement, and legal
processes.

As we have already argued, the first step in this direction

must be to enact nondiscriminatory, systematic, rationalized laws to replace our moralistic criminal laws. In addition, criminal laws must be made commensurate with, or else part of, the civil laws used to control middle-class violations; these laws must be administered by truly protective civil procedures that are systematically, impartially, and rationally directed at serving the interests of the defendants while protecting the interests of the community. Just as these interests must be balanced and optimized, so the blame for violations of the criminal law must be balanced in the light of our modern conceptions of man and society. Both the community and the perpetrators of the violations must be assessed their just measure of blame, to be determined by the best available social-science evidence concerning the causation of criminal actions. These assessments of blame must become a prescribed part of the law, not simply a matter of judges' using their discretion concerning mitigating circumstances. In addition, any forms of restitution or compensation must be assessed by judges in direct proportion to the assessments of blame—and in proportion to the needs of victims and the ability of the blameworthy to pay. As noted previously, the judicial procedures used to administer these new laws must also be rationalized and made nondiscriminatory.

Perhaps the most crucial need of all, however, is that the penalties for violating our criminal laws must be radically changed. At present, legal procedures as a whole serve to stigmatize individuals caught up in the legal "net," whether guilty or not. Their social position and their self-conceptions are altered in such a way that any bent they may have toward criminal activities is strengthened. And punishment by imprisonment serves only to reinforce these tendencies and to train the convicted man to become more criminal.

Stigmatization begins with arrest—a police action that marks a man for life. At this point, a man's social identity is transformed from the "right side" of life to the "wrong side," and whether he is ever found guilty is largely irrelevant. When a man is arrested it becomes a matter of public record that he has been charged by the authorities with a crime; he is now publicly charged with being a criminal. This charge immediately becomes available to the mass media, which frequently report arrests under the presumption that a charged man is a guilty man. If a crime has received publicity, the arrest is announced with fanfare and the name of the man charged released to the public; the police, district attorneys, and other officials have never been known to be reticent about having their "successes" publicized. The public, of course, knows nothing about the arrested man except what the officials and the media choose to relate. By one prejudicial act, law-enforcement officials and the mass media have succeeded in destroying any link of trust between that man and the rest of his society; and the destruction of that trust makes it impossible for many others to treat him like a fellow human being. It is an event of this kind that leads people to express an unwillingness to hire anyone with an arrest record, whether convicted or not.[34] It leads businesses and government agencies to refuse to hire anyone with an arrest record. This tragic situation exists within our society despite the fact that less than one-third of those arrested will be convicted.[35] The police and their supporters argue that this percentage is so low because too many legal protections of the rights of criminals prevent our system of justice from convicting those who are "really" guilty. But that is precisely the point: to the police and much of the public, arrest constitutes guilt, regardless of all the fine legal distinctions and protections.

Perhaps even more important than the immediate public stigmatization produced by arrest is the official stigmatization. One arrest catalogues a man as a permanent suspect—one who cannot be trusted—in an increasingly inclusive and efficient system of police records—the primary source of information for police operations. The record of one arrest makes a man potentially subject to police surveillance, investigations,

[34]Richard D. Schwartz and Jerome Skolnick, "Two Studies of Legal Stigma," in The Other Side: Perspectives on Deviance, ed. Howard S. Becker (New York: The Free Press, 1964).

[35]See, for example, Courtlandt C. Van Vechten, "Differential Criminal Case Mortality in Selected Jurisdictions," American Sociological Review 7 (December 1942), pp. 833–839.

roundups, and arrests on suspicion of a similar offense for the
rest of his life. The record of one arrest is publicly available
"proof" that a man cannot be trusted, that he is, indeed, a
"criminal." Even the record of an arrest for a minor traffic
violation may help to destroy a man's social position many
years later.

Because arrest and the public disclosure and documentation of arrest do have severe stigmatizing consequences,
new laws must restrict the grounds for making arrests, the
keeping and use of records of arrest, and the public announcement of arrests. Insofar as our criminal laws and legal procedures are made increasingly civil, arrest should and would
become a last resort. Rather than being arrested, an individual should be subpoenaed for a hearing. While it has no doubt
been a shock to the police and other law-enforcement officials,
the recent practice of setting minimal bail bonds or of eliminating them entirely has not led to any significant increases in
flight, even though the charge still results in all of the effects
of stigmatization and conviction will lead to severe punishment.
The use of civil procedures in place of arrest will probably
produce the same result, at least under new laws and with new
consequences. Arrests, then, should only be made when the
individual has not met the legal requirements to appear for a
hearing or has not carried out the requirements of the civil
procedure.

Regardless of the type of procedure used, the stigmatization process cannot be destroyed until the investigative procedures and the multiple forms of jeopardy based on the
permanent police records are ended. First of all, there is no
significant evidence whatsoever, other than that provided by
the police themselves, that criminal offenses are the result of
any personality factors, anything peculiar to the "substantial
self"[36] of the individual. Rather, these offenses are clearly
related to the social situations in which individuals find themselves. Secondly, the police evidence concerning recidivism

[36]See my discussion of the "substantial self" in Jack D. Douglas, *The
Social Meanings of Suicide* (Princeton: Princeton University Press, 1968).

is largely the result of the social situation—distrust, hatred, unemployment—produced by the stigmatization process. The evidence supposedly justifying the use of the record system is itself principally the result of using the record system.

Court records, certainly, are necessary to keep track of such matters as trials, decisions, and appeals. While we must examine the use of court records and carefully restrict their use by laws, it is possible that we shall want to adopt a more efficient system of identification records. It is even possible that we shall in time find that certain extreme forms of behavior, such as child molestation, are in fact repeated simply because of personality factors or situational factors unrelated to the enforcement process itself, in which case we would probably want the police to use records to keep track of such people. Also, records will have to be maintained while cases are being adjudicated and for some short period after they have been closed in the event suits are brought against the police. But the police use of a vast system of permanent records must be ended. They should be legally destroyed after that short period, and they should not be available for police investigations during that period. We must free men from their pasts, rather than officially stigmatizing them.

What must also be stopped is the public announcement of police charges against individuals and the publicity given the announcement by the mass media. Neither serves any purposes other than building the reputation of the police department and increasing the audience of the mass media. New laws must make it too costly for the police and mass media to publicize arrests. Without infringing free speech, both the police and the media must be made liable by civil suit for any damage done to the social reputations of individuals later found innocent. With most individuals found innocent, it is likely that new laws curtailing publicity on arrests would make it far too risky to endanger a man's reputation on the basis of anything but firm evidence.

The effectiveness of all these recommended changes hinges on the one most important change of all: the change from the use of imprisonment as a punishment for offenses to

the use of compensation and restitution. This fundamental reform, which would be instituted as part of the program to
change from moralistic criminal laws to rationalized civil laws,
is essential if the other needed reforms are to work. As long
as men face *any* risk of being dehumanized by being placed in
a cage for many years, and especially as long as this dehuman-
ization process is reserved almost exclusively for lower-class
individuals, there cannot possibly be any shared sense of
justice in our society. Moreover, the horror of this stigmatizing
punishment inevitably turns men into desperadoes who see the
rest of society as their enemy. If we continue to dehumanize
men by making them "public enemies," if we continue to make
it all but impossible for those men to be rehumanized, they
must continue to treat us as their enemies.

We must attack this problem at the most basic level: we
must change the effective social meanings of past offenses.
Certainly the proposals of government aid in bonding those
with "records," so that it will be possible for them to "prove"
themselves in responsible jobs, will be useful in decreasing
the feeling of risk involved in hiring persons with a police
record. But this can only be a stopgap measure. Of far more
importance, we must protect the social reputations of those
who have been previously convicted. We must make all members of society as legally liable for discrimination in housing
and employment on the basis of a "record" as we do for discrimination on the basis of religion or race or sex. Such discrimination must be subject to individual civil action for
damages and to government action to protect the individual's
rights. Legal officials must also be liable for revealing any
"records."

It is the job of the social scientists to teach the public
what we believe we have already learned: individuals who commit criminal offenses do so primarily because of the socially
defined situations which they and other members of society
construct and not because they are "evil at heart." By doing
this, we shall lay the foundation for destroying the stigmatization process. It is the job of legal officials to destroy that ancient
stigmatization process which has made all of us the victims of

the offenders' social fate. The attempts to end crime by officially institutionalizing that process have failed completely.
We must now destroy the process and transform the whole
social context within which offenses are handled if we want
to stop the vicious, spiraling relationship between stigmatization by total institutions, the resulting sense of injustice, the
resort to more crime, and the response of further increases in
tyrannical controls.

In the past century or two, imprisonment has been second
in importance only to the social meanings of "criminal" in the
stigmatization process. Yet, no single aspect of our present
legal procedures has failed more completely and more obviously than our attempts to end crime and rehabilitate criminals
by imprisonment. Imprisonment creates a thorough sense of
injustice because it is invoked erratically, arbitrarily, and un-
fairly. Imprisonment is the most depersonalizing, dehumanizing,
and cruel practice in our society. Furthermore, it almost universally forces both men and women into situational homosexuality. And, as we have become more aware of its cruelty
and irrationality, it has increasingly dehumanized us—its perpetrators.

Moreover, imprisonment, as we have noted, serves mainly
as a learning experience in criminal techniques and attitudes.
And this learning experience is so successful that the great
majority of released prisoners return one or more times. In
spite of the humanitarian goals of prison reformers, who have
sought to rehabilitate prisoners by experimenting with types of
prisons and types of therapy, most attempts at rehabilitation
have failed completely. Even though complex official statistics
are notoriously subject to manipulation—and to nourishing the
illusions of well-meaning reformers—studies of recidivism rates
have shown little change even for costly programs, where
some "Hawthorne effect" (lower rates because of the honor
of being studied) might be expected. It is absurd to believe that
any form of "therapy," which is a cooperative process that
can only be helpful under conditions of mutual trust, can work
in a situation of total mistrust between guards and their prisoners. It is equally absurd to believe that therapists are not seen

as representatives of the prison authorities. Therapists are sometimes more hated because prisoners believe therapists' reports are responsible for their not getting parole.

The failure of imprisonment has been so obvious that it has not escaped the attention of prison authorities themselves. The recognition of this failure has been a prime stimulus in accelerating the development of halfway houses which combine restraint and freedom. The restraint continues presumably because the prisoners are considered potentially dangerous to society. They live and work part-time on the outside; thus, prisonization is minimized. Retraining takes place in the natural social settings that the prisoners will be living in after "paying their debt to society." While halfway houses are certainly better than prisons, they must be viewed as stopgap measures.

In conjunction with our changing conceptions of the causes of violations, we must revise our fundamental ideas concerning the consequences for violations. As discussed earlier, moralistic punishment and imprisonment do not deter crimes but, rather, have the opposite effects of not only causing them but of locking the offenders into patterns of crime. To end this process we must discard the idea of punishment and all possibilities of prisonization. Instead, we must move rapidly toward establishing new forms of sentences more comparable to those meted out in civil suits; instead of stigmatization and imprisonment, offenders must be "sentenced" to make compensation and restitution to the victims. Compensation, or simple repayment, obviously better fits cases in which the victim is judged partially at fault and in which he experiences no personal injury; restitution, or compensation plus punitive payments for damages, better fits cases involving more individual fault or personal injury.[37] In most cases, the establishment of these new forms of sentences will be seen as more just by perpetrators and victims alike, and both will be able to avoid the terrible consequences of stigmatization and imprisonment.

[37]See Stephen Schafer, *The Victim and His Criminal* (New York: Random House, 1968).

Most Western nations already use various forms of compensation and restitution, involving as well the greater recognition of society's general liability for criminal offenses. This movement is gaining momentum in the United States, and, though social "compensation" is done under the aegis of "welfare," it is now given to victims in some cases of need in New York and California. We must accelerate this movement and generalize it so that it will cover most cases now dealt with under our criminal laws. Most resistance to this new system of justice comes not from a desire for revenge or for cruel punishments but from a belief that it will not work. When the public becomes more aware of how totally stigmatization and imprisonment have failed, it will be more receptive to compensation and restitution. If the public came to see that it is mainly the horror of imprisonment itself that forces the "wanted man" into flight to avoid prosecution and incarceration, then it would be better able to grasp the fact that compensation and restitution will work. When the public recognizes that this system not only will be far more effective in controlling offenses but will cost taxpayers far less, then its support will be vigorous. In time, we can expect that most forms of imprisonment will seem as useless and ridiculous as imprisonment for debt seems to us today.

A control system based on civil procedures for administering justice through compensation and restitution will prove all the more workable to the degree that it is combined with crime-prevention programs. Employment counseling and post-trial programs of education will be a great deal more effective when we are rid of the sense of injustice produced by present practices. In those cases in which flight does prove a problem, or in which the offender's natural situation is too conducive to committing further offenses, then halfway houses, involving minimal constraint, would prove helpful. In a very small percentage of cases it will probably be necessary to maintain a form of maximum isolation from the rest of society simply because the offender cannot be controlled by any other means. In such instances, Americans should investigate the possibilities of "banishment" in which the recalcitrant offenders are

allowed to run their own society, providing humane living conditions are maintained; banishment would absolve the rest of
us from the guilt of dehumanizing our fellow human beings.

But none of these reforms will work to better control offenses and add to our sense of justice unless law enforcement
is rationalized and simultaneously brought more directly under
the control of the public. We have already seen how the police
create a deep sense of injustice among the urban poor. We
have seen in the recent events documented by the Walker
commission report on Chicago that the police, who are themselves trapped by the present system involving moralistic laws
and imprisonment, an angry poor, and public access to guns,
are coming into increasingly bitter and open conflict with the
changing moral forces in our society.[38] As the scientific and
technological revolution speeds up, social changes will not
only intensify, they will bring the police into greater and greater
conflict with new moral forces, especially those from the educated middle class, unless the present system is rationalized.
If it is not, police power will have to be expanded even further
to overcome these new moral forces and we will inevitably
become a police-controlled society—a police state.

One of our most pressing needs is for greater access to
information on the operations of the police, who, for the most
part, now function as secret societies. Except for rare official
investigations, the police control all access to information
about their operations. Most research on the police is carefully screened. What little reliable information we have on the
police is either the result of reports by former insiders, and
these are generally harsh indeed,[39] or the occasional willingness
of individual police officials to cooperate. No man is free so long
as he is subject to investigation and seizure by police organizations that operate in secret.

All of us today are, in varying degrees, the prisoners of
our police procedures. It is a rare man who does not harbor

[38]National Commission on the Causes and Prevention of Violence, *Rights in Conflict* (New York: New American Library, 1968).
[39]See Arthur Niederhoffer, *Behind the Shield: The Police in Urban Society* (Garden City, N.Y.: Doubleday, 1967).

some sense of resentment against the police for this *open-air imprisonment*. Many of us have been shocked in recent years to learn how great and how secret the federal and local police powers are. Many millions who have openly opposed such governmental activities as the Vietnam war have fears that the F.B.I. and other agencies have secret files on them in anticipation of future investigations. Even some of the sociologists involved in research for the President's crime commission discovered how tightly the curtain of secrecy can be drawn when the public image of the federal law-enforcement authorities is endangered.

If we are to regain and protect our freedoms from the official control organizations, we must enact and enforce strong laws that guarantee total disclosure of all police operations. We must also establish autonomous investigative and control organizations, with powers equal to those of the control agencies, to carefully monitor and control the control agencies. Since freedom is avowedly our most prized possession, we must spare no cost to protect it and the penalties for infringing it must be severe indeed. Officials who progressively destroy our freedoms will always be far more dangerous to us all than the criminals who endanger our property and our personal safety. The vast majority of Americans would rather be free though unsafe than safe but unfree.

Criminal Justice
in America

ABRAHAM S. BLUMBERG

We owe an everlasting intellectual debt to Emile Durkheim for his insightful notion that crime is an inevitable feature of social structure: "Crime is normal because a society exempt from it is utterly impossible."[1] Durkheim's classic formulation provides us with a timeless sense of perspective in contemplating the meaning and pervasiveness of crime and deviance in the human situation. It also transcends the recurring hysteria epitomized in the current catchall political slogans of "crime in the streets" and "law and order."

Criminologists with an interest in history are quick to recognize that ours is not the best of times nor the worst of times in comparison with other epochs in producing criminals, assorted villains, social deviants, grim deeds of violence, murder, and genocide. While the technology available for inflicting harm upon others has expanded enormously, it is probably safer to walk the streets of an American city today than those of medieval Italy.[2] Durkheim's analysis is confirmed, inter alia, by compelling historical evidence, and it should, therefore, not surprise us that most if not all of us have violated legal norms

[1]Emile Durkheim, *The Rules of Sociological Method* (New York: The Free Press, 1964), p. 67.
[2]See William M. Bowsky, "The Medieval Commune and Internal Violence: Police Power and Public Safety in Siena, 1287–1355," *American Historical Review* 73, no. 1 (October 1967), pp. 1–17.

on more than one occasion without being labeled or officially adjudicated as delinquents and criminals.[3]

No matter which version of the official crime statistics one accepts, it is quite evident that few of us are brought to book— that is, apprehended, processed in the official enforcement and court machinery, and judged to be criminals and delinquents. Any society that committed the energy, resources, and personnel necessary to root out and punish all "wrongdoers" would create enough mass paranoia, violent conflict, and savage repression to become a charnel house before passing into oblivion. On the other hand, every society produces its quotient of crime and deviance and an accompanying apparatus to sort out those malefactors deemed most suitable for processing—usually those persons readily vulnerable to a successful labeling and adjudication procedure.[4]

The selection of suitable candidates for the adjudication process is not some version of a roulette game. On the contrary, it has fairly well-defined limits that have been traditionally imposed by the social stratification system. The "clients" served by our enforcement, court, prison, parole, and other "rehabilitation" systems are overwhelmingly drawn from the lower classes.

Modern crime may be said to occur in three broadly distinct forms, each seeming to phase into and, at times, be interlocked with the other. The most profitable form, and the one involving the least amount of risk, is *upperworld crime.* It is the least susceptible to the official enforcement machinery, and it is only rarely represented in the *Uniform Crime Reports* of the F.B.I. Upperworld crime is carefully planned, like a military campaign, in the walnut-paneled executive suites of corporations with billions of dollars in assets, in statehouses, and in country clubs. Often the criminal venture is simply thought

[3]James S. Wallerstein and Clement J. Wyle, "Our Law-Abiding Lawbreakers," *Probation* 25 (March–April 1947), pp. 107–112; Austin L. Porterfield, *Youth in Trouble* (Fort Worth: Leo Potishman Foundation, 1946).

[4]Kai T. Erikson, *Wayward Puritans* (New York: John Wiley & Sons, 1966); Howard S. Becker, *Outsiders: Studies in the Sociology of Deviance* (New York: The Free Press, 1963).

of by the participants as shrewd business strategy calculated to produce a greater profit or to perform a "real service" for the consumer, the voter, or some other constituency—not infrequently at their expense. "The Great Electrical Conspiracy" involving General Electric and Westinghouse, among others; the peculations of Billie Sol Estes and the activities of the corporate and federal officials without whose help he could not have succeeded in stealing millions; the cunning of tax evaders and the chicanery of some who put money in Swiss banks; the frauds and larceny connected with the federal highway program; and the drug scandals are but a few examples of the exorbitantly profitable criminal activities that take place at the upperworld level.[5] Enforcement agencies, the Food and Drug Administration, the Antitrust Division, among others, are relatively feeble and often ineffectual in dealing with the social harm ultimately inflicted by these white-collar criminals, and their prosecution is far from being an ordinary occurrence.

Related to upperworld crime is *organized crime;* the ties between the two are especially close in the sphere of politics where the political machine often acts as business broker between the two. Local political machines, which ordinarily control local police and court officials, afford the protection organized crime requires in order to function. Its activities cut across state lines and national boundaries and range from legitimate enterprises, such as labor unions, to those catering to appetites and pursuits forbidden by penal codes—gambling, usury, drugs, pornography, and prostitution. Unfortunately, little except surmise and conjecture is known about organized crime and organized criminals—except that they are seldom grist

[5]See Richard Austin Smith, "The Incredible Electrical Conspiracy," *Fortune* 63 (April 1961), pp. 132–137, and (May 1961), pp. 161–164. See also Fred J. Cook, *The Corrupted Land* (New York: Macmillan, 1966), for a detailed account of some of these examples of upperworld crime. Also, Gustavus Myers, *Great American Fortunes* (New York: Modern Library, 1936), and Matthew Josephson, *The Robber Barons* (New York: Harcourt, Brace & World, 1962), for further illustrations of upperworld crime committed in the accumulation of some of America's most respected fortunes. Also, Walter Goodman, *All Honorable Men* (Boston: Little, Brown, 1963), and John G. Fuller, *The Gentlemen Conspirators* (New York: Grove Press, 1962).

for the processing mill of the conventional police, the prosecutor's office, and the local courts.

The third and least honorific form of crime is often the
least remunerative, the least protected; it is committed mostly
by lower-strata persons because of their limited range of skills
and circumscribed options for action. Except for some confidence men and other professional-career criminals whose
activities may bring them into contact with upperworld and
organized criminals, the crimes of the lower classes are of the
commonplace variety ranging from shoplifting to armed robbery
and homicide. It is usually the most visible kind of criminal
activity and, in this sense, it can be termed *visible crime;* as
such, it is the most vulnerable to the official instruments of law
enforcement. For example, one-third of all arrests in America
are for some version of the prosaic charge of "drunkenness"
or "public intoxication," the usual variations being "drunk in a
public place," "drunk and disorderly," or an old favorite, "drunk
and resisting arrest." Violations committed by the lower classes
constitute the great bulk of crimes duly reported in the annual
Uniform Crime Reports.

In summary, our enforcement and court bureaucracies are
in large measure organized and geared to detecting, sorting
out, and adjudicating the kinds of crimes and delinquencies
most often and most visibly engaged in by the socially marginal
strata.[6] That fact produces serious consequences for the criminal-justice system in America and for those unfortunate enough
to be caught up in it.

As Walter Schaefer some time ago pointed out, "the quality of a nation's civilization can be largely measured by the
methods it uses in the enforcement of its criminal law."[7] By this
yardstick, today's system of criminal justice in America is
symptomatic of the impoverishment of our quality of life. The
grievances of the minority poor in our urban slums, which

[6]L. P. Tiffany, D. M. McIntyre, Jr., D. L. Rotenberg, *Detection of Crime*
(Boston: Little, Brown, 1967); Donald J. Newman, *Conviction* (Boston: Little,
Brown, 1966).
[7]Walter V. Schaefer, "Federalism and State Criminal Procedure," *Harvard
Law Review* 70, no. 1 (November 1956), p. 26.

precipitate civil disorders and riots, are often exacerbated by the very governmental institutions intended to serve them. The role of the police, for example, as a pressure in the lives of the poor has often been cited. But too little has been said about the oppressive features of other aspects of the criminal process —especially the criminal courts where many believe they cannot find justice. Nor can those outside the slums afford to be smug about this situation, for the same functionaries and adjudication agencies not infrequently subject members of the vast middle strata of America to strikingly similar treatment. The enforcement and adjudication process in our criminal-justice system boils down to this: intolerably large case loads, which must be disposed of by an organizational bureaucracy of limited resources, are encouraging police, prosecution, and court personnel to be concerned largely with strategies that lead to a guilty plea. Because our system of justice has become almost totally committed to the disposing of cases without trial, the due process idea of justice for most people simply no longer exists.

The Bronx County Bar Association not too long ago condemned our "mass assembly-line justice" that "was rushing defendants into pleas of guilty and into convictions in violation of their legal rights." And recently, a most frank, revealing, and damning statement about the largest criminal court system in America, New York City's, appeared in The New York Times:

> The life of a Criminal Court judge has been described as "generally degrading" and the system of justice has been condemned as "dehumanizing" by one of the city's newest judges, former License Commissioner Joel L. Tyler.

> "You sit on that bench," Judge Tyler said, "and you get this terrible sense that you can't help anyone who could be helped. Sometimes you look at a young man or woman and you feel that if someone could really get hold of them maybe something good could come of their lives.

> "But the system is just too big, the individual is nothing, the lawyers are ciphers and the judge turns out to be a virtual mechanic more often than not."

In the course of a two-hour interview, Judge Tyler criticized the handling of narcotics addicts ("It's fantastic, crazy—we march them into the sea like lemmings"); the lawyers for the Legal Aid Society, who handle most arraignments ("They don't fight hard enough"); and the facilities of some of the parts of the Criminal Court ("The traffic courts are a disgrace; the Brooklyn Criminal Court is a rat hole").

After a couple of weeks in Traffic Court, Judge Tyler was assigned to what is known as the "backup part" in Manhattan Criminal Court, at 100 Centre Street. A backup part is a small room behind the large courtroom.

It doubles as a robing room for judges, and such violations as prostitution and public drunkenness are often tried there.

"When I got there I knew I was going to quit," the judge said. "A dirty little 2 by 4 room, hot as hell—imagine trying a criminal case in a place like that. . . ."

But Judge Tyler said that the frustrations of his job went far deeper than the lack of proper physical facilities.

"First," he said, "you get so many cases stacked up you don't have time to really consider the individual.

"At arraignment you may have a minute with each person. Most of them are narcotics addicts, and if you let them go, you know they will be right back on the stuff. If you hold them on bail—most don't make it—they are thrown eventually into a program that is of doubtful value. . . ."

Does he have any hope for the administration of criminal justice here?

"Not much, but enough to kick about it," he said. "The older judges, some of them, tell me that they started like I did, mad as hell, wanting to reform things, but finally they realized you can't beat the system. When I get to that point I'll hand in my papers."[8]

Defendants in our criminal courts can expect, at best, to be given short shrift (three- to five-minute hearings are the

[8]The New York Times, August 25, 1968, p. 26.

norm), to be treated perfunctorily or even with arrogant harshness. Administrative ingenuity has been hard-pressed to resolve an almost irreconcilable conflict: between the intense pressures to process large numbers of cases on the one hand and the stringent ideological and legal requirements of due process of law on the other hand. To meet production requirements in our criminal courts, a tenuous resolution of the dilemma has emerged: a variety of bureaucratically ordained and controlled shortcuts, deviations, and outright violations of the rules are employed by all court personnel, ranging from lawyers and prosecutors to probation officers and judges. Fearfully anticipating criticism on ethical as well as legal grounds, all the significant participants in the court's structure are bound into an organized system of complicity. The rhetoric of official rules governing the behavior of police, prosecutors, judges, and probation officials is not a reliable guide to their actual behavior, which consists of patterned, covert, and informal evasions of due process in order to meet production requirements.[9]

The meticulous rules of due process are designed to render justice to every man. Drawn from the painful experience of history, they constitute the bedrock of procedural measures calculated to protect individuals from oppressive government, from each other, and from ruthless officialdom. The rules include, among other provisions, a presumption of innocence and a truly adversary proceeding, in the course of which an accused person, assisted by counsel, receives a full, fair, and open judicial hearing or trial. The hearing must be a real one, not a show or a contrived pretense. The proceedings from arrest to sentencing must be free from any taint of coercion or threat, no matter how delicate or benign these may appear. For the police, the prosecutor, and the criminal court judge, however, the rules of due process introduce elements of contingency and uncertainty. Enforcement agents, therefore, tend to rework these rules for organizationally prescribed ends that

[9]Abraham S. Blumberg, *Criminal Justice* (Chicago: Quadrangle Books, 1967); Jerome H. Skolnick, *Justice Without Trial* (New York: John Wiley & Sons, 1966); Aaron V. Cicourel, *The Social Organization of Juvenile Justice* (New York: John Wiley & Sons, 1968).

will reduce the elements of chance, of contingency, of failure in their respective work milieus, consistent with the dominant bureaucratic values of efficiency, high production, and the maximization of individual careers.

The word "bureaucracy" is not used as a word of opprobrium, but is employed in its technical sense to mean the harnessing of men, skills, and resources in order to produce the goods and services we want. Bureaucratization is a universal trend; we could not produce a Chevrolet or an aspirin without it. Some of the characteristics of a bureaucracy are: centralized control of the means of production; diffusion of responsibility and the division of work into specialties; the downgrading of the individual (the skills hired are of greater significance than the person possessing them); the cult of efficiency or the submission to higher authority (a bureaucrat carries out his orders in conformance with set policies and work routines—although not always enthusiastically); and secrecy (most of the decision-making process is shielded from outside view). Yet, the very nature of these fundamental features of a bureaucracy dooms due process in our criminal courts and tends to compromise it in the enforcement procedure. Overcentralization produces means to an end and the means become ends in themselves (efficiency for the sake of efficiency, production for the sake of production); workaday treatment of clients that the bureaucracy is supposed to serve leads to buck-passing ("Who is in charge here?"); the relative insulation from the electorate of court officials—prosecutors, judges, career civil servants—breeds arrogance. All these factors, together with the behind-the-door practice of making decisions, contribute to the sordid state of our criminal process.

Much of our process of criminal justice is not only cloaked in secrecy, it is imbued with myths. And one of the most persistent myths is that "ours is the accusatorial as opposed to the inquisitorial system." Our great commitment of resources, however, is invested in the prosecution, with virtually none for the defense. This one fact overrides the accusatorial elements and converts the system into an inquisitorial model. The burden of proof is said to be on the state to procure independent evidence to establish an individual's guilt; we therefore proudly claim to have rejected all methods of coercion, be they subtle or savage, in securing convictions.

Another myth is that the system of bargain justice, or pleading guilty to a lesser charge—"plea copping," or what I prefer to call "justice by negotiation"—meets the standards of due process of law because the defendant freely and willingly admits his guilt in open court. Still another myth is that judges are not part of the bargain-plea process, that they are not aggressively involved in procuring pleas. Most Americans also believe that the policing, prosecuting, judging, evaluating, and defending functions are haphazardly decentralized and do not have any firm interconnection; that, too, is a myth. The most damaging myth—most damaging, certainly, to naïve defendants—is that criminal lawyers are engaged, within the context of an adversary proceeding, in *defending* clients. Finally, the myth endures that probation and psychiatry, as "helping" professions in the court setting, serve both the defendant and the court organization by furnishing objective, impartial evaluations and reports.

Bargain justice has become the central feature of our criminal-justice process because it is cheap, administratively convenient, and meets the needs of bureaucracy to appear efficient in dealing with an impossible work load. Guilty pleas save time, expense, and wear and tear on everyone involved —the police, the prosecutors, the judges, and the lawyers. Equally important, the high conviction rate produces a favorable public image for the police, prosecutors, and judges. The defense lawyer seems to have earned his fee, having apparently snatched his client from a more severe fate, and the client—the defendant—has been rewarded for "cooperating" by being allowed to plead to a lesser charge. Of course, initially the police and prosecutor have deliberately "overcharged" him in order to assure that he is able ultimately to plead guilty to something; any given offense may give rise to a multiplicity of charges, ranging from serious felonies to minor misdemeanors. The ultimate charge, then, to which a defendant pleads, is the critical fulcrum of the bargaining

process. Everyone, in other words, including the guilty defendant, can wring benefits even from so coercive and impersonal a system as bargain justice.

But what of the individual who may be innocent? What
of the innocent defendant enmeshed in a court structure largely
organized around processing an impossible case load toward
guilty pleas? He usually fares no better than the guilty. Any
bureaucratic organization is judged in terms of its output; its
future budgets are dependent upon output. It is for that reason
that many of our metropolitan courts have become assembly
lines that process virtually all their cases—some as high as
90 per cent—toward some sort of plea. The innocent, faced
with the same prosecution and court structure of a crushing
calendar and limited resources, is in an extremely hazardous
position. Our assembly-line system is one of "justice without
trial" characterized by a negation of innocence with everyone
caught up in it perceived to be guilty of some crime.

Police, prosecution, courts, and other agencies of criminal
law enforcement are not truth-seeking clinics. These agencies
create a work environment for themselves that is comfortable
and responsive to the universal need of all bureaucracies: to
appear omniscient and omnipotent. Far too often, whenever
the needs of the client conflict with those of the bureaucracy
and its functionaries, it is the organization's needs and priorities that prevail. The American system of bargain justice
is a contrived, synthetic, and perfunctory substitute for real
justice. It has no universal standards of justice beyond the
thin shell of legalism that protects all its participants from
appellate review. Its routine procedures and methods readily
lend themselves to favoritism, venality, coercion, arbitrariness,
and total disregard for the rights of the individual. What passes
for full, fair, and open hearings are the superficial and hasty
negotiation sessions over the defendant's fate conducted in
secret by his court representative and the prosecutor, sessions
in which the reasons for the final guilty plea are forever
shrouded in mystery and, consequently, are rarely subject to
review. We have no way of knowing what criteria were employed for determining the plea and the sentence, for determining the operative, critical variables in each case. We

have no way of knowing by whom these criteria were employed and for what purpose, beyond the often self-serving statements of the court officials that appear as part of the public court record at the time the plea is made. Too often plea and sentence are contingent upon how enmeshed the defense lawyer is in the organizational fabric of the court—the extent of his "influence" and "fixing" ability. Too often the defendant who has "cooperated" with the system is the one who fares best.[10] And too often, the entire system is politically manipulated, especially that part of it pertaining to the lucrative bail-bond business which enriches the bondsmen and their political sponsors while victimizing the poor and the socially unpopular.[11]

The rules of due process as expanded and strengthened by the United States Supreme Court—the right to counsel, the right to remain silent, the limitations on confessions—are predicated on the existence of an adversary system of criminal justice. The rules envision a "combative" procedural system wherein the prosecuting and defense attorneys will clash in the arena of a courtroom and, after the dust has settled, the data that determine guilt or innocence will have emerged. Unfortunately, this model system of criminal justice does not exist. It is based on the erroneous assumption that the accused will ultimately have "his day in court." He rarely does. What actually happens is that all the agencies in our system of criminal justice—from the police to the judge—are going through the motions of readying a case for trial that seldom occurs. In most communities, only about 6 per cent of criminal cases at the felony level ever go to trial. The rest are bargain-plea cases.

Any systematic examination of the workings of our criminal-justice system must begin with the police, for it is the police who have become the most critical and perhaps even

[10]Abraham S. Blumberg, "The Practice of Law as a Confidence Game," *Law and Society Review* 1, no. 2 (June 1967), pp. 15–39.
[11]See Ronald Goldfarb, *Ransom: A Critique of the American Bail System* (New York: Harper & Row, 1965), for an excellent analysis of the manner in which an archaic bail system corrupts and often defeats the possibility of justice.

the most powerful component of the enforcement and adjudication structure. The police, the prosecutor's office, and the
grand jury serve as the three initial screening organizations
through which a criminal case is sifted; not one of them provides much real protection for an accused person because their
standards for proof of guilt—designed primarily to push the
case along to the next step in the screening process—are
minimal and rather superficial.[12] Most of us do not fully grasp
the implications of the awesome power possessed by the police in using their discretion to make an arrest. Even in a simple
situation involving a defendant of modest means, who may
ultimately be exonerated, it can cause the loss of a job, a
period of detention, the indignities of fingerprinting and being
photographed, psychic pain, and, finally, the expenditure of
hundreds of dollars for a bail bond and a lawyer. Indeed,
arrest itself is a form of summary punishment. And this power
of arrest is all the more disquieting when it is realized that
approximately 50 per cent of all criminal cases are screened
out of the judicial process at the preliminary arraignment as
not meriting further attention.[13]

The discretionary power of the average patrolman on
matters involving crime and justice in our society is greater
than that exercised by any judge in any courtroom in the
United States. In a recent Chicago study conducted in connection with a legal-services program for youthful offenders
it was established that out of 500 arrest situations the police
had arrested only 100 persons and finally presented a total of
40 cases for possible court action. The criteria employed by
the police in reaching a decision on which persons were
proper subjects for arrest and processing are known only to
the police. The net result of this situation is that police perform
important judicial functions in many more instances than do

[12]Abraham S. Goldstein, "The State and the Accused: Balance of Advantage in Criminal Procedure," *Yale Law Journal* 69 (June 1960), pp. 1148–1199.
[13]The President's Commission on Law Enforcement and Administration of
Justice (hereafter cited as President's Commission), *The Challenge of Crime in
a Free Society* (Washington, D.C., United States Government Printing Office,
1967), p. 133.

our judges.[14] That, of course, is the critical variable which is the source of tension, resentment, confrontation and violence occurring between the police and other groups in our society. No other professional group in America, whose formal training is so limited and whose qualifications are often so problematic, is granted the immense latitude and discretion the police have in dealing with the lives and welfare of people.

In exercising his discretion, the policeman simply reflects the social attitudes and the racial and ethnic biases of the larger, middle-class white community. These social opinions and perspectives are manifested by the aggressive conduct of police toward young people whom they often consider "hoods";[15] by a treatment of Negroes so hostile that it has, on occasion, become the catalytic agent for race riots;[16] by their victimization of slum dwellers and a tendency to use excessive force and violence in dealing with lower-class men, white or black;[17] and by acting as self-righteous, self-appointed petty tyrants among the alcoholic and derelict residents of skid row.[18] These are just some examples of the working style of police in their exercise of discretion.[19]

[14]Norval Morris, "Politics and Pragmatism in Crime Control," *Federal Probation* (June 1968), pp. 9–16; Arthur L. Stinchcombe, "Institutions of Privacy in the Determination of Police Administrative Practice," *American Journal of Sociology* 69, no. 2 (September 1963), pp. 150–160.

[15]Irving Piliavin and Scott Briar, "Police Encounters with Juveniles," *Americal Journal of Sociology* 69 (September 1964), pp. 206–214.

[16]Robert Conot, *Rivers of Blood, Years of Darkness* (New York: Bantam Books, 1967); Stanley Lieberson and Arnold R. Silverman, "Precipitants and Conditions of Race Riots," *American Sociological Review* 30, no. 6 (December 1965), pp. 887–898.

[17]Albert J. Reiss, Jr., "Police Brutality—Answers to Key Questions," *Transaction* 5, no. 8 (July–August 1968), pp. 10–19.

[18]Egon Bittner, "The Police on Skid-Row: A Study of Peace Keeping," *American Sociological Review* 32, no. 5 (October 1967), pp. 699–715.

[19]For detailed discussions of the impact and consequences of police discretion, see Joseph Goldstein, "Police Discretion Not to Invoke the Criminal Process: Low-Visibility Decisions in the Administration of Justice," *Yale Law Journal* 69 (March 1960), pp. 543–594; William A. Westley, "Violence and the Police," *American Journal of Sociology* 59 (July 1953), pp. 34–41; Egon Bittner, "Police Discretion in Emergency Apprehension of Mentally Ill Persons," *Social*

The often unsupervised conduct of the police affords them the opportunity to usurp the other roles in the criminal process —prosecutor, jury, judge, and, sometimes, even executioner. Police and prosecution were once bound by a constitutional arrest standard of "probable cause"—a reasonable belief that a crime has been committed and that the accused is the perpetrator. Though even probable cause as an arrest standard is not enough evidence to establish guilt, police and prosecution today seldom observe the demanding due process requirement of probable cause. The standard is thought by police to threaten their "efficiency" and as a consequence they often perfect strategies that evade the rules and support their charge.[20]

State legislatures, taking cognizance of the fact that police were not observing the standard of probable cause anyway, passed the "stop and frisk" legislation that established the much lower standard of "reasonable suspicion" as a basis for interrogating persons in the street. When a policeman reasonably believes that he is in danger, he now has the authority to stop and frisk anyone for a possible weapon. Thus state laws, subsequently upheld by the United States Supreme Court, have given the police statutory comfort and support for that which they were doing anyway when they were evading the rules of probable cause. It is particularly noteworthy that the President's Commission on Law Enforcement and Administration of Justice indicated in its report that the stop-and-frisk power is employed by the police primarily against the inhabitants of our urban slums, against racial minorities, and against the underprivileged. Police will make "field interrogations" of persons, the commission found, simply because their clothing, hair, gait, or other mannerisms squared with preconceived

Problems 14 (Winter 1967), pp. 278–292; Herman Goldstein, "Police Discretion: The Ideal Versus the Real," *Public Administration Review* 23 (September 1963), pp. 140–148; Richard C. Donnelly, "Police Authority and Practices," *Annals* 339 (January 1962), pp. 90–110. Ed Cray, *The Big Blue Line* (New York: Coward-McCann, 1967), is especially critical of police malpractice.

[20]Skolnick, *Justice Without Trial,* chap. 10.

police notions of who is "suspicious"—quite often, blacks.[21] The police practice of illegal arrests on "suspicion" or for "investigation" rather than probable cause was fairly widespread prior to the passage of stop-and-frisk legislation, especially in neighborhoods inhabited by the poor and racial minorities.[22] Most of these arrests—about 300,000 a year—are made either as a fishing expedition or as part of an "aggressive patrol" tactic to demonstrate police "rep" and "muscle." And most of them terminate without any formal charge being brought.

A police manual of instructions on how to frisk merits recording. The subject of a police search, which usually takes place in public, is told to stand facing a wall with his hands raised. Then: "The officer must feel with sensitive fingers every portion of the prisoner's body. A thorough search must be made of the prisoner's arms and armpits, waistline and back, the groin and area about the testicles, the entire surface of the legs down to the feet."[23] No "petty indignity" or "minor intrusion" this—which may now be employed by any policeman in the United States suddenly in the throes of "reasonable" suspicion. Any policeman at any time may feel that he is in danger, and anyone at any time may be stopped and frisked. Having been given this authority, police now possess virtually unlimited power over the lives of the rest of us. As Justice William O. Douglas, the lone dissenter in the High Court's stop-and-frisk decision, said: "To give the police greater power than a magistrate is to take a long step down the totalitarian path. . . . If the individual is no longer to be sovereign, if the police can pick him up whenever they do not like the cut of his jib, if they can 'seize' and 'search' him in their discretion, we enter a new regime."[24]

[21]The President's Commission, *Task Force Report: The Police* (Washington, D.C.: United States Government Printing Office, 1967), pp. 178–185; see also C. A. Reich, "Police Questioning of Law-abiding Citizens," *Yale Law Journal* 75 (June 1966), p. 1161.

[22]Arnold S. Trebach, *The Rationing of Justice* (New Brunswick: Rutgers University Press, 1964), pp. 4–6.

[23]Terry v. Ohio 391 U.S. 1 (1968).

[24]Ibid.

A significant portion of the criminal law pertains to the regulation of sexual appetites, gambling, and drugs. Action taken by police in regard to all three depends upon the state of pressures placed upon their department, from within and from without. Like any other bureaucracy, the police are under constant pressure—sometimes self-induced—to justify their budget. No argument for public funds is more persuasive than a battery of bureaucratic statistics, which, valid or not, also have a way of offsetting anticipated criticisms. As an illustration, in August 1967 the New York City Police Department, always sensitive to the fluctuations of the public's pulse on matters of morality, rounded up more than 2,500 prostitutes on charges of "loitering"—prostitution, under the new state penal law, being no longer a crime but a "violation," an offense of a very minor order. Since it is not a crime simply to "loiter" to commit an act of prostitution, the arrests were considered by the judge who dismissed the charges as "illegal and made in violation of the mandate of the loitering statute and in violation of the rights of all the defendants." A police spokesman indicated at the time that to arrest for a "violation" would be "unprofitable and uneconomic"; nevertheless, the incident points up the extent to which a large urban police force will go to demonstrate "activity." Bureaucratic values of "efficiency" tend to override the human values involved—even when those human values happen to be supported by the Constitution. Too often the character of police enforcement becomes a function of private police morality, bureaucratic concerns of meeting production quotas, and an appearance of providing maximum services for the tax dollar.

Police departments do, of course, lay an incredible emphasis on "activity," on "batting averages" or the number of "collars." And one reason why they do so is because "activity" is a yardstick to measure eligibility for promotion or assignment to less onerous duties. Not surprisingly, in the frantic and often feverish milieu in which police work is performed, mistakes are made. In December 1967, 100 peaceful demonstrators were arrested in New York City, interrogated, and photographed before they were released from custody without charges—all as a result of what was later described by a police official as an "honest mistake" in identifying the group arrested. Victor Rosario will never forget another mistake. Arrested on an assault charged by his common-law wife and her lover, he was packed off to Bellevue and subsequently to Matteawan State Hospital for the Criminally Insane where he spent four years because he told a bizarre story to the police, the prosecution, the judge, and the psychiatrists: that he had seen his wife's lover drink his own blood mixed with beer in order to prove he was more manly than Rosario. Because no one took the time to verify the facts, Rosario was consigned to the madhouse. At the very least, the concept of "machismo" —concern with preserving manliness in Puerto Rican culture —should have alerted police, prosecution, judge, and psychiatrists to the possibility of truth in Rosario's explanation for the assault.[25] Efforts to maintain organizational equilibrium amidst the stresses from without and within, together with the usual production and "efficiency" requirements of a bureaucracy, produce a work style on the part of police that compromises their objectivity and capacity for fact-finding.

Not only does the pressure for quotas and activity cause mistakes, the entire system of assembly-line justice engenders a defensiveness on the part of the police, prosecution, and criminal courts. Together they represent a closed community manifesting a hostile attitude toward "outsiders" and "critics." It is the police, however, who are the most visible, and it is their actions and their conduct that make them the greatest crystallizers of public opinion about our law-enforcement system, particularly among those in the poorer classes. As the report of the National Advisory Commission on Civil Disorders put it:

> The policeman in the ghetto is a symbol not only of law, but of the entire system of law enforcement and criminal justice. As such, he becomes the tangible target for grievances against shortcomings throughout the system. Against assembly-line justice in teeming lower

[25]Thomas S. Szasz, *Law, Liberty and Psychiatry* (New York: Macmillan, 1963), pp. 166–168.

courts; against wide disparities in sentences; against antiquated correctional facilities; against the basic inequities imposed by the system on the poor—to whom, for example, the option of bail means only jail. The policeman in the ghetto is a symbol of increasingly bitter social debate over law enforcement.[26]

The district attorney's office is the organization with which the police conduct most of their official business, other than appearing as a complainant or witness in court. Acting as a sort of law teacher and guide to the police, prosecutors tend to interpose their own knowledge and expertise between the police and the court. Frequently police, in their zeal, overcharge a particular defendant; it is the district attorney's office that formulates the policeman's raw data into more legally cohesive and logical complaints.

All district attorney offices have bureaucratic characteristics similar to those of the police: commitments to maximum production, the cult of efficiency, the ever-present batting average. And these are characteristics that depersonalize defendants. In the quality of their personnel and performance, all D.A. offices run the gamut from the brilliant to the mediocre; in the main, however, the quality is merely adequate. One New York City assistant district attorney, in a rather revealing statement before the United States Supreme Court, summed up the situation in many of the nation's prosecution offices. In explaining to the justices how it was that a narcotics defendant had pleaded guilty and had served a sentence even though his arrest and conviction were illegal, the assistant district attorney declared: "I have a very humiliating confession to make—ours is a large office. . . . [It was] a run-of-the-mill case that got lost in the shuffle." Unfortunately, to the personnel of most district attorney offices, all too many cases are run-of-the-mill.

Since most defendants are poor, approximately 70 per cent of the entire criminal court case load involves persons who are legally indigent and who must be helped by the Legal Aid Society. But even the privately represented defendant has

[26]Report of the National Advisory Commission on Civil Disorders (New York: Bantam Books, 1968), p. 299.

little more in the way of resources that would help him. Private investigations by the defense to obtain supportive factual or medical or psychiatric data are not only expensive, they are almost impossible to obtain. The state spends money to assist the prosecution, not the defense. At the outset, therefore, the advantage of presentation in a case is weighted heavily in favor of the prosecution—a circumstance that makes plea bargaining inevitable, if not mandatory, for almost all defendants.

Plea bargaining occurs between the defendant and his counsel on the one side and three different divisions of our law-enforcement system on the other: the district attorney's office, the judge's office, and, if it has been called upon to investigate the defendant prior to his pleading, the probation department. Ordinarily, the office of the prosecution has a crude index as to what a particular case is "worth" based on such diverse variables as how easily the charges can be proved beyond a reasonable doubt, how much harm the complainant has suffered, what the restitution possibilities are, and how long the yellow sheet (rap sheet or prior record) of the accused is. There is also one overriding dimension that is seldom discussed and that has to do with fads and fashions in crime— what offenses are currently more opprobrious than others. In short, does this case merit special attention? Is it worth a great deal in terms of publicity?[27] Thus, for example, drug offenses at times will be treated lightly; deemed to be worth little, law-enforcement officials will permit lesser pleas in connection with selling and possessing drugs. But, should there be a public furor over narcotics, then drug cases appreciate greatly in terms of plea bargaining. Bargaining a charge of rape, to cite another example, usually depends on the circumstances of the case and how much, if any, publicity it has received; ordinarily the defendant is allowed to plead guilty to the lesser charge of assault, which carries less severe penalties and obviates public disgrace. Regardless of the variables involved, the plea that is accepted is one currently regarded as afford-

[27]See David Sudnow, "Normal Crimes: Sociological Features of the Penal Code in a Public Defender Office," *Social Problems* 12 (Winter 1965), pp. 255–276.

ing an "adequate scope of punishment." This is the imprecise criterion on which our system of bargain justice in criminal cases is based.

A defendant's ultimate desire for a negotiated plea may simply be attributed to the decline of our jury system. Whatever that system's merits or drawbacks, the fact is that defendants shun a jury trial because juries are notoriously conviction prone.[28] The outcome of any jury trial often turns on the question of whom a jury will believe—the assertions of law-enforcement officials and their witnesses, or the accused and his witnesses; the answer, with frequent regularity is: the police and those offering testimony in their behalf. This predilection of juries lies at the root of an accused's reluctance to risk a jury trial, even though Americans like to emphasize that all individuals have a right to a trial. And ironically, despite the fact that Americans do indeed consider the right to a jury trial a central feature of their system of jurisprudence,[29] if the accused pleads guilty—thereby forgoing a trial—the prosecution and defense will often remind the judge, by way of mitigating the sentence, that the accused has not caused the state to go to the expense of a time-consuming trial. On the other hand, the defendant who has been convicted in a trial receives rather less generous treatment than one who has negotiated, and his chances of receiving probation are virtually nil.

A further weapon employed by the prosecution to make an accused person think twice about a jury trial is the multiple-count indictment. A single act may subject an individual to several criminal charges. A bargain plea, however, eliminates all the risks of a jury trial while reducing the original multiple charges to somewhat less serious offenses.

[28] In New York's criminal courts, for example, only about 5 per cent of all cases went to trial by jury between 1950 and 1964. Of these jury-tried cases, conviction rates ranged from a low of about 70 per cent annually to a high of about 92 per cent. The same high percentages continued in the 1964-to-1969 period.

[29] In Duncan v. Louisiana 391 U.S. 145 (1968), the Supreme Court expanded the right to trial by jury at the state level, indicating that even in cases of "serious misdemeanors" trial by jury is an essential feature of due process of law and cannot be dispensed with in the American scheme of justice.

The prosecutor has still other coercive devices at his disposal. He is usually able to control the pace with which a case moves through the judicial mill, and has a good deal of discretion and influence in connection with bail practices. Dangling the alternative of jail or bail is another means of softening up a defendant for the bargain process—as anyone who has spent time in the crowded jails of any city will attest. The prosecutor can also exert pressure on a defendant simply because he has the option to prosecute or not to prosecute, and also because it is a matter of his discretion alone whether a lesser plea is accepted or whether it is not. In addition, the prosecution has a rather awesome advantage in exercising its prerogative of "calendaring"—making sure that certain cases go before certain judges. The use of the court calendar to determine which judge gets which case is often the critical factor in how a defendant fares.

These are the obvious pressures available to the prosecutor. However, he possesses informal and latent resources in the nature of allies and agents who seek many of the same goals he seeks. These are the judges, defense lawyers, court psychiatrists, and probation officials whose formal and informal relations with him have greater claims on how he fulfills his duties than that of any particular defendant. Accused persons come and go in the court system, but its structure and its personnel are relatively permanent. Any individual stridencies, tensions, and conflicts provoked by a particular case must be overcome and good relations preserved at all costs. The defendant, then, is a secondary factor in the prosecutor's office.

As for the judge, who will be discussed in more detail shortly, he also acquires a vested interest in a high rate of negotiated pleas, despite the fact that he is required to be impartial and committed to preserving the rights of all offenders. He shares the prosecutor's earnest desire to avoid the time-consuming, expensive, and unpredictable adversary trial. He, too, sees an impossible backlog of cases with their mounting delays as possible public evidence of his inefficiency and failure as an administrator as well as a judge. A bargain plea of guilty so easily enables him to envision the accused as an already repentant individual who has not only "learned his lesson" but deserves more lenient treatment for not causing the fuss of a trial.

The defense lawyer, whether of the "legal-aid" variety or privately retained, is also ultimately concerned with strategies leading to a bargain plea. It is the impersonal elements involving the economics of time, labor, and expense, together with his commitment to the court organization, that win the allegiance of most defense attorneys, not the needs of the accused. These defense lawyer "regulars" of the criminal courts are frequently former staff members of the prosecutor's office, and they utilize their know-how and their contacts with former colleagues to effect bargain justice.

An accused and his kin, as well as others outside the court community, are unable to apprehend the nature and dimensions of the close and continuing relations between the lawyer "regular" and the prosecutor's office. Their camaraderie is based on real professional and organizational needs of a quid pro quo. The adversary features that may be manifested in this procedural relationship are for the most part muted and exist, even in an attenuated form, almost entirely for external consumption. The principals—defense lawyer and assistant district attorney—rely upon one another's cooperation for their continued professional existence, and so the differences and the bargaining between them are usually "reasonable" rather than real or fierce.[30] Any defense attorney has an ongoing "account"—an unwritten ledger of favors received and returned—with the prosecutor's office that he can draw upon from time to time in order to meet the exigencies posed by a particular case. In many instances, the legal-aid group in the court can negotiate a comparatively fair plea for an indigent defendant because of the close relationship between the group and the prosecutor's office.

The defense lawyer in the criminal court is, in effect, a double agent: he performs an extremely vital and delicate

[30]Arthur Lewis Wood, *Criminal Lawyer* (New Haven: College University Press, 1967).

mission for both the court organization and the accused. He ties the entire criminal-justice system together—and makes it more palatable for the defendant. He assumes different roles at different stages in his client's case, using them all alternately and sometimes in combination. The real professional is a consummate actor who at the preliminary stages of a criminal case will make every conceivable legal motion and use every conceivable legal opportunity to demolish the prosecutor's case. Beyond the preliminary stages, his options become much more limited and his role changes to that of negotiator or fixer —the man of influence with access to the seats of power, the possessor of secret knowledge, the path-smoother who at the same time must begin to "cool out" his client in case of defeat.

To understand how a defense attorney's fees are fixed and collected is to understand his role in a criminal case. The problem of fixing and collecting the fee significantly influences the criminal-court process itself, and not just the relationship between the lawyer and his client. In essence, a lawyer-client confidence game is played. In varying degrees, all law practice involves a manipulation of the client and a stage management of the lawyer-client relationship so that at least the *appearance* of help and service will be registered. The basic vendible commodity of the defense counsel is presumed access to secret knowledge and the seats of power and influence.[31] This lack of a visible product offers a special complication to the criminal lawyer with respect to his fee and in his relations with his client. The relationship is further complicated, of course, because the hostility generated within the accused as a consequence of his arrest, incarceration, possible loss of a job, and other traumas connected with his case is directed, by means of displacement, toward his lawyer. Therefore, because his defense "services" are intangible, because most defendants are not only poor but likely to be singularly unappreciative if sentenced to jail, the criminal lawyer collects his fee in *advance*. And in recognition of the defense lawyer's crucial role in helping dispose of the

[31] See Jerome E. Carlin, *Lawyers' Ethics* (New York: Russell Sage Foundation, 1966).

court case load, judges and prosecutors will cooperate with him in many important ways, but particularly in helping him collect his fee. For example, they will agree to adjourn the case of an accused in jail awaiting plea or sentence if the attorney requests such action. While explicitly this may be done for some innocuous or seemingly valid reason, the real purpose is to assist the attorney in applying pressure for his fee, which he knows will probably not be forthcoming if the case is concluded. Sometimes this state of affairs is delicately signaled by the defense attorney in his requesting for an adjournment because "Mr. Green, a missing witness, has not appeared." Adjournments for this and similar purposes—sometimes as many as eight or nine in a case—may keep a defendant's case on the calendar for four to seven months.

Ordinarily, judges are not supposed to be involved in the plea-bargaining process between the prosecution and the defense counsel. The judge, it is thought, is simply required to review the fairness and reasonableness of a plea, and to ascertain that no coercion was exerted in obtaining it. A judge, it is also thought, never makes any commitments with regard to the sentence he will impose in return for a specific plea. Despite these proscriptions, lawyer-regulars in our criminal courts are always in three-way communication with the district attorney's office and the judge's chamber in order to smooth out any differences that may arise in connection with a specific plea by their client. Defense lawyers also have a political "account" with most judges and prosecutors, a factor that augments their professional *value* in any bargaining process. There is, therefore, a continuous procession of lawyer-regulars in the corridors between the prosecutor's office and the judge's chambers for the purpose of establishing, sub rosa, the plea and the sentence. Even so, it is not surprising to observe the frequent number of spontaneous, last-minute, private conferences at the judge's bench in which minor details of a lesser plea have to be ironed out. Too often a judge has not been privy to the details of a bargain plea already worked out between the lawyer-regular and the prosecutor's office, but he will, nevertheless, usually endorse it. There then follows a fairly typical scene in which a judge tries to muster all the authority of his office in order to gloss over a badly staged "cop-out." For the court record, the judge must redirect the scene so that the lesser plea will stand and the court's business can proceed.

Most judges in our criminal-court system epitomize seven different types of behavioral patterns. Individually, they can be described as follows:

1. The Scholar
2. The Hack
3. The Political Adventurer
4. The Pensioner
5. The Hatchet Man
6. The Tyrant
7. The Contract Man

The scholar and the hack are the workhorses of the court. Their organizational role of disposing of most of the court's work load is performed in strikingly different fashion, however. The hack is simply a plea-taking machine; he handles cases much as a checker handles groceries in a supermarket. The scholar, on the contrary, keeps his hand in publishing in law journals, is sought out by other judges and lawyers for advice, and wheels and deals to overcome the case load. And he does so with style, finesse, intelligence, and even brilliance. A legal craftsman, he is seldom reversed for his rulings. A not uncommon sight in his courtroom is the interruption of a tumultuous trial for the purpose of accepting pleas of guilty in fifteen to twenty other cases, to hear motions on matters affecting cases before him, to sentence defendants in cases previously heard, or to consult suddenly with lawyers, probation officials, or members of the district attorney's staff. His fellow judges view the fact that he frequently works on Saturday, Sunday, holidays, and at odd hours of the night with consternation and misgivings; his passion for work is regarded with suspicion. However, all in the court community admit that he "gets results." He is sought after by the lawyer-regulars because of his reputation for being an eminently "practical" man who is more than willing to compromise in return for a plea. He is also sensitive to political cues and any number of individuals are constantly seeking his intervention, counsel, and assistance. Often, he utilizes his reputation for leniency and practicality to dispose of a whole backlog of cases, which are, for this reason, funneled to his courtroom for disposition.

The hack is a more traditional political figure on the bench. Basically, his career aspirations are limited, but he, too, greatly enjoys his work, which he is incapable of handling in other than a routine fashion. His easygoing, nonpunitive attitudes, coupled with his personal desire to make his mark in the organization, allow him to dispose of a large number of cases. Yet except for a capacity to do more than his fair share in pruning the docket, he is otherwise a somewhat pedestrian character and is not, consequently, viewed as a professional threat by other judges, as is the scholar. For the hack, the judgeship is simply a comfortable slot; it answers financial and other ego needs that would not otherwise be available to him. In every major urban court in the nation, it is usually two or three judges who carry the bulk of the work load, and invariably it is the scholar and the hack who perform the task.

The judge who is a political adventurer is a man with important political connections and grandiose designs for the future. As a result, his performance on the bench is usually lackluster and of no consequence. His incumbency will be short-lived, the bench serving as a momentary stepping stone to other political offices. The political adventurer has no profound interest in law, and certainly not in criminal law; he is far more concerned with building a personal political organization and most of his efforts will be directed not toward trying to effect justice but toward manipulating the court organization for his own ends. He rarely misses an opportunity to register favorable newspaper and media publicity about himself and his judicial chores as part of his overall plan to further his career. Of course, the career schemes of some fail and they find themselves consigned to a lower-court destiny; the resulting bitterness and querulousness can transform them into "pensioners" or "tyrants."

The pensioner is a judge who has been rewarded rather late in his political life with a sinecure on the bench. He prefers to be left undisturbed, to spend as little of his time as possible in court, and to lead an almost anonymous existence. He takes virtually no interest in the administrative activities of the court. Usually judicial pensioners have put in long years of patient service to the political club at the local precinct level. They have rendered professional services to the party, the neighborhood clubhouse, and its swarm of favor seekers, and their ascent to the bench is a way of simultaneously discharging a political obligation while placing an individual in a public position where he can do little political harm.

The hatchet-man member of the bench is usually a graduate of the district attorney's office. He has close ties to that office, the political clubhouse, and other power blocs in municipal government. It is his function to hear those ticklish cases that place the municipal administration on the defensive —in other words, cases of malfeasance or breach of trust by public officials and petty civil servants. Further, he is also presented with all cases of persons who have either failed to cooperate with the prosecuting authorities or committed a crime sufficiently scandalous to have earned the avid attention of the news media. It is up to the hatchet man, therefore, to stage-manage an impression of swift justice, impassively, clinically, and uniformly administered, in order to reflect credit on the court organization.

The tyrant is the deeply hostile, frustrated, ambition-ridden individual who has been defeated in his career aspirations. He is at a dead end, and knows it. Possessed of an unbounding contempt and scorn for others, his arrogance is incredible. He is the terror of his courtroom—loathed and hated by lawyers, defendants, and probation officers, merely tolerated by district attorneys. Largely rejected by his colleagues, this egocentric exploits his judicial post as a vehicle for presenting a spectacle calculated to attract the attention of the press. He glories in publicity, even if it is negative.

The most destructive aspect of his conduct, however, is his discharge of the professional and legal obligations of his office. He completely dominates the courtroom proceedings and manipulates them toward his own ends or toward what he perceives to be the truth. He controls the court stenographer, virtually dictating what material is to be included or excluded from the record. He manipulates juries through smiles, smirks, and unrecorded off-the-cuff comments that may discredit a witness or a defendant's testimony. He intimidates defendants and privately threatens lawyers. Thus, robed in organizational authority, he is able to satisfy the needs of a personal pathology.

The contract man plays an important judicial role in every large criminal court. All enforcement and adjudication functionaries tend to see life as a series of exchanges—bargains that must be struck in order to assure tranquil, orderly operations. Usually one judge is assigned the delicate task of translating arrangements and bargains struck by the local political machine into judicial reality. (In connection with the police function, the contract man is one particular high-ranking person in the precinct.) The contract man's duties, therefore, may range from granting trivial "favors" to executing a major fix. The contract man seldom deals in money, but rather in political quid pro quos that have been initiated by the local political machine. The contract man will be quite visible at the clubhouse, although judges are supposed to remain aloof from politics, for it is there that he receives his orders. He is important because he carries out the sensitive assignments in connection with all court matters in which the local politicos are interested. He is the true nexus between the machine and the politically susceptible judges on the bench; as a rule, therefore, both minor and major arrangements are cleared and transmitted through him.

All seven judicial types, however, despite the differential character of their performance, contribute to the functioning of the court organization. The division of labor in the court is not as random or as fortuitous as it may appear. Each judicial type contributes in his own way to the total institutional arrangement, performing a systemic mission in terms of his own drives, needs, and personality. As long as a judge's idiosyncrasies and whims do not materially interfere with the attainment of organi-

zation objectives, they will be permitted to continue undisturbed.

The probation officer becomes an agent in an accused's
processing sooner or later, depending at which stage his services are invoked by the judge. A probation officer sees himself
as a professional "caseworker in an authoritative setting";
for probation officers and court psychiatrists must, insofar
as established rules and procedures are concerned, accept
and act upon the stated facts of a defendant's case as presented
by the police and district attorney. This restriction has specific
consequences in their relations with an accused. In other
words, important aspects of a defendant's background are
perceived by them in terms and meanings defined by the police
and district attorney. As a consequence, a defendant, whether
before or after he has pleaded, is considered by a probation
officer and a psychiatrist as already "in treatment"; to both,
the court is a clinic, an analogy particularly pleasing to the
psychiatrists since many of them believe that criminals are
sick. What the accused is usually unable to understand fully
is that he does not enjoy a worker-client or a doctor-patient
relationship with either of these functionaries. Harboring a
somewhat fuzzy notion that these are "helping" professions,
he tends to speak much more freely about himself than he
would to others, and in the process he sometimes says too
much for his own good. He overlooks the fact that what he says
is not confidential and that this can have consequences in the
ultimate disposition of his case. For the court organization
relies heavily on probation and psychiatric reports, especially
in those cases in which no other firm or compelling legal,
political, personal, or other criteria exist as the basis for disposition. Probation and psychiatric reports, although laden with
labels of the most vague diagnostic nature—"psychopathic,"
"immature," "depraved," "weak-willed," "inadequate," "ego-
centric-aggressive," "primitive," "unconventional," "shiftless,"
"antisocial"—furnish the pseudo-scientific peg upon which
many criminal court decisions are made. To an important
degree, the justifications and rationales advanced in the re-

ports on the accused are grounded in information precast and fashioned by police and prosecutor; probation and psychiatric reports merely reaffirm and recirculate the same unflattering data, but they couch and refurbish it in the special jargon of social workers and psychiatrists. The so-called "independence" or "impartiality" of probation officers is inevitably tainted by their absorption into the organizational motives and designs of the entire court system.

The probation officer also has an important duty to perform after the accused has pleaded guilty and begun to have some second thoughts about the matter. This function may best be described as "cooling the mark out." Losers and defeated persons must somehow be "cooled out"—pacified and reassured—in order to avoid any unseemly social explosion. The defense lawyer, probation officer, psychiatrist and next of kin all perform important cooling-out duties; even the police, prosecutor, and judge may find it occasionally expedient to perform them as an accused, in changing his initial plea of "not guilty" to one attesting guilt, is processed toward a reconceptualization of himself.

The courtroom cop-out ceremony is an exceedingly important aspect of our criminal-court system. It is during this ritual that the accused states publicly for the first time that he is guilty of a specific crime. Moreover, he not only is made to assert his guilt openly, he must also recite the details of the crime. Furthermore, he must indicate that he is entering his guilty plea freely, willingly, and voluntarily and that he is not doing so because of any promises or bargains or in consideration of any commitments made to him by anyone. This last is intended as a blanket statement to shield the police, the prosecutor's office, the defense attorney, the probation office, or the judge from any possible charges of exerting coercion or undue influence in violation of due process requirements. It also serves to preclude any appeals court reversal of the case on these grounds, and to obviate the utility of any second thoughts that the accused may develop in connection with his plea.

In the United States, the adversary system has always been an ideal; it has little if any validity. What we have in its place is the bargain system—a synthetic substitute that is part of the larger institutional blight characterized by what Galbraith calls our "failure to invest in people." The bureaucratic fetish for production in our criminal-court system merely promotes the ferreting out and prosecution of those cases most easily processed.[32] As a result, we have spent much of our limited resources in talent and money in the prosecution of addicts, alcoholics, prostitutes, homosexuals, and gamblers. They are readily available and they produce the desired publicity and the desired statistical data. But this fetish for production and quotas corrupts all functionaries in our enforcement and adjudication system. Further, it victimizes those least able to defend themselves. Quite obviously, it would require a massive application of funds and other resources to better balance the scales of American criminal justice. In the face of ventures that drain our limited resources, and thereby permit us to have only second-rate education systems and sleazy health and welfare services, it would be unrealistic to expect in the near future a major commitment to effect necessary changes in our system of criminal justice.

To begin to unscramble a system that propels almost everyone caught up in it, innocent and guilty alike, toward a guilty plea, we have to redefine the nature and limits of the criminal sanction itself. We have for years been trying to control alcoholism, drug addiction, gambling, abortion, and some sexual behavior through the use of the criminal sanction. But our efforts to cope with these social problems through the lavish application of the criminal law have been a total failure. Removal of these problems from the courts, and their reassignment to the more proficient aegis of other professional institutions, would free the courts for more urgent and more appropriate judicial activity.

We must also redefine the nature and limits of police work, since, in the short run, it is impractical to expect that the caliber of our police or the milieu in which they operate will change appreciably. Much police work—almost 80 per cent of it—is

[32]William J. Chambliss and John T. Liell, "The Legal Process in the Community Setting," *Crime and Delinquency* 12 (October 1966), pp. 310–317.

of the social-worker, caretaker, baby-sitter, errand-boy variety of activity.[33] In short, the police function must be reviewed and narrowed to the kind of crime-control and peace-keeping activities that a redefinition of the criminal sanction would involve. Not only would the control of alcoholics, gamblers, and addicts be reviewed as a police function, but traffic control and aiding injured, lost, and helpless individuals would be reassigned as civil occupations.

Obviously, any reassignment of activities currently under the jurisdiction of the police would necessitate sizable outlays of money. Indeed, much of the work we have given the police has been a cost-cutting device to avoid developing and paying for proper civil billets. For example, various paramedical occupations should have been created long ago to deal with public first-aid emergencies. With the police being responsible for "everything," they are naturally vulnerable for the mistakes that must inevitably occur in carrying out the impossible. A reordering, therefore, of police priorities to give crimes of violence greater attention, accompanied by an increased use of civilian personnel to perform police paper work and other duties not directly related to law-enforcement and peace-keeping functions, is imperative.

It is also imperative that we place new laws on the books that more clearly define police authority—as well as police procedures and the limits of police discretion, especially in relation to street encounters and interrogation. And, further, an urgent need exists for formal procedures that would encourage the rapid processing and evaluation of citizen complaints. Coupled with this need is the desirability of establishing community advisory groups to work with the police both in implementing their programs and in helping them recruit mature, well-motivated individuals who represent the community.

Since the system of bargain justice, or justice by negotiation without trial, is likely to continue for some time to be the major feature of our criminal-justice system, some suggestions

---

[33]See Elaine Cumming, Ian M. Cumming, and Laura Edell, "Policeman as Philosopher, Guide and Friend," *Social Problems* 12 (Winter 1965), pp. 276–286.

for supervision of the process are in order. Not too much would be required in additional resources to charge an independent body, not enmeshed in the organizational framework of our court system, with the responsibility of reviewing guilty pleas. This group, or person, could function in a capacity similar to that of a Swedish ombudsman or an inspector-general; it would be a public agency wholly independent of the present highly structured, closed community of the criminal courts and it would scrupulously supervise each guilty plea in order to determine whether minimum standards of justice had been met. Among other duties, the agency would:

1. Determine whether the indictment had been read and the charges clearly explained to the defendant; it would also determine whether the accused had been clearly advised of his right to a jury trial.
2. Question a defendant who indicates a desire to plead guilty on his reasons for wanting to do so.
3. Request the prosecution to summarize any evidence against the defendant other than a confession.
4. Examine carefully the exact circumstances of a defendant's arrest and of all police practices and activities that preceded and followed it.
5. Scrutinize each lesser plea transaction to determine whether any secret arrangements were made under duress or in the expectation of some promised benefit.
6. Assess the health, age, education, race, and other factors, such as intelligence, that might negate the notion that a defendant confessed or pleaded guilty voluntarily.
7. Evaluate the effects of any period of confinement prior to pleading, its duration, and the living conditions during such detention.

While it is true that under present requirements police, prosecutors, defense lawyers, probation personnel, judges, and others are ordinarily obligated to make some or all of the foregoing inquiries and assessments, they cannot be relied upon to do so in many routine cases. Further, they are all so elaborately entangled with one another in occupational and organizational terms that their objectivity and evaluations are compromised. Unless funds are found to finance investigations, psychiatric services, and well-trained, independent adversary defense counsel for accused persons, our system of criminal justice will continue to be prejudiced, impersonal, high-handed, expedient, and unjust.

If the slogan of "law and order" is to mean anything, it must be translated into a viable system of judicial and administrative practices that will override the injustices and inequities generating the anger and desperation now helping to produce criminality. Unless the poor and the weak, who constitute the bulk of our criminal case load, receive the kind of protection and resources now available only to the affluent, the knowledgeable, and the powerful, it is useless to prate about "law and order." The existing administration of the criminal adjudication system in America promotes and reinforces class warfare by indicating to those at the bottom that they have no real stake in our society. Until more resources are committed to the defense of the vulnerable, bargain justice will continue to be our shoddy substitute for due process.

PART II

The Nature and "Causes" of Crime

Crime and Its Impact
in an Affluent Society

LEROY C. GOULD

Americans are concerned about crime. Expressing this concern, the President's Commission on Law Enforcement and Administration of Justice opened its 1967 report on the state of crime in the United States with the following words:

> There is much crime in America . . . far too much for the health of the Nation. Every American knows that. Every American is, in a sense, a victim of crime. Violence and theft have not only injured, often irreparably, hundreds of thousands of citizens, but have directly affected everyone. Some people have been impelled to uproot themselves and find new homes. Some have been made afraid to use public streets and parks. Some have come to doubt the worth of a society in which so many people behave so badly. Some have become distrustful of the Government's ability, or even desire, to protect them. Some have lapsed into the attitude that criminal behavior is normal human behavior and consequently have become indifferent to it, or have adopted it as a good way to get ahead in life. Some have become suspicious of those they conceive to be responsible for crime: adolescents or Negroes or drug addicts or college students or demonstrators; policemen who fail to solve crimes; judges who pass lenient sentences

I wish to extend my appreciation and thanks to Kai Erikson and Lloyd Rogler for critically reading an early draft of this chapter and to Morgan McCall for research assistance.

or write decisions restricting the activities of the police; parole boards that release prisoners who resume their criminal activities.[1]

Because Americans are concerned about crime, however, does not mean that their concern is justified. The public's fears are often misguided, and one of the purposes of a governmental commission is to place fears in perspective. Presumably, therefore, one of the tasks of the President's crime commission was to assess the problem of crime in the United States and come to some conclusion about whether it is as serious as most Americans seem to believe.

The crime commission did not reach a consistent conclusion. It made statements, such as the quotation above, indicating that the crime problem is completely out of hand. Yet in other sections of the report, it made statements indicating public concern is misguided.[2] The commission noted, for example, that "the public fears most the crimes that occur the least—crimes of violence. People are much more tolerant of crimes against property, which constitute most of the crimes that are committed against persons or households or businesses."[3] And, the commission went on to explain, the "fear of crimes of violence is not a simple fear of injury or death or even of all crimes of violence, but, at the bottom, a fear of strangers. The personal injury that Americans risk daily from sources other than crime are enormously greater."[4] And finally, the commission concluded, "the fear of crime may not be as strongly influenced by the actual incidence of crime as it is by other experiences with the crime problem generally";[5] in par-

[1]President's Commission on Law Enforcement and Administration of Justice (hereafter cited as President's Commission), *The Challenge of Crime in a Free Society* (Washington, D.C.: United States Government Printing Office, 1967), p. 1.

[2]These reservations did not appear in the main volume of the commission's report, but in the supplement, *Crime and Its Impact—An Assessment* (Washington, D.C.: United States Government Printing Office, 1967), prepared by the commission's task force on assessment.

[3]Ibid., p. 88.
[4]Ibid.
[5]Ibid., p. 89.

ticular, the commission was troubled about distorted crime reporting in the mass media.

Despite these reservations, the crime commission felt obliged to remark:

The [commission] cannot say that the public's fear of crime is exaggerated. It is not prepared to tell the people how fearful they should be; that is something each person must decide for himself. People's fears must be respected; certainly they cannot be legislated.[6]

IS CRIME INCREASING IN THE UNITED STATES?

The crime commission was not willing to say that Americans' fears about crime are unfounded. The commission did say, however, that their fears are misguided. In addition, the commission reminded its readers that the problem of crime is not new to the United States and may even have been worse in years past:

There has always been too much crime. Virtually every generation since the founding of the Nation and before has felt itself threatened by the spectre of rising crime and violence.

A hundred years ago contemporary accounts of San Francisco told of extensive areas where "no decent man was in safety to walk the street after dark; while at all hours, both night and day, his property was jeopardized by incendiarism and burglary." Teenage gangs gave rise to the word "hoodlum"; while in one central New York City area, near Broadway, the police entered "only in pairs, and never unarmed." A noted chronicler of the period declared that "municipal law is a failure . . . we must soon fall back on the law of self preservation." "Alarming" increases in robbery and violent crimes were reported throughout the country prior to the Revolution. And in 1910 one author declared that "crime, especially its more violent forms, and among the young, is increasing steadily and is threatening to bankrupt the Nation."[7]

The commission also could have mentioned that crime is not, as some people seem to think, unique to America. Crime

6Ibid., p. 88.
7Ibid., p. 19.

is present throughout the world and evidently always has been. As one writer observed in the nineteenth century:

> Crime is present not only in the majority of societies of one particular species but in all societies of all types. There is no society that is not confronted with the problem of criminality. Its form changes; the acts thus characterized are not the same everywhere; but, everywhere and always, there have been men who have behaved in such a way as to draw upon themselves penal repression.[8]

RECENT TRENDS IN AMERICAN CRIME RATES

The commission was aware, however, that it is not crime in other nations that Americans are afraid of; they are afraid of crime in their own communities. And they are not concerned with whether crime is more or less prevalent today than it was a century ago; they are worried about whether it is more prevalent now than it was at some earlier point in their own lifetime.

With this more limited time perspective in mind, the commission tried to answer the question of whether or not crime has increased in the past three decades. Even for this time span the commission could not give a definitive answer because a complete, reliable source of national crime statistics has never existed. However, some incomplete data do exist, in particular that contained in the *Uniform Crime Reports,*[9] and it is these statistics that the crime commission was forced to use.

The annual *U.C.R.,* begun in 1931 by the International Association of Chiefs of Police and now maintained by the Federal Bureau of Investigation, contains statistics on seven serious crimes: willful homicide, forcible rape, aggravated assault, robbery, burglary, larceny ($50 and over), and motor-vehicle theft. Although these statistics are incomplete, because some law-enforcement jurisdictions do not participate in the reporting system, enough data are available to make national es-

[8]Emile Durkheim, *The Division of Labor in Society,* trans. George Simpson (New York: The Free Press, 1960), p. 102.

[9]United States Department of Justice, Federal Bureau of Investigation, *Uniform Crime Reports* (Washington, D.C.: United States Government Printing Office, 1931 to the present).

timates of crime for the years 1933 through 1965.[10] These estimates, however, pertain only to the seven "Index Crimes" and include only "crimes known to the police."

Since 1933, the rate of homicide has declined and the rates of forcible rape and aggravated assault have increased (Figure 1). Robbery, prevalent in 1933, declined in frequency until about 1945; it has been increasing irregularly since then, although the 1933 high has not been reached again. Overall, the *U.C.R.* index of crimes against the person shows a general decline in these four types of crimes from 1933 through 1943 and a general increase since 1944.

Even if these figures are accepted as accurate, however, problems of interpretation still exist because the four crimes do not demonstrate the same trends. Noting, for example, that most of the recent increases in crimes against the person are due to increases in assaults, and that the number of homicides has actually decreased, it is hard to say whether the incidence of serious crimes against the person has been rising or falling. To answer this question, one must be willing to equate assaults with homicides or at least, in terms of seriousness, be willing to say that a certain number of assaults is as serious as one homicide. Few people would be willing to make such a comparison; certainly, the crime commission was unwilling.

National rates of crimes against property are all higher today than they were in 1933, although the rate of motor-vehicle theft is only slightly above the 1933 level (Figure 2). In general, crimes against property decreased from 1933 through 1942 and increased thereafter.

[10]The procedure for making national estimates, as well as for formulating definitions of some of the categories in the "Index Crimes," has varied over the years, making it impossible to use the yearly volumes of the *Uniform Crime Reports* to assess crime trends since 1933. In order to solve this problem, the *U.C.R.* Division of the F.B.I., in cooperation with the President's crime commission, compiled revised national crime estimates for all Index Crimes, using current definitions of the crimes and consistent estimating procedures. These estimates, although not published in numerical form, appear in graphic form in *The Challenge of Crime* and are available from the F.B.I. I have used these revised figures throughout this chapter.

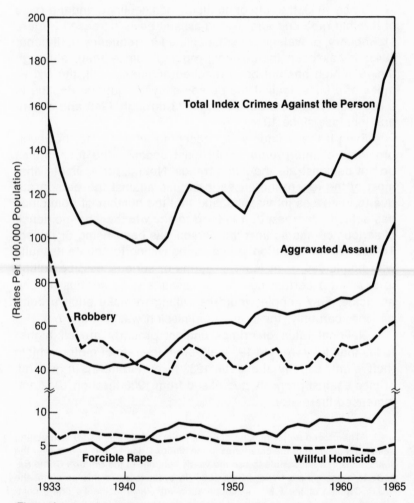

Figure 1
Index Crime Trends, 1933–1965. Reported Crimes Against the Person.
Note: The scale for willful homicide and forcible rape is enlarged to show trend. *Source:* President's Commission, *The Challenge of Crime,* p. 22.

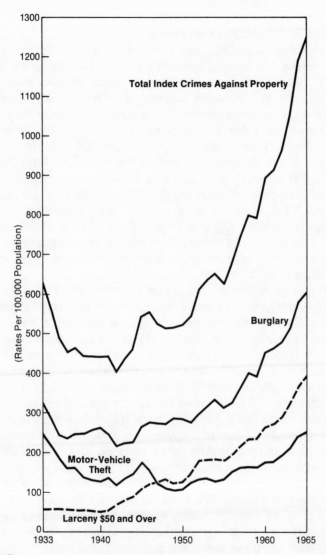

Figure 2
Index Crime Trends, 1933–1965. Reported Crimes Against Property.
Note: The scale for this figure is not comparable with that used in
Figure 1.   *Source:* President's Commission, *The Challenge of Crime,*
p. 23.

PROBLEMS IN INTERPRETING
THE *UNIFORM CRIME REPORTS*

These crime statistics, while relatively straightforward, are nonetheless misleading. For example, the figures do not—and the F.B.I. does not claim that they do—include all crimes committed, even in the seven categories in the index. The index reports only "crimes known to the police"; it does not reflect the many crimes that the police never hear about nor those few crimes that, while known to police, are not reported to the *Uniform Crime Reports* Division of the F.B.I. The F.B.I. makes an earnest effort to get complete and accurate data from all police jurisdictions;[11] even so, the reporting system is voluntary and the F.B.I. is never sure that all crimes that are in fact "known to the police" come to be included in the *U.C.R.* Understandably, of course, there is no record of those crimes that never come to the attention of a law-enforcement office in the first place.

Because of these difficulties in interpreting the *Uniform Crime Reports,* the President's crime commission instituted a national survey[12] to find out just how many people have been victims of crime. While this survey was itself incomplete, because it excluded businesses and other organizations that can also be the victims of crime, it nevertheless had an advantage over the *U.C.R.* because it included reports of crimes against individuals that did not come to the attention of the police and therefore would never be listed in the *U.C.R.* totals. So that comparisons could be made between the national survey carried out in 1965 and the *U.C.R.* figure for 1965, the crime commission, with the cooperation of the F.B.I., prepared an *adjusted U.C.R.* index for 1965 that excluded, wherever possible, crimes against organizations. The national survey showed that a number of crimes—rape, robbery, assault, burglary, and larceny—are apparently underreported in the *Uniform Crime Reports* index, that rates for homicide are about the same in the two

[11]President's Commission, *Crime and Its Impact,* p. 23.
[12]Ibid., pp. 17–19. The survey was conducted by the National Opinion Research Center of the University of Chicago.

indexes,[13] and that rates of motor-vehicle thefts are somewhat overreported by the *U.C.R.* (Table 1).

This last finding highlights another problem that the F.B.I. faces in compiling an accurate index. Not every report of a theft that comes into a police station is bona fide; people often lose or misplace what they think is stolen, and sometimes they try to collect on insurance policies by making a fraudulent report. The police, to be sure, are aware of these errors and most departments try to screen out false crime reports. This can never be done with absolute accuracy, nor can it be assumed that all law-enforcement offices are equally rigorous in their screening.

Underreporting in the F.B.I. index, however, is evidently a more serious matter than overreporting. What are the reasons for underreporting? The President's crime commission tried to obtain the answer by asking the victims it surveyed whether they had reported the crime to the police when it occurred, and if not, why not.[14] The reason most often given for not reporting crimes was that the victim believed the police could not be effective or would not want to be bothered (Table 2). Also frequently mentioned was the feeling that the issue was a private matter or that reporting the crime would unnecessarily hurt the offender.

Regardless of why crimes are not reported, however, the President's crime commission survey of victims indicates fairly conclusively that crime is even more common than had previously been suspected. In some cases, like forcible rape and burglary, the true rate of crime may be as much as three times the reported rate, and in all seven crime categories, except motor-vehicle theft and homicide, some underreporting is apparent in the *Uniform Crime Reports.*

The fact that the *U.C.R.* does not list all crimes committed does not mean that crime is increasing. Nor does it mean that it is decreasing. All it means is that not all crime is reported.

[13]The number of homicides reported in the victim survey were too few to be statistically reliable.

[14]President's Commission, *Crime and Its Impact,* p. 18.

Table 1

Comparison of 1965 Crime Rates Between National Survey and *U.C.R.*
(Per 100,000 population)

Crimes	National Survey	U.C.R. Rate for Individuals	U.C.R. Rate for Individuals and Organizations[1]
Willful homicide	3.0	5.1	5.1
Forcible rape	42.5	11.6	11.6
Robbery	94.0	61.4	61.4
Aggravated assault	218.3	106.6	106.6
Burglary	949.1	299.6	605.3
Larceny ($50 and over)	606.5	267.4	393.3
Motor-vehicle theft	206.2	226.0	251.0
Totals			
Crimes of violence	357.8	184.7	184.7
Crimes against property	1,761.8	793.0	1,249.6

[1] F.B.I., *Uniform Crime Reports,* 1965, p. 51. The *U.C.R.* national totals do not distinguish crimes committed against individuals or households from those committed against businesses or other organizations. The *U.C.R.* rate for individuals (middle column) is the national rate adjusted to eliminate burglaries, larcenies, and vehicle thefts not committed against individuals or households. No adjustment was made for robbery.

Source: President's Commission, *Crime and Its Impact,* p. 17.

This underreporting, however, makes it hazardous to interpret the trends in American crime as revealed in the *Uniform Crime Reports,* for as long as significant underreporting occurs, it is possible that crime trends will reflect nothing more than changes in the willingness of victims to report crimes to the police.[15] In other words, until all people report all crimes when they occur and the police are sure that what is reported is in fact a crime, the *Uniform Crime Reports* will be an incomplete index of crimes. And until it is complete, it will be impossible to know whether its report on the level of crime in this country is accurate.

[15] The crime commission discussed this and related problems in crime statistics in some detail. *Crime and Its Impact,* pp. 21–25.

Table 2
Victims' Most Important Reason for Not Notifying Police[1] (In percentages)

Crimes	Per Cent of Cases in Which Police Not Notified	Reasons for Not Notifying Police				
		Felt It Was Private Matter or Did Not Want to Harm Offender	Police Could Not Be Effective or Would Not Want to Be Bothered	Did Not Want to Take Time	Too Confused or Did Not Know How to Report	Fear of Reprisal
Robbery	35	27	45	9	18	0
Aggravated assault	35	50	25	4	8	13
Simple assault	54	50	35	4	4	7
Burglary	42	30	63	4	2	2
Larceny ($50 and over)	40	23	62	7	7	0
Larceny (under $50)	63	31	58	7	3	(*)
Auto theft[2]	11	20	60	0	0	20
Malicious mischief	62	23	68	5	2	2
Consumer fraud	90	50	40	0	10	0
Other fraud (bad checks, swindling, etc.)	74	41	35	16	8	0
Sex offenses (except forcible rape)	49	40	50	0	5	5
Family crimes (including desertion, nonsupport)	50	65	17	10	0	7

*Less than 0.5%.
[1]Willful homicide, forcible rape, and a few other crimes had too few cases to be statistically useful, and they are therefore excluded.
[2]Auto theft was not reported in only five instances.
Source: President's Commission, Crime and Its Impact, p. 18.

PER CAPITA AND PER PROPERTY CRIME RATES

A further problem with the *Reports* is the way in which crime statistics are presented. This problem has to do with the choice of a base for computing crime *rates.* This base is the population, and crime rates are reported as a certain number of offenses per 100,000 people. At first glance, this does not seem to be at all unusual. To present only the total number of crimes without taking population growth into consideration, many would say, would result in spurious trends in the amount of crime. Unless the number of crimes is increasing faster than the population, the argument goes, increases in crime may be due to nothing more than population growth; proportionately, then, crime would not be on the increase.

But what does this argument mean? It means that the crime problem is conceived in terms of people only; it is conceived in terms of the proportion of the population that commits crimes. As this proportion increases, the crime problem increases; as it falls, the crime problem diminishes.

There are, of course, other ways in which the crime problem could be viewed. One would be the amount of damage it causes to public confidence in, and respect for, law and order. Another would be the amount of loss to victims. Still another would be that the crime problem is related to the number of opportunities to commit crime or, a fourth view, to the amount of crime committed in proportion to opportunity. In each of these four cases, it does not make much sense to calculate crime rates on a per capita base.

While an appropriate base for each of these ways in which to appraise the crime problem is easier to imagine than to calculate, it seems quite likely that computations of crime rates based on each of these alternatives would show different trends. For example, the amount of property in this country has risen much faster than the population in recent years; it is possible, therefore, that a crime rate based on the availability of property to be stolen (which is one measure of the opportunity to commit property crimes) would show a decline, whereas the per capita rate of property crime shows an increase.

To test this particular notion, I have assembled data on three forms of property crime for which there are fairly consistent national statistics on both the number of crimes and the amount of property available to be stolen. The three crimes are motor-vehicle theft, bank robbery, and bank burglary. (Inasmuch as bank robbery and bank burglary are both thefts of the same kind of property, namely, cash in banks, I have combined the statistics on these two crimes.) Data on the number of motor-vehicle thefts are from the *Uniform Crime Reports* and cover the years 1933 through 1965;[16] data on bank robberies and bank burglaries, for the years 1921 through 1965, are supplied by the American Bankers Association.[17] *Historical Statistics of the United States* and *Statistical Abstracts of the United States* provide information on the number of registered motor vehicles, which is the property base for computing the rate of motor-vehicle thefts, and the amount of cash and coin in banks, which constitutes the property base for calculating the rate of crime against banks.[18]

The property rate of motor-vehicle theft was considerably lower in 1965 than it was in the earlier period (Figure 3); in fact it was lower than almost the whole period from 1933 through 1945. Per capita motor-vehicle theft rates, however, were higher in 1965 than at any other time since 1933. What is striking about both of these curves is the general decline of rates during the 1930's, the sharp rise during the years of the Second World War and sharp decline immediately following the war, and the general rise in rates since 1950.

[16]Corrected figures have been used; see footnote 11. Motor-vehicle theft is probably the most accurately reported property crime in the *U.C.R.* index. See Tables 1 and 2.

[17]These data, which have been previously unpublished, appear in George Camp, "Nothing to Lose—A Study of Bank Robbery in America" (Ph.D. dissertation, Yale University, 1967), pp. 144–145.

[18]United States Department of Commerce, Bureau of the Census, *Historical Statistics of the United States, Colonial Times to 1957,* and the continuation to 1962 (Washington, D.C.: United States Government Printing Office, 1960 and 1965); idem, *Statistical Abstract of the United States* (Washington, D.C.: United States Government Printing Office, 1963, 1964, and 1965).

Bank robbery and bank burglary (Figure 4) were prevalent in the early 1930's, declined abruptly during the late 1930's, and then began a rather steady rise in the 1940's. Unlike motor-vehicle theft, however, bank robbery and burglary did not increase during the war years, and they began their general rise earlier, in 1944 instead of 1950. The data for bank robbery and burglary, which go back further in time than the data for motor-vehicle theft, show that the rate of these crimes reached a peak during the Depression years of 1932 or 1933. (The years 1921 through 1929 in Figure 4 are not exactly comparable with the later years because the American Bankers Association did not include burglaries in its statistics during the 1920's.) Like motor-vehicle theft, bank robbery and burglary rates were considerably lower in 1965 than in the 1930's when a property base instead of a per capita base is used to calculate the crime rate.

Figures 3 and 4, then, reveal two things. First, they describe a very noticeable cyclical trend in the rates of these two property crimes: high in 1933, falling off in the 1940's, and on the increase since. Calculated on the basis of population, these crimes were about as prevalent in 1965 as they were in 1933; calculated on the basis of property, they occurred with considerably less frequency in the 1960's than in the early 1930's.

Whether or not crime has been increasing over the past three decades depends, therefore, on how the problem is viewed. If the question is simply, "Has the total number of crimes been increasing," it could be said with a reasonable degree of confidence that the answer is "Yes," at least for six of the seven crimes listed in the *Uniform Crime Reports*.[19] (Willful homicide has shown no increase, in absolute numbers, since 1933.) Viewed on a per capita basis, some crimes appear to have declined, others to have risen, and still others to have been variable. Viewed on a per property basis, crimes against

---

[19]Based on fragmentary data, some crimes not listed in the index—such as gambling and safe-cracking—have not shown any increase or have actually declined. See President's Commission, *Crime and Its Impact,* p. 21, and Leroy C. Gould et al., "Crime as a Profession," mimeographed (Washington, D.C.: Office of the Attorney General, Law Enforcement Assistance Administration, 1967), pp. 28–29.

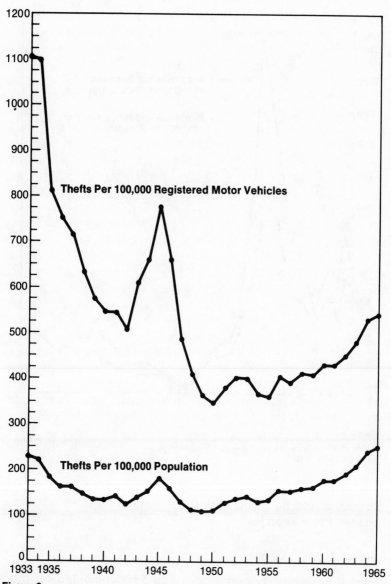

Figure 3
Motor-Vehicle Thefts per Capita and per Motor-Vehicle Registration
(1933–1965).

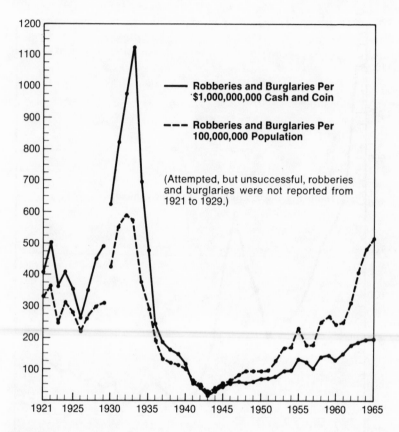

Figure 4
Bank Robbery and Burglary per Capita and per Cash and Coin in
Banks (1921–1965).

property have evidently declined. (A per property base, of
course, would be inappropriate for computing rates of crimes
against the person.)

THE CONCEPT, "CRIME"

Even if per property crime rates could be computed for more
than cars and cash, it seems unlikely that many Americans
would accept such rates as a meaningful index of property

crime. To do so would be to depart from what seems to be the common American conception of "crime." For most Americans, the concept of "crime" is inseparable from the concept of the "criminal," and inseparable from their concept of "criminal" is the notion that criminals are a class set apart from the rest of society. The key to the American conception of crime is that it is something criminals do, and what is important is not how many crimes are committed per unit of property but how many criminals are loose in society. With this conception, Americans would naturally understand per capita crime rates better than per property crime rates.

Even so, per capita rates of crime are not good measures of the proportion of the population that is criminal. In the case of crimes known to the police, the rates do not correct for the fact that some criminals commit many crimes, others only a few, and still others only one. Rates based on the number of offenders known to either the police or the courts do not correct for the fact that many criminals never get caught.

The tendency to think of crime as something pertaining to criminals, rather than to some other unit in society, has a long history in America. The Puritans, who saw crime in theological terms, thought of crime as being the evil product of predestined damnation.[20] Later, the medically oriented came to see crime as arising from some inherited abnormality.[21] Still later, psychologists attempted to describe crime in terms of mental or personality defects. And finally, sociologists sought the origins of crime in those social situations—neighborhood, school, family, peer group—that presumably predispose people to be either criminals or law-abiding citizens. What is peculiar to all these notions of crime is that criminality, much like disease, is accepted as a characteristic of individual persons, not a characteristic of groups, communities, or societies.

Any careful consideration of the concept of "crime," how-

---

[20]See Kai T. Erikson, *Wayward Puritans* (New York: John Wiley & Sons, 1966), esp. chap. 5.

[21]For a good review of changing conceptions of the causes of crime, see Elmer H. Johnson, *Crime, Correction, and Society*, rev. ed. (Homewood, Ill.: Dorsey Press, 1966), chaps. 7 and 8.

ever, points up the fact that a crime, in its broadest sense, contains many elements that are not only social in nature but have
little to do with the criminal himself. Aside from the individual
who commits a crime, there must be, first of all, a community
that has defined the commission of that act as criminal. Second, there must be someone in the community who has observed the act and who has applied the community's definition
to it. Third, a crime implies that there has been a victim. And
finally, a crime, at least a crime that is punished, implies that
someone in the community is responsible for punishment.

A crime in its broadest sense, therefore, is a social phenomenon involving complex interactions between a number of
individuals and social institutions. It involves interaction between the criminal and his victim. It involves interaction between the criminal and the law. It involves interaction between
the victim and the law. It involves interaction between the criminal and the society's agents of social control. And it involves
interaction between the victim and society's agents of social
control. A crime, then, is not simply an act that is against the
law; it is an act that society has defined as illegal, perpetrated
against someone—the victim—perceived by some member of
that society, and acted upon by the society's agents of social
control.

Although this definition of crime is similar to definitions
suggested by other students of deviant behavior,[22] there are
those who will find fault with it.[23] What about a case in which
a person commits an act which is proscribed by the community
but which is not perceived by anyone except the actor himself
and is not punished? Is this a crime? By the above definition,
no. But this is analogous to the question of the tree falling in
the forest where no one is present to hear it fall. Is there any
sound? The answer, of course, depends upon the definition of

[22]See in particular: Erikson, *Wayward Puritans,* esp. chap. 1; Howard S.
Becker, *Outsiders: Studies in the Sociology of Deviance* (New York: The Free
Press, 1963), esp. chap. 1; and Aaron V. Cicourel, *The Social Organization of
Juvenile Justice* (New York: John Wiley & Sons, 1968).

[23]Cf. Jack P. Gibbs, "Conceptions of Deviant Behavior: The Old and the
New," *Pacific Sociological Review* 9 (Spring 1966), pp. 9–14.

sound. If the definition includes only the physical process of generating pressure waves in the air, then the answer would be yes, there was sound. If, on the other hand, the definition encompasses a more extensive process—the creation of pressure waves in the air, the activation of sensory mechanisms in the ear, and the mental recognition of these sensory stimuli— then there was no sound. It is a matter of definition.

In defining crime, the argument is not whether the definition offered here (or any other definition for that matter) is correct, but whether it is useful. My only claim is that this definition will be more useful and more appropriate for a sociological analysis of crime than definitions now commonly in use. Not only does this definition move from a psychological to a sociological level of analysis, it also broadens the scope for a legitimate causal explanation of crime. Once the concept of "crime" is removed from the "disease" model in which it has been embedded for so long, notions about the causes of crime may be entertained that do not impinge directly upon the criminal, the one who has the "disease." To include in the concept of crime, for instance, the notion of a victim leads to questions about how and under what circumstances the victim may be a party to the crime; indeed, under what circumstances may victims be the cause of crime? Similarly, the notion that crime includes interaction between the criminal, the victim, and the law leads immediately to questions about the role of law in the genesis of crime, not just in defining it, but in causing it. In a like manner, once a society's agents of control are included in the definition of crime, their role in the crime becomes more relevant.

None of these aspects of crime have gone completely unnoticed. Criminologists, to one degree or another, have considered them all. What is odd is that they have, for so long, made such little use of them. When they have talked about these aspects they have done so, usually, without altering the old conception of crime. These factors are considered not as properties of crimes but as independent variables that may help explain why certain people—criminals—commit crimes.

The definition of crime suggested here requires a change in the basic criminological unit of analysis; the unit of analysis is no longer a person but a group of people—a community or a society. Crime, under this definition, is not simply an individual act of transgressing the law, but a social act involving the interaction between the person who transgressed the law, the law-enforcement agencies, and the law itself. Since it is the particular interaction of all these elements that constitutes a "crime," the social unit of which all these elements are a part becomes the appropriate unit for theoretical and empirical analysis.

Changing the unit of analysis in this way has a very significant practical consequence: it removes a number of methodological difficulties that have traditionally hampered criminological research. When crime is defined as the commission of illegal acts, it is very hard to observe or measure crime with any degree of accuracy. Using statistics gathered by control agencies as measures of the occurrence of individual criminal acts presents serious problems. Many criminal acts never come to the attention of these agencies, some crimes are more likely than others to come to their attention, and the criminal acts of some persons—the poor or those from minority groups—are more likely to become public than the criminal acts of others.[24] In other words, there is no assurance that official crime statistics in any way approximate the real distribution of criminal acts in the population and many reasons to suspect that they generally do not.

Changing the definition of crime removes many of these problems because the new definition considers only criminal events that have come to the attention of law-enforcement agencies and that normally go into crime statistics.[25] Under

[24]For a more detailed discussion of these problems, see Leroy C. Gould, "Who Defines Delinquency: A Comparison of Self-Reported and Officially Reported Indices of Delinquency for Three Racial Groups," *Social Problems* 16 (Winter 1969), pp. 325–336.

[25]For a further discussion of the same point, see John I. Kitsuse and Aaron V. Cicourel, "A Note on the Use of Official Statistics," *Social Problems* 11 (Fall 1963), pp. 136–137.

this definition, the *Uniform Crime Reports* are an acceptable index of crime in America. Though this index is incomplete in that it does not include all crimes, it is nonetheless important, and it is the single official source of national reported crime data.

THE IMPACT OF PROPERTY ABUNDANCE ON PROPERTY CRIME

Assuming that it is legitimate to study reported crime, and that the *U.C.R.* index is a reasonable measure of it, are there regularities in these crime data that can be explained? If there are, a second question to be answered is: do these regularities suggest that crime results from deficiences in human nature? While most Americans seem to think that crime does result from some form of human pathology, and that it reflects a breakdown in public morality, it is far from easy to support this hypothesis on the basis of the *Uniform Crime Reports.* As noted earlier the *Reports* show no consistent trend in crimes against the person during the last 32 years, and the rates of crimes against property have varied—high in the early 1930's, low in the 1940's, and high again in the 1950's and 1960's. If crime is a symptom of human pathology, then it might be expected that a greater similarity would exist between the rates of different kinds of crimes, especially crimes of violence. If public morality is faltering, then the rates of all crimes should be rising.

Nonetheless, the incidence of most crimes in the F.B.I. index has shown an increase since about 1950. It might, therefore, be argued, and many Americans make this point, that the crime problem is currently getting out of hand. Yet the question still remains: is this recent rise indicative of a breakdown in public morality or of an increase in personal pathology?

It should be remembered that most of the recent increase in crime is attributed to a step-up in the number of crimes against property, and there are many variables that might affect the rate of property crime other than personal pathology. One of the most obvious is the abundance of property. The more property there is, the more property everyone will have and, for that reason, the less likely it is to be stolen because people already have what they might otherwise be tempted to take. Conversely, it might be argued that the more property there is, especially if it is poorly distributed, the more likely it is to be stolen simply because there is more to be taken.

An examination of property-crime data, however, shows that neither of these hypotheses is true, at least for motor-vehicle theft and bank robbery and burglary, the two forms of property crime for which accurate data exist on both abundance of property and number of thefts. Although a strong relationship does indeed exist between property abundance and theft, the relationship is not as simple as that suggested in the two hypotheses. Instead of being a linear relationship, that is, a relationship in which the theft rate changes directly and consistently with changes in the abundance of property, the relationship is curvilinear (Figures 5 and 6). In particular, it is U-shaped. In other words, when property is generally scarce, small changes in its quantity are inversely related to changes in the number of thefts while these changes become directly related when property becomes generally abundant.

The numerical measurement appropriate for this kind of correlation[26] shows that property theft is closely connected to property abundance.[27] For motor-vehicle theft the correlation is .98, and for bank robbery and bank burglary the correlation is .92. Expressed another way, the abundance of motor vehicles predicts the number of motor-vehicle thefts with 95 per cent accuracy and the abundance of cash and coin in banks predicts the number of bank robberies and burglaries with 85 per

[26]The appropriate measure is the multiple correlation coefficient (R) for the multiple regression equation $y = a + bx + cx^2$, where y is the number of thefts and x the abundance of property.

[27]Property abundance, however, must be expressed in relative rather than absolute terms. Specifically, unit changes in the amount of property where there is little property must be weighed more heavily than unit changes where there is a lot of property. A log transformation expresses this relative aspect of property abundance by taking the size of the property base into account. Therefore, property abundance, in these correlations, means: $\log_{10}$ motor-vehicle registrations or $\log_{10}$ cash and coin in banks.

cent accuracy.[28] Since a time lag has been built into these correlations between changes in property abundance and changes in number of thefts[29] (the time lag is one year for motor-vehicle theft and six months for bank robbery and burglary), it is appropriate to use the word "predict." In other words, knowledge about the number of registered motor vehicles in any one year during this 32-year period would have predicted the number of thefts the following year with an accuracy of 95 per cent, and knowledge about the amount of cash and coin in banks would have predicted the number of bank robberies and burglaries six months later with 85 per cent accuracy.

But what about property crime in general? Will this same U-shaped curve explain the relationship between the abundance of other forms of property and other forms of property theft? Presumably it will, at least for those forms of property crime listed in the *U.C.R.* index. Figure 7 shows the curvilinear relationship between consumer-consumption expenditures[30] (a general index of property abundance) and the amount of property crime listed in the *U.C.R.* index.[31] The multiple correlation is .97.

[28]A correlation coefficient must be squared before it can be interpreted as a measure of predictability. It is, of course, more conventional to say that a correlation coefficient squared equals the "amount of variance explained." It seems appropriate to interpret R^2 here as a measure of predictability, however, since the regression analysis incorporates a time lag between changes in abundance of property and number of thefts.

[29]The choice of these particular time-lag intervals was based on a larger time-lag analysis discussed elsewhere: Leroy C. Gould, "The Changing Structure of Property Crime in an Affluent Society," *Social Forces* 48 (September 1969), pp. 50–60.

[30]The *Historical Statistics* and *Statistical Abstracts* provide an index of goods and services in the private sector. I have also used durable-goods production and disposable income as general measures of property abundance and find similar relationships to total property crime, although the relationships are not quite as strong.

[31]I have not included larceny ($50 and over) because of the serious distortion caused by inflation since 1933. I have, however, included robbery even though the *Uniform Crime Reports* list this crime as a crime against the person (because of the threat of violence). For purposes of this analysis, robbery is treated as a property crime since the objective of the crime is to acquire property rather than to inflict injury.

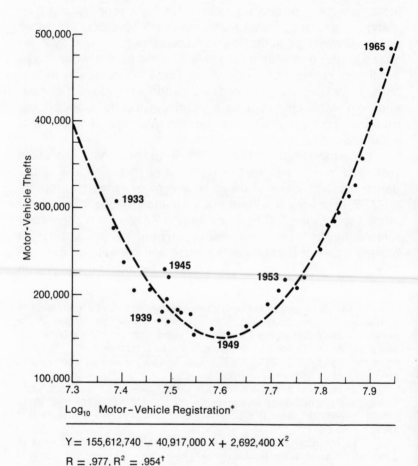

$$Y = 155,612,740 - 40,917,000\,X + 2,692,400\,X^2$$
$$R = .977, R^2 = .954†$$

Figure 5
Curvilinear Relationship Between Motor-Vehicle Thefts and the Abundance of Motor Vehicles.

*See footnote 28.
†See footnote 27.

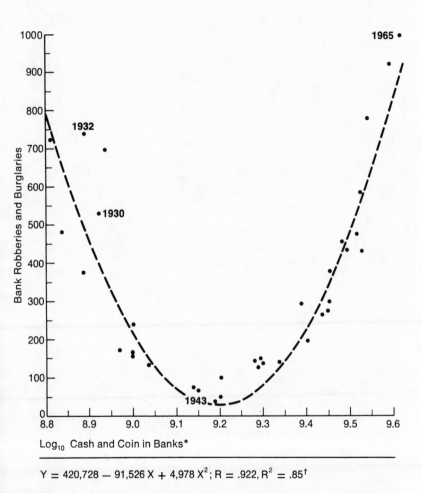

$$Y = 420{,}728 - 91{,}526\,X + 4{,}978\,X^2\,; R = .922, R^2 = .85^\dagger$$

Figure 6
Curvilinear Relationship Between Bank Robbery and Bank Burglary
and the Abundance of Cash and Coin in Banks.

    *See footnote 28.
    †See footnote 27.

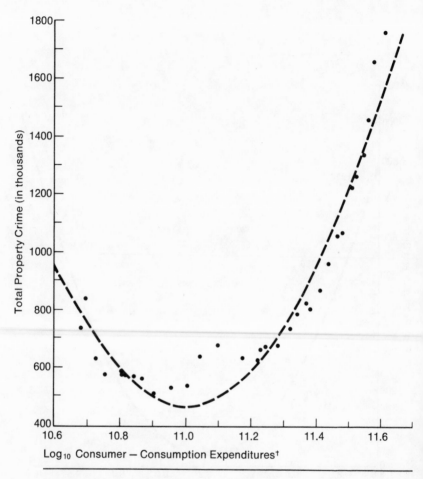

$$Y = 374{,}997{,}920 - 68{,}111{,}000\,X - 3{,}096{,}600\,X^2$$

$$R = .97, \qquad R^2 = .94^{\ddagger}$$

Figure 7
Curvilinear Relationship Between the *U.C.R.* Index of Property Crimes*
and Consumer-Consumption Expenditures.

    *Robbery, burglary, and motor-vehicle theft.
    †See footnote 28.
    ‡See footnote 27.

Although this analysis has dealt with only three kinds of property crime, and with only one of a number of possible indexes of the availability of property to be stolen, it nevertheless shows two important things: that the amount of property available for these different kinds of property crime is strongly related to the amount of crime, and that this relationship is not linear but curvilinear. Or to put it another way: in the first part of the period under study—early 1930's to mid-1940's—increases in the abundance of property were followed by *decreases* in the amount of theft, whereas in the latter part of the period increases in the abundance of property were followed by *increases* in the amount of theft. This shift in the relationship between property abundance and property theft suggests a fundamental change in the social structuring of major property crimes during the past 30 years. What is this change? What could account for it?

THE EFFECTS OF SCARCITY AND ABUNDANCE

The most immediately discernible difference between the 1930's and the early 1940's and the years that follow is that the former period was one of general economic doldrums while the latter has been one of affluence. The early period encompassed the Great Depression and the Second World War; the latter has offered almost uninterrupted prosperity. This suggests that property crime is contingent upon general economic conditions involving the relative scarcity or abundance of property.

The question persists, nevertheless, whether the specific relationship found between theft and property abundance is not a special example of a more general correlation between crime and the economy. Would the relationship, for example, between the number of private airplanes and theft of private airplanes today, when private airplanes are scarce but the economy is good, reflect the same kind of interconnection observed between the abundance of automobiles and automobile theft in the 1930's? If the relationship is the same, then it could be concluded that theft rates are geared specifically to the abundance of the property and not to the overall economy; if the relationship is not the same, then it must be concluded that it is the state of the economy and not the abundance of property that influences theft rates.

Unfortunately, no figures are available for airplanes or other forms of scarce property that can be used to test directly these alternatives. Indirectly, however, evidence is available to support the contention that the relationship depends upon the abundance of property rather than on the general health of the economy. It is true, for instance, that one of the most widely used indicators of economic activity—unemployment—was practically unrelated to property crime during the years encompassed by this study.[32] Furthermore, the strong relationships between property abundance and theft against that property show a time span peculiar to each form of property. The low point in the theft curve for bank robbery and burglary came in 1943, while the low point for motor-vehicle thefts did not occur until 1949. These low points are consistent, however, with differences in the availability of the two forms of property during the 1940's. The amount of cash and coin in banks, which did not vary much from 1920 to 1940, has grown rapidly ever since 1941 and 1942, dates which just precede the upturn in bank robbery and burglary rates. Motor vehicles, because of wartime restrictions on production, did not become plentiful until late in the 1940's. It was not, for example, until 1947 that the 1941 level of per capita automobile ownership was regained, and it was not until 1950 that the enormous postwar growth in automobile ownership began to level off. This increase in ownership coincides closely with the upturn in motor-vehicle theft rates. To state the point another way, theft against a form of property which is scarce, in this case automobiles, even though economic conditions are generally favorable,

[32]The correlation (r) between the percentage of the labor force unemployed and motor-vehicle theft is -.05. Between the percentage of unemployed and bank robbery and burglary, $r = .26$; it equals -.22 between the percentage of unemployed and the *Uniform Crime Reports* index of property crime (burglary, robbery, and motor-vehicle theft). The corresponding multiple correlations (for the equation $y = a + bx + cx^2$) are: motor-vehicle theft, .05; bank robbery and burglary, .27; and total property crime, .26.

seems to be influenced more by the scarcity of the property than by the state of the economy.

PROFESSIONAL AND AMATEUR THIEVES

The notion that the relationship between property thefts and amount of property available becomes positive once property becomes sufficiently abundant does not necessarily mean that the same kinds of people will be involved in the thievery during times of abundance that are involved during times of scarcity. In motor-vehicle thefts and bank robberies, the evidence suggests that these crimes are committed predominantly by different kinds of people today than before World War II.

The most striking change in the population of motor-vehicle thieves in recent years is the extent to which it has become dominated by youths. While no data show this precisely, because many thieves are never caught, available statistics on arrests for motor-vehicle theft,[33] as shown in Figure 8, indicate that most car thieves today are juveniles. It is true that many youths were also part of this population before and during the Second World War; the proportion of adults, however, was larger in those years. Moreover, the proportion of adults varied inversely with the availability of motor vehicles. In the years 1933 to 1941, when motor-vehicle registrations were rising, the proportion of adults arrested for motor-vehicle theft declined. This proportion continued to drop for two more years; it then jumped dramatically during the later years of the war when motor-vehicle registrations were on the decline. The proportion of adult car thieves remained high during the postwar years; then, beginning in 1950, it decreased steadily until 1957 and has remained at about that level ever since. What this change in the average age of motor-vehicle thieves means is that the crime itself has changed from one committed primarily for economic gain to one prompted by the simple thrill of joy-riding.

Bank robbery is another matter.[34] The nature of this population of thieves has also changed, but bank robbery has not

[33]F.B.I., *Uniform Crime Reports,* 1933–1965.
[34]No systematic study of bank burglars has been made.

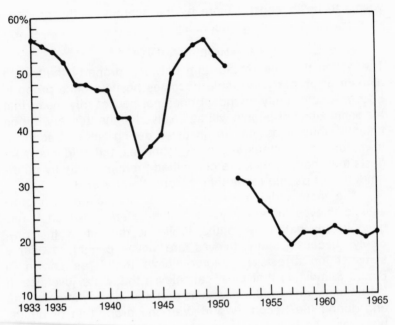

Figure 8
Per Cent of Those Arrested for Motor-Vehicle Theft in the U.S. Who
Are 21 Years Old or Older. *Note:* Figures for this graph are from the
F.B.I., *Uniform Crime Reports,* 1933–1965.

become, like auto theft, a crime of youth. It has become what
might be called a crime of desperation.

A recent and extensive study of bank robbery in the United
States, which included interviews with a random sample of
bank robbers incarcerated in federal prisons, disclosed two
important characteristics about bank robbers.[35] First, it showed
that prior to 1940 they were professional, full-time criminals
who robbed banks for a living; bank robbery, like other forms
of crime, was a livelihood. Since about 1945, a new, essentially
amateur, criminal element has entered the ranks of bank robbers. Forty-five per cent of bank robbers now in prison were
not pursuing a criminal career prior to robbing a bank. (Since

[35]Camp, "Nothing to Lose."

nearly 90 per cent of all bank robbers are caught, these figures are representative of all bank robbers.) The second important point revealed by the study was that, amateur or not, those holding up banks today are not doing it as a means of supporting themselves but to get out of a jam.

What now characterizes both the professional and the non-habitual criminals who rob banks is the desperation which motivates the act. In approximately one-fourth of the bank robberies, this desperation stems from a threat to the individual's person or livelihood—impending business failure, financial foreclosure, unpaid gambling debts. In the rest of the robberies, the desperation arises from an inability to get ahead in one's profession, either legitimate or illegitimate. What is significant, however, is that bank robbery is not viewed as a normal means of livelihood, even by the longtime criminals who turn to bank robbery; it is viewed as a source, though a risky one, of emergency cash.

Both car theft and bank robbery, then, have ceased to be crimes of regular economic gain. Instead of stealing cars to be resold for profit, as auto thieves used to do, most car thieves today are youths who steal cars for an evening's entertainment. Bank robbers, instead of being people who regularly steal money from banks for a living, are people who suddenly need a large amount of cash to meet one particular economic crisis and are willing to risk robbing a bank to get it.

Changes in theft rates, therefore, at least for the kinds of property crimes examined in this study, are influenced by economic conditions; they are not influenced by conditions of personal pathology. To be sure, it is the human response to economic conditions that ultimately determines the amount of crime. But there is nothing to suggest that this response is particularly pathological. In those who steal for a living, the response seems to be much like that of any legitimate businessman or professional responding to changes in market supply and demand. Just as a businessman looks for new products to sell when the market for old products becomes saturated, so a professional auto thief looks for something new to steal, say color television sets or mink coats, when the market for stolen automobiles becomes saturated. Similarly, just as a businessman might move his investments from stocks to bonds when the stability of the stock market comes into doubt, so a professional bank robber might turn to other crimes, such as home-improvement fraud, when these crimes offer less risk than bank robbery.

Those who do not steal for a living respond differently to economic conditions. Since this kind of criminal steals property to use himself, he is not influenced by the black market for stolen goods. Instead, he is influenced by his own deprivation. In particular, he is motivated to steal material things when he cannot afford to buy them legitimately, but nevertheless wants them. This happens not when things, like automobiles, are scarce, but when they are abundant; it happens when most people have the desired property but a few do not and thus sense their deprivation all the more keenly because they are among the few who are without.[36] While it could be argued that it is pathological to steal merely in order to get something that cannot be obtained legitimately, the pathology would nonetheless seem mild if it could be cured by simply making the fruits of an abundant economy more equally available to all.

THE EASE OF COMMITTING PROPERTY CRIMES

One final characteristic of property crimes that has changed in recent years should be mentioned: the ease with which these crimes can be committed today. It is a simple matter to illustrate this fact with motor-vehicle thefts and bank robberies and burglaries. When cars were scarce and money was not plentiful, it was harder to steal these commodities than it is now. Not only were there far fewer cars around to be stolen in the 1930's, but those who then had cars watched them more carefully and locked them more diligently than car owners do today. Also,

---

[36]The reasons suggested here as to why amateur criminals steal are essentially the same as those suggested by Robert K. Merton, *Social Theory and Social Structure*, rev. and enl. ed. (New York: The Free Press, 1957), esp. chap. 4. Merton did not, however, distinguish between professional and amateur criminals.

automatic transmissions facilitate driving today, and this innovation is of particular significance since automobiles are now often stolen by youths who are inexperienced drivers; many young people could not even drive a stolen car away if they had to manipulate a clutch and gearshift.

The ease with which a bank can now be robbed is even more striking. Unlike the banks of thirty or forty years ago, which separated tellers from customers—and robbers—with iron bars and which were likely to have armed guards on the premises, banks today are more or less wide open; the iron bars are gone, they are easily "cased," often isolated, and poorly protected.[37] Banks now seldom employ armed guards, and more than half of them do not even have adequate alarm systems—that is, alarms that sound in a police station or in the office of a protection agency.[38]

With so much property so ill-protected, it is little wonder that rates of property crime are rising. What is surprising, though, is that they are increasing at such a modest pace and that crimes per unit of property are actually far lower today than they were during the 1930's. Evidently the distribution of goods throughout the population is somewhat less unequal; otherwise, rates of theft by amateurs would be much higher than they are. In any event, theft by amateurs today seems to be less of a national problem than was theft by professional criminals 35 years ago.

Crimes against the person, to be sure, are not necessarily related to crimes against property. Moreover, crimes against the person have not been uniformly increasing. Rape and assault have increased but homicide has decreased. Crimes against the person, however, represent such a small per cent of all crimes that their contribution to the overall crime rate is dwarfed by the huge number of property crimes. It is property crime, then, and especially the dramatic increase in the per capita rate of property crime in recent years, that has contributed most to the belief that crime is "getting out of hand."

[37]Camp, "Nothing to Lose."
[38]Ibid., p. 55.

CRIME CONTROL

If this analysis is correct, it follows that Americans are not only misguided in their fear of crime and their assumptions about its causes, but they are equally misguided in the ways in which they go about controlling it. Law-enforcement agencies, for example, spend little time trying to modify the social conditions that encourage crime;[39] they concentrate instead on the task of catching criminals. While this approach may have been well advised in the early 1930's, when the bulk of crime was committed by a relatively few people who considered crime their profession, it may not make so much sense today when most crimes are committed by amateurs. Taking one professional criminal out of circulation in 1930 may well have "solved" many crimes, but removing one of today's amateurs from the ranks of criminals solves only one crime, or at best a few. Nevertheless, police still persist in tackling crime by the old-fashioned "case" method.

Typically, the police move into action on a crime only after receipt of a complaint from a victim that an offense has taken place—a robbery committed, a store burglarized, a car stolen. Their first step is an investigation by a uniformed patrolman who classifies the offense and records a minimal description of what happened. The patrolman's report then makes its way to one of several specialized detective details where it is routed to an individual detective or detective team. Each report constitutes a case, which is then assigned to a detective who becomes responsible for "clearing" it. This may mean—and in many instances does mean—little more than checking the facts with the complainant, usually the victim himself, and noting that unless new facts develop the case is likely to remain unsolved. Occasionally new facts do materialize and the case is solved, but this circumstance is the exception rather than the rule. Most crimes are never solved.

The case approach to crime is the process of responding

---

[39]The activities of some regulatory agencies, such as the Securities and Exchange Commission and the Food and Drug Administration, are a notable exception.

to reports of particular offenses, one by one, and of treating each report as a case to be solved. While this approach to crime has never been particularly successful—crime in the majority of instances does pay—it nonetheless constitutes the public and professional conception of good law-enforcement practice. The stereotype of a good detective is someone, like Sherlock Holmes, who investigates individual crimes through assiduous and ingenious methods that lead to the capture of the criminal.

The case approach, superficially, seems entirely reasonable, for the police do exist, after all, primarily because individual crimes take place. The approach has the further merit of assuring victims and the community at large that the police are busy and giving serious attention to law violations. But on close analysis, the concentration on cases, one by one, is in many respects unfortunate. It is an inefficient way to catch criminals and it effectively removes law-enforcement agencies from the business of controlling the overall structure of crime.

Without law-enforcement intervention, the structuring of crime is left to criminals. Though some criminals, on their own, will arrange their "businesses" in ways that are of some advantage to society, there is no guarantee that this will be done—and usually it is not. For example, criminals can and do organize gambling to make games "honest"; for customers get paid for their winnings and disputes with players are resolved with a minimum of violence. On the other hand, criminal organizers of gambling have never been known either to keep the house profits low or to discourage people from gambling who cannot afford to lose.

Some hold to the belief that ultimately we would be better off with no gambling at all. Yet the fact remains that people do gamble, and obviously legitimate gambling establishments are not sufficient to supply this service in all its desired forms. Indeed, the free-enterprise economy itself produces the motivation for gambling and even depends upon it to a considerable extent. The basic issue, then, is to mitigate the adverse consequences of gambling in a manner similar to the controls placed over the stock market—which is, after all, a form of legitimate gambling. As regulated brokers' fees and margin requirements have helped to make playing the stock market less dangerous to the consumer—and consequently to society—so would governmental regulation of other forms of gambling help to make them less dangerous.

Similarly, this nation has given practically no consideration to controlling crime by making it more difficult to steal. With a proliferation of checks, credit cards, serve-yourself retail stores, inadequately protected banks, and unlocked and unprotected merchandise of all kinds, it is not surprising that property crime is increasing. A small amount of effort directed at making these objects of crime less accessible might have a much greater effect on the crime rate than twice that effort poured into the current practice of tracking down and catching the culprit after the theft has been committed. In like fashion, money invested in programs to reduce poverty, especially among those who have begun to share the material desires of the middle class, could have large rewards in reduced crime. As these people come to participate successfully in the legitimate retail market for goods, their traffic in the illegitimate market should diminish.

The point is that much more could be done to regulate, control, and reduce crime. But this will not be done so long as American society continues to direct its attack only against those who commit crimes. If, indeed, crime involves political, legal, and economic institutions, as well as criminals and victims, then its reduction and control must ultimately depend in some part on changing the role these institutions and victims play in the crime process.

THE HIDDEN COSTS IN CRIME CONTROL

The control and reduction of crime, however, probably could not proceed without social costs. One of these costs, as some sociologists such as Durkheim and Erikson[40] have pointed out, would be the potential loss of one important mechanism of social solidarity. Inasmuch as crime serves to unify the public

---

[40]Durkheim, *The Division of Labor,* and Erikson, *Wayward Puritans.*

through the public's response to and concern about it, these sociologists argue, to reduce crime too much would threaten the unity of a nation. But this unity would also be threatened if crime control included, as some people have advocated,[41] a policy of political tolerance for some forms of crime—such as crimes of vice. For the public to be outraged about crimes that its government condones would probably be for the public to be outraged about government itself. Therefore, it would seem appropriate that governmental policy on crime should avoid official tolerance as well as overzealous control as both would threaten long-range social unity.

Reducing the amount of crime would also have more tangible social consequences. One of these would be the increase in unemployment, by decreasing the number of personnel needed in law-enforcement and correctional agencies and by placing on the job market those criminals formerly engaged in illegitimate occupations. Another consequence would be additional deprivation for those who can now purchase stolen goods but who are too poor to buy these items in the legitimate marketplace. This is not to say that these particular social consequences could not be dealt with by other and better means, or that they in any way justify leaving the problem of crime alone. This is only to say that crime is a complicated phenomenon that is an integral part of our society, and to change its structure radically will inevitably have undesirable results for some people—criminals who profit from it, the poor who are subsidized by it, and law-enforcement officials whose careers depend upon it. It is not unlikely, therefore, that these people, or at least some of them, will be less than enthusiastic about any vast changes in the status quo.

CONCLUSIONS

The impact of crime on society, then, involves not only those forces that induce some members of society to commit criminal acts, it also involves those institutions in society responsible

---

[41]Cf. Donald R. Cressey, *Theft of the Nation: The Structure and Operations of Organized Crime in America* (New York: Harper & Row, 1969).

for controlling these acts. Further, the impact of crime extends
to those victimized by it, and who thus would like to see it
eliminated, and to those profiting from it, and who thus would
like to see it perpetuated. And, ultimately, crime in any society
involves some of the very forces that serve to hold society
together.

The role of crime in society, moreover, is not static. As the
analysis of the relationship between property crime and the
availability of property demonstrates, the structure of crime
can change over time, responding to changes in the economic
conditions of society. These changes affect both the amount
of crime being committed and those committing the crimes.

Because crime commands such an important place in our
society, it and its social ramifications must be better understood. But this understanding must be achieved dispassion-
ately; it cannot evolve from any public paranoia about "the
crime problem getting out of hand." Crime may not be getting
out of hand at all, and even if it should be, the reasons why
may have nothing to do with the public's concern.

Americans are justified in being concerned about crime,
yes. Yet their concern is out of proportion to the menace crime
presents. Increases in crime in recent years are related more
to an expanding economy than to a breakdown in human in-
tegrity or to a collapse of the moral order. While there are those
who even go so far as to say that growing materialism is itself a
sign of social decay, most Americans accept and enjoy their
material advances. They find it hard to accept the notion,
therefore, that this progress has been achieved with social
costs, one of which is an increase in crime. The increase in
crime in America will continue, however, until we either place
less importance on accumulating material possessions or more
equitably distribute these possessions throughout society.

The Social Reality of Crime

RICHARD QUINNEY

The history of contemporary sociology is characterized by a progressive loss in faith—faith in the existence of anything beyond man's imagination. As a consequence, sociologists are being led to new assumptions about their craft and the substance of their labors. New orientations to old problems are making this a dynamic period for sociology.

Perhaps in no other sphere of sociological study is intellectual revisionism more apparent than in that of crime. In the following pages, I shall attempt to indicate how current thoughts and trends in the sociological study of crime can culminate in a theory of crime. The theory I will present—*the theory of the social reality of crime*—rests upon theoretical and methodological assumptions that are consistent with the happenings of our time. The purpose of the theory is to provide an understanding of crime that is relevant and meaningful to our contemporary experiences.

ASSUMPTIONS ABOUT EXPLANATION IN THE STUDY OF CRIME

Until fairly recent times, studies and writings in criminology have been oriented almost wholly to the observer's standard of what constituted crime. Such a conception of crime was consistent with the criminologist's interest in "the criminal."

In the last few years, however, with the realization that definitions of crime are relative to particular legal systems, students of crime have relied increasingly upon the legal definitions of a society as the standards for the study of crime. In other words, a nonlegal conception of crime has tended to be replaced by a relativistic—that is, legalistic—conception. The focus of attention of a considerable number of criminologists has thus been turned to the study of how criminal definitions are constructed and applied in a society.

The change in orientation among students of crime has resulted in the development of two schools of thought. On the one hand is the argument that the proper study of crime still consists of the study of the offender and his behavior; on the other is the conviction that attention should be devoted primarily to the study of how the criminal law is formulated, enforced, and administered. There is no reason, however, why the two schools of thought should become deadlocked in polemics. While interest in the study of criminal definitions is long overdue and provides a welcome corrective to the absurdities that resulted from the study of only the offender, the two approaches actually complement one another. Furthermore, it is possible for the two approaches of criminal behavior and criminal definition to be synthesized in such a way as to provide a new theoretical framework for the study of crime.

A synthesis into a theory of the two major substantive orientations in criminology rests upon certain assumptions about theoretical explanation. These assumptions are in regard to (1) ontology, (2) epistemology, (3) causation, and (4) theory construction.

ONTOLOGY

What is the world really like? I mean, what is it we pretend to separate ourselves from when we go about our observations? Contrary to the position of positivists, I am adopting a nominalistic position. Accordingly, we can accept no universal essences. The mind is unable to frame a single concept that corresponds to an objective reality. There is no certainty of an objective reality beyond man's conception of it; thus, the question of an objective reality may be dispensed with. There is no reason why we must believe in the objective existence of anything. Our concern, rather, is with the formulation of theories that are meaningful for the explanation of our experiences.

EPISTEMOLOGY

Implied in the ontological assumption is the epistemological assumption that we as observers cannot "copy" anything that may be regarded as an objective reality, since we are skeptical of the existence of such a reality. Our observations, instead, are based upon our own mental *constructions,* not upon essences beyond our experiences. Expressed in a more dramatic way: "Beauty is in the eye of the beholder." Our concern, therefore, is not with any correspondence between "objective reality" and observation, but between observation and the utility of such observations in understanding our own subjective, multiple social worlds.

CAUSATION

The objective of much of the theoretical explanation in criminology, based on a set of positivistic assumptions, has been to find the "causes" of crime. While the search for causes continues in the study of crime, modern usage of the causation concept as found in the philosophy of science is considerably different from that employed by criminologists.[1] The strategy in regard to causation that I propose for a theory of crime is consistent with the stated assumptions about the nature of the world and the way in which we understand it, as well as with current usage in the philosophy of science.

My first point in reference to causal explanation in criminology is that causal explanation need not be the sole interest

[1]For discussions of the usage of causation in modern philosophy of science and in the physical sciences, see Percy W. Bridgman, "Determinism in Modern Science," in *Determinism and Freedom in the Age of Modern Science,* ed. Sidney Hook (New York: P. F. Collier, 1961), pp. 57–75; Mario Bunge, *Causality: The Place of the Causal Principle in Modern Science* (New York: World Publishing, 1963); Werner Heisenberg, *Physics and Philosophy: The Revolution in Modern Science* (New York: Harper & Row, 1958).

of criminologists.[2] The objective of any science is not to formulate and verify theories of causation, but to construct an order among observables. Explanations as generalized answers to the question "why?" may be presented in other than causal form. For example, explanations in terms of probability statements, functional relations, and developmental stages can be formulated into propositions that do not depend upon causal explanation. A science of human behavior is obviously possible without the notion of causation.

Second, a statement of causation is not necessarily a statement of the nature of reality, but is a *methodological construction* of the observer. This conception of causation as a methodological construction is neatly expressed by a philosopher of science: "Causes certainly are connected by effects; but this is because our theories connect them, not because the world is held together by cosmic glue."[3] Thus, any defined causal relationship has to be regarded as a construct imposed by the scientist in his attempt to give meaning to what he has formulated as a significant theoretical problem. Our confusion in causal explanation has usually stemmed from inadvertently turning the causation construct into a description of reality.[4] Causation is initially a heuristic device, a methodological tool, not a description of the substance of our observations.

[2]Alternatives to causal explanation in criminology have been suggested in Hermanus Bianchi, *Position and Subject Matter of Criminology: Inquiry Concerning Theoretical Criminology* (Amsterdam: North-Holland, 1956); Nathaniel Cantor, "The Search for Causes of Crime," *Journal of Criminal Law, Criminology and Police Science* 22 (March–April 1932), pp. 854–863; Peter Lejins, "Pragmatic Etiology of Delinquent Behavior," *Social Forces* 29 (March 1951), pp. 317–321; David Matza, *Delinquency and Drift* (New York: John Wiley & Sons, 1964); Walter C. Reckless, *Criminal Behavior* (New York: McGraw-Hill, 1940). Acceptance of causal analysis in contemporary criminology is found in Travis Hirshi and Hanan C. Selvin, *Delinquency Research: An Appraisal of Analytic Methods* (New York: The Free Press, 1967).

[3]Norwood Russell Hanson, *Patterns of Discovery* (Cambridge: Cambridge University Press, 1965), p. 64.

[4]Regarding the confusion between nominal and real constructs in general, see Robert Bierstedt, "Nominal and Real Definitions in Sociological Theory," in *Symposium in Sociological Theory,* ed. Llewellyn Gross (New York: Harper & Row, 1959), pp. 121–144.

A third consideration in the formulation of causal explanations in the study of crime is that care must be taken not to use the causation construct in the same manner in which it is used in the physical sciences. Because of the basic differences between physical and social phenomena, the causation concept in the social sciences differs radically from the construct in the physical sciences. Causative explanations of crime have tended to be based on the mechanistic conception of causation found in the explanations of physical phenomena, a conception that, paradoxically, is outmoded in modern physical science. What is required in the explanation of crime, *if* a causative explanation is formulated, is a conception of causation that is attuned to the nature of social phenomena.

The world of social phenomena, as studied by the social scientist, is a world that has meaning for the human beings living within it.[5] The world of nature, however, as studied by the physical scientist, does not mean anything to the physical objects within it. Therefore, the constructs of the social scientist have to be founded upon the *social reality* created by man. As Schütz has noted in this connection, "The constructs of the social sciences are, so to speak, constructs of the second degree, that is, constructs of the constructs made by the actors on the social scene, whose behavior the social scientist has to observe and to explain in accordance with the procedural rules of his science."[6] Social scientists may well conceive of a *substantive causal process,* a process that is not only part of a social reality constructed by man but is also distinct from the first-order causal constructs formulated as methodological devices by the physical scientist. Thus, causation could be used substantively in an explanation of crime in the special sense of *social causation.* To the extent that man defines situations, that is, constructs his own world in relation to others,

[5]Robert M. MacIver, *Social Causation* (New York: Ginn and Co., 1942); Pitirim A. Sorokin, *Sociological Theories of Today* (New York: Harper & Row, 1966), pp. 12–34.

[6]Alfred Schütz, "Concept and Theory Formation in the Social Sciences," in *Philosophy of the Social Sciences,* ed. Maurice Natanson (New York: Random House, 1963), p. 242.

the student of social life may conceive of a social causation as part of a social reality.

THEORY CONSTRUCTION

The appropriate structure of a theory is far from certain in sociology. Much effort has been devoted to the establishment of methods for research, but little attention has been given to the development of methods for the construction of theory. Partly because of the lack of criteria for theory construction, Homans has suggested that a theory must consist of propositions that state relationships and form a deductive system.[7] Such a narrow standard ignores explanations that may be formulated in other than deductive form. Other types of explanation, it can be argued, may contain propositions that are not deductive but probabilistic, functional, or genetic.[8] Hence, a set of propositions need not necessarily be deductive, in the sense that another set of propositions must be deduced from it, in order for the original set of propositions to be regarded as a theory.

More important for theory construction is that propositions be consistent with one another and be integrated into a system.[9] That is, the conclusions obtainable from one proposition must not contradict the conclusions from another, and any conclusions obtained from the theory must be derivable within the given system of propositions. Beyond these standards for theory construction are the testability of the propositions, the validity of the propositions as determined by subsequent research, and the utility of the system of propositions for understanding the problem that originally inspired the formulation of the theory.

[7]George Casper Homans, "Contemporary Theory in Sociology," in *Handbook of Modern Sociology*, ed. Robert E. L. Faris (Chicago: Rand McNally, 1964), pp. 951–977.

[8]See Robert Brown, *Explanation in Social Science* (Chicago: Aldine, 1963); Morris R. Cohen and Ernest Nagel, *An Introduction to Logic and Scientific Method* (New York: Harcourt, Brace & World, 1934), pp. 197–222; Abraham Kaplan, *The Conduct of Inquiry: Methodology for the Behavioral Sciences* (San Francisco: Chandler, 1964), pp. 327–369.

[9]David Miller, *Scientific Sociology: Theory and Method* (Englewood Cliffs, N.J.: Prentice-Hall, 1967), pp. 9–10.

The structure of my theory of crime in'
ositions that are consistent with one and
into a theoretical system. Associated w'
are one or more specific statements that e
form, the relationships noted within the
the propositions are arranged according ⸺
sition units. The propositions express relations thaᴛ ⸺
coexistent and sequential. Implied in the model of the theory
is the assumption that patterns of phenomena develop over a
period of time.[10] Each proposition unit within the model requires explanation, and each unit relates to the others. Ultimately, however, crime is understood within the entire context
of the theoretical system.

ASSUMPTIONS ABOUT MAN AND SOCIETY
IN A THEORY OF CRIME

Some general perspective must be maintained in the study of
any social phenomenon. Two very general perspectives that
have been used by sociologists, and most social analysts for
that matter, have been in reference to the *static* and the *dynamic* nature of society. While either perspective is equally
plausible, sociologists have tended to favor the perspective
that concentrates on the static aspect of society.[11] This emphasis, in turn, has had the effect of relegating the forces and
events that do not appear to be conducive to stability and
consensus, such as deviance and crime, to the pathologies of
society.

The theory of the social reality of crime, however, is based
on the dynamic nature of society. Underlying the theory are
assumptions regarding the autonomous nature of man and the
disorderly character of society. These assumptions can be

[10]For discussions of sequential theories, see Howard S. Becker, *Outsiders: Studies in the Sociology of Deviance* (New York: The Free Press, 1963),
pp. 22–25; Clarence Schreg, "Elements of Theoretical Analysis in Sociology,"
in *Sociological Theory: Inquiries and Paradigms,* ed. Llewellyn Gross (New
York: Harper & Row, 1967), pp. 242–244.

[11]See Robert A. Nisbet, *The Sociological Tradition* (New York: Basic
Books, 1966); Reinhard Bendix and Bennett Berger, "Images of Society and
Problems of Concept Formation in Sociology," in *Symposium,* pp. 92–118.

...d into those of (1) process, (2) conflict, (3) power, and social action.

PROCESS

The dynamic aspect of social relations may be referred to as social process. While analytical descriptions of society may be couched in static terms, that is, in terms of the structure and function of social relations, we must be aware that social phenomena are in a constant state of flux.[12] The concept of process allows us to maintain a dynamic view of social phenomena.

The social-process assumption applies to all social phenomena that have duration and are undergoing change—that is, to all the phenomena that are of interest to the sociologist. A social process is a continuous series of actions leading to a particular kind of result. To use MacIver's definition, social process is "a system of social change taking place within a defined situation and exhibiting a particular order of change through the operation of forces present from the first within the situation."[13] Social processes are thus a part of concrete social settings that give specific actions definition and provide them with their specific quality.

The methodological implication of the process assumption is that any social phenomenon may be viewed as part of a complex network of events, structures, and underlying processes. As in the "modern systems approach," social phenomena are seen as generating out of an interrelated whole.[14] Any particular phenomenon, in turn, is viewed as contributing to the dynamics of the total process.

CONFLICT

In any society conflicts of various kinds—between persons, social units, or cultural elements—are inevitable and are to be

[12]Howard Becker, *Systematic Sociology on the Basis of the Beziehungslehre and Gebildelehre of Leopold von Wiess* (New York: John Wiley & Sons, 1932).

[13]MacIver, *Social Causation*, p. 130.

[14]Walter Buckley, "A Methodological Note," in Thomas J. Scheff, *Being Mentally Ill* (Chicago: Aldine, 1966), pp. 201–205.

expected as normal consequences of social life. Conflict is especially prevalent in those societies differentiated by several value systems and diverse normative groups. An assumption of consensus on all or most values and norms in such societies is contradicted by our experience.

The conflict model of society is in sharp contrast with the consensus model of society. The consensus model conceives of social structure in terms of a functionally integrated system held together in a state of equilibrium. The conflict model views societies and social organizations as being shaped by diversity, coercion, and change. The differences between these two contending, but complementary, conceptions of society have been best described by Dahrendorf.[15] According to him, we assume in the consensus (or integrative) model of society that: (1) society is a relatively persistent, stable structure of elements; (2) society is a well-integrated structure of elements; (3) every element in a society has a function, that is, renders a contribution to its maintenance as a system; and (4) a functioning social structure is based on a consensus of values among its members. In the assumptions of the conflict (or coercion) model of society, on the other hand, we assume that: (1) society is at every point subject to processes of change; (2) society displays at every point dissensus and conflict; (3) every element in a society renders a contribution to its change; and (4) society is based on the coercion of some of its members by others. In the conflict model, then, society is held together by force and constraint and is characterized by ubiquitous conflicts which result in continuous change. In the conflict model "values are ruling rather than common, enforced rather than accepted, at any given point of time."[16]

While a general condition of conflict may be present in the total society, as conceived in the conflict model, the likelihood still exists that a stability and consensus on values prevails among subunits in the society. Specific groups with

[15]Ralf Dahrendorf, *Class and Class Conflict in Industrial Society* (Stanford: Stanford University Press, 1959), pp. 161–162.

[16]Dahrendorf, "Out of Utopia: Toward a Reorientation in Sociological Analysis," *American Journal of Sociology* 67 (September 1958), p. 127.

their own cultural elements are found in most societies. To put it another way, there may be internal social differentiation within a society, with conflict existing between the social units, at the same time that integration and stability characterize specific social groups. As Robin Williams has written, "Although the total larger society may be diverse internally and may form only a loosely integrated system, within each subculture there may be high integration of institutions and close conformity of individuals to the patterns sanctioned by their own group."[17]

Conflict need not necessarily imply the disruption of society. Some sociologists have been interested in the *functions* of social conflict, "that is to say, with those consequences of social conflict which make for an increase rather than a decrease in the adaptation or adjustment of particular social relationships or groups."[18] To them, conflict is one of the processes that promotes cooperation, establishes group boundaries, and unites social factions. Furthermore, social conflict may lead to the emergence of new patterns that may in the long run be beneficial to the whole society or to aspects of it.[19] Any doubt about the functional possibilities of social conflict has been dispelled by Dahrendorf in the following manner: "I would suggest, in any case, that all that is creativity, innovation, and development in the life of the individual, his group, and his society is due, to no small extent, to the operation of conflicts between group and group, individual and individual, emotion and emotion within one individual. This fundamental fact alone seems to me to justify the value judgment that conflict is essentially 'good' and 'desirable.' "[20] Con-

[17]Robin Williams, *American Society,* 2nd ed. (New York: Alfred A. Knopf, 1960), p. 375.

[18]Lewis A. Coser, *The Functions of Social Conflict* (New York: The Free Press, 1956), p. 8.

[19]Coser, "Social Conflict and the Theory of Social Change," *British Journal of Sociology* 8 (September 1957), pp. 197–207.

[20]Dahrendorf, *Class and Class Conflict,* p. 208. The importance of conflict in society is also discussed, among other places, in George Simmel, *Conflict,* trans. Kurt H. Wolff (New York: The Free Press, 1955); Irving Louis Horowitz,

flict, therefore, may not always be viewed as the disruptive agent in a society, but may at times be more meaningfully conceived as a cohesive force.

POWER

In contrast with the integration conception of society, which assumes that common values are shared in the society, the conflict conception assumes that coherence is assured in any social organization through coercion and constraint. That is to say, the conflict conception assumes that *power* is the basic characteristic of social organization. "This means," as Dahrendorf has pointed out, "that in every social organization some positions are entrusted with a right to exercise control over other positions in order to ensure effective coercion; it means, in other words, that there is a differential distribution of power and authority."[21] Thus, conflict and power are inextricably linked in this conception of society. The differential distribution of power produces conflict between competing groups, and conflict, in turn, is rooted in the competition for power. Wherever men live together, there is conflict and a struggle for power.

Power, then, is the ability of persons and groups to determine the conduct of other persons and groups.[22] Power is utilized not for its own sake but as the vehicle for the enforcement of scarce values in society, whether the values are material, moral, or otherwise. The use of power affects the distribution of values and values affect the distribution of

---

"Consensus, Conflict and Cooperation: A Sociological Inventory," *Social Forces* 41 (December 1962), pp. 177–188; Raymond W. Mack, "The Components of Social Conflict," *Social Problems* 12 (Spring 1965), pp. 388–397.

[21]Dahrendorf, *Class and Class Conflict,* p. 165.

[22]Max Weber, *From Max Weber: Essays in Sociology,* trans. H. H. Gerth and C. Wright Mills (New York: Oxford University Press, 1946); Hans Gerth and C. Wright Mills, *Character and Social Structure* (New York: Harcourt, Brace & World, 1953), esp. pp. 192–273; C. Wright Mills, *The Power Elite* (New York: Oxford University Press, 1956); George Simmel, *The Sociology of George Simmel,* trans. Kurt H. Wolff (New York: The Free Press, 1950), pp. 181–186; Robert Bierstedt, "An Analysis of Social Power," *American Sociological Review* 15 (December 1950), pp. 730–738.

power. As Easton has indicated, the "authoritative allocation of values" is an essential process in any society.[23] In any society, institutional means are used to officially establish and enforce sets of values for the entire population.

Power and the allocation of values are basic to the formation of *public policy*. Diverse groups with specialized *interests* become organized to such an extent that they are able to influence the policies that are to affect all persons. These interest groups exert their influence at every level and branch of government in order to have their own values and interests represented in public-policy decisions.[24] The ability of any interest group to influence public policy is dependent upon the group's position in the political power structure. Therefore, access to policy-making channels varies from one group to

[23]David Easton, *The Political System* (New York: Alfred A. Knopf, 1953), p. 137. Similar ideas are found in Harold D. Lasswell, *Politics: Who Gets What, When, How* (New York: McGraw-Hill, 1936); Harold D. Lasswell and Abraham Kaplan, *Power and Society* (New Haven: Yale University Press, 1950).

[24]Among the vast amount of literature on interest groups, see Donald C. Blaisdell, *American Democracy Under Pressure* (New York: Ronald Press, 1957); V. O. Key, Jr., *Politics, Parties, and Pressure Groups* (New York: Thomas Y. Crowell, 1959); Earl Latham, *Group Basis of Politics* (Ithaca, N.Y.: Cornell University Press, 1952); David Truman, *The Governmental Process* (New York: Alfred A. Knopf, 1951); Henry W. Ehrmann, ed., *Interest Groups on Four Continents* (Pittsburgh: University of Pittsburgh Press, 1958); Henry A. Turner, "How Pressure Groups Operate," *Annals of the American Academy of Political and Social Science* 319 (September 1958), pp. 63–72; Richard W. Gable, "Interest Groups as Policy Shapers," *Annals of the American Academy of Political and Social Science* 319 (September 1958), pp. 84–93; Murray S. Stedman, "Pressure Groups and the American Tradition," *Annals of the American Academy of Political and Social Science* 319 (September 1958), pp. 123–129. For documentation of the influence of specific interest groups, see Robert Engler, *The Politics of Oil* (New York: Macmillan, 1961); Oliver Garceau, *The Political Life of the American Medical Association* (Cambridge: Harvard University Press, 1941); Charles M. Hardin, *The Politics of Agriculture: Soil Conservation and the Struggle for Power in Rural America* (New York: The Free Press, 1962); Grant McConnell, *Private Power and American Democracy* (New York: Alfred A. Knopf, 1966). Also, Harry A. Mills and Royal E. Montgomery, *Organized Labor* (New York: McGraw-Hill, 1945); Warner Schilling, Paul Y. Hammond, and Glenn H. Snyder, *Strategy, Politics and Defense* (New York: Columbia University Press, 1962); William R. Willoughby, *The St. Lawrence Waterway: A Study in Politics and Diplomacy* (Madison: University of Wisconsin Press, 1961).

another. Furthermore, access to the formation of public policy
is unequally distributed as a result of the nature of the structural arrangements of the political state: "Access is one of the
advantages unequally distributed by such arrangements; that
is, in consequence of the structural peculiarities of our government some groups have better and more varied opportunities
to influence key points of decision than do others."[25] Groups
that have the power to gain access to the decision-making
process also have the power to influence the policy that will
inevitably control the lives of all.

A major assumption in the conception of society that I
am proposing, therefore, is that of the importance of interest
groups in the shaping of public policy. The formation of public
policy represents the interests and values of those groups that
are in positions of power. Rather than a pluralistic conception
of the political process, in which it is assumed that all groups
make themselves heard in the process of policy decision-
making, I am relying upon a conception that assumes an
unequal distribution of power in the formulation and administration of public policy.[26]

SOCIAL ACTION

An assumption of man that is consistent with the conflict-power
conception of society is one that asserts that man's actions are
purposive and meaningful, that man engages in voluntaristic
behavior. This humanistic conception of man is in contrast
with the oversocialized conception which views man as a crea-

[25]Truman, *The Governmental Process,* p. 322.

[26]Evaluations of the pluralistic and power approaches are found in Peter
Bachrach and Morton S. Baratz, "Two Faces of Power," *American Political
Science Review* 56 (December 1962), pp. 947–952; Thomas I. Cook, "The Politi-
cal System: The Stubborn Search for a Science of Politics," *Journal of Philosophy* 51 (February 1954), pp. 128–137; Charles S. Hyneman, *The Study of
Politics* (Urbana: University of Illinois Press, 1959); William C. Mitchell, "Politics as the Allocation of Values: A Critique," *Ethics* 71 (January 1961), pp. 79–
89; Talcott Parsons, "The Distribution of Power in American Society," *World
Politics* 10 (October 1957), pp. 123–143; Charles Perrow, "The Sociological
Perspective and Political Pluralism," *Social Research* 31 (Winter 1964), pp.
411–422.

ture who is constantly attempting to conform, trying to avoid punishment, and desiring to win the approval of his fellows. Man alone, after all, is capable of considering alternative actions, of breaking from the established social order.[27] Once the individual has an awareness of self, acquired as a member of society, he is able to choose his actions. The extent to which a person does conform depends in large measure upon his own self-control.[28] It is also true that nonconformity may actually be a part of the process of finding self-identity; it is thus *against* something that the self can emerge.[29]

A conception of man based upon his ability to reason and choose courses of action allows us to view man as changing and becoming, rather than merely being.[30] The kind of culture that man develops shapes to a considerable degree the ability of the human being to be creative. Man may develop the capacity through his culture to have greater freedom of action.[31] Not only is he shaped by his physical, social, and cultural experiences, but he is able to select what he is to experience and develop. Emerging in contemporary culture is the belief in human possibilities and potential, that man can be realized to a far greater extent.[32] This belief must be incorporated into a conception of contemporary human behavior.

[27]For essentially this aspect of man, see Peter Berger, *Invitation to Sociology: A Humanistic Perspective* (Garden City, N.Y.: Doubleday, 1963), chap. 6; Max Mark, "What Image of Man for Political Science?" *Western Political Quarterly* 15 (December 1962), pp. 593–604; Dennis Wrong, "The Oversocialized Conception of Man in Modern Sociology," *American Sociological Review* 26 (April 1961), pp. 183–193.

[28]Tamotsu Shibutani, *Society and Personality: An Interactionist Approach to Social Psychology* (Englewood Cliffs, N.J.: Prentice-Hall, 1961), esp. pp. 60, 91–94, 276–278. Also see S. F. Nadel, "Social Control and Self-Regulation," *Social Forces* 31 (March 1953), pp. 265–273.

[29]Erving Goffman, *Asylums* (Garden City, N.Y.: Doubleday, 1961), pp. 318–320.

[30]Richard A. Schermerhorn, "Man the Unfinished," *Sociological Quarterly* 4 (Winter 1963), pp. 5–17; Gordon W. Allport, *Becoming: Basic Considerations for a Psychology of Personality* (New Haven: Yale University Press, 1955).

[31]Herbert J. Muller, *The Uses of the Past* (New York: Oxford University Press, 1952), esp. pp. 40–42.

[32]Julian Huxley, *New Bottles for New Wine* (New York: Harper & Row, 1957).

The *social-action* frame of reference, which serves as the basis of this humanistic conception of man, is drawn from the work of such writers as Weber, Znaniecki, MacIver, Nadel, Parsons, and Becker.[33] It was originally suggested by Max Weber: "Action is social in so far as, by virtue of the subjective meaning attached to it by the acting individual (or individuals), it takes account of the behavior of others and is thereby oriented in its own course."[34] Hence, according to the social-action perspective, human behavior is *intentional,* has *meaning* for the actors, is *goal-oriented,* and takes place with an *awareness* of the consequences of behavior.

Because man engages in social action, a *social reality* is created. That is, man in interaction with others constructs a meaningful world of everyday life.

It is the world of cultural objects and social institutions into which we are all born, within which we have to find our bearings, and with which we have to come to terms. From the outset, we, the actors on the social scene, experience the world we live in as a world both of nature and of culture, not as a private but as an intersubjective one, that is, as a world common to all of us, either actually given or potentially accessible to everyone; and this involves intercommunication and language.[35]

Social reality consists of both the social meanings and the products of the subjective world of persons. Man, accordingly, constructs activities and patterns of actions as he attaches meaning to this everyday existence.[36] Social reality is thus both a *conceptual reality* and a *phenomenal reality.* Hav-

[33]Florian Znaniecki, *Social Actions* (New York: Farrar, Straus & Giroux, 1936); MacIver, *Social Causation;* S. F. Nadel, *Foundations of Social Anthropology* (New York: The Free Press, 1951); Talcott Parsons, *The Structure of Social Action* (New York: The Free Press, 1949); Howard Becker, *Through Values to Social Interpretation* (Durham, N.C.: Duke University Press, 1950).

[34]Max Weber, *The Theory of Social and Economic Organization,* trans. A. M. Henderson and Talcott Parsons (New York: The Free Press, 1947), p. 88.

[35]Alfred Schütz, *The Problem of Social Reality: Collected Papers I* (The Hague: Martinus Nijhoff, 1962), p. 53.

[36]See Peter L. Berger and Thomas Luckman, *The Social Construction of Reality: A Treatise in the Sociology of Knowledge* (Garden City, N.Y.: Doubleday, 1966).

ing constructed social reality, man finds a world of meanings and events that is real to him as a conscious social being.

THEORY OF THE SOCIAL REALITY OF CRIME

The theory of the social reality of crime contains six propositions and a number of statements within the propositions. The first proposition is a definition of crime. The next four propositions consist of the explanatory units of the theory. The final proposition collects the previous propositions into a composite formulation of the social reality of crime. Included is a model of the construction of the social reality of crime. The propositions and their integration into a theory of crime are consistent with the assumptions about explanation and the assumptions about man and society outlined above.[37]

PROPOSITION 1 (Definition of Crime): *Crime is a definition of human conduct that is created by authorized agents in a politically organized society.*

This is the essential starting point in the theory—a definition of crime—which itself is based on the concept of definition. Crime is a *definition* of behavior that is conferred on some persons by other persons. Agents of the law (such as legislators, police, prosecutors, and judges), as representatives of certain segments of a politically organized society, are responsible for the formulation and administration of criminal law. Persons and behaviors, therefore, become criminal because of the *formulation* and *application* of definitions of crime.

In viewing crime as a definition, we are able to avoid the commonly used "clinical perspective" which concentrates on the quality of the act and which assumes that criminal behavior

[37]For earlier background material, see Richard Quinney, "A Conception of Man and Society for Criminology," *Sociological Quarterly* 6 (Spring 1965), pp. 119–127; idem, "Crime in Political Perspective," *American Behavioral Scientist* 8 (December 1964), pp. 19–22; idem, "Is Criminal Behavior Deviant Behavior?" *British Journal of Criminology* 5 (April 1965), pp. 132–142.

is an individual pathology.[38] Crime, according to the first proposition of the social reality of crime, is not inherent in behavior, but is rather a judgment made by some about the actions and characteristics of others.[39] This proposition allows us to focus upon the formulation and administration of the criminal law in relation to the behaviors that become defined as criminal. Crime is seen as a result of a process that culminates in the defining of persons and behaviors as criminal. It follows, then, that the greater the number of definitions of crime, formulated and applied, the greater the amount of crime.

PROPOSITION 2 (The Formulation of Definitions of Crime): *Definitions of crime are composed of behaviors that conflict with the interests of those segments of society that have the power to shape public policy.*

Definitions of crime are formulated according to the interests of those segments (various social groupings) of society that have the power to translate their particular interests into public policy. The interests—based on particular desires, values, and norms—that are ultimately incorporated into the criminal law are those treasured by the dominant interest groups in the

[38]See Jane R. Mercer, "Social System Perspective and Clinical Perspective: Frames of Reference for Understanding Career Patterns of Persons Labelled as Mentally Retarded," *Social Problems* 13 (Summer 1966), pp. 18–34.

[39]This perspective in the study of social deviance has been developed in Becker, *Outsiders;* Kai T. Erikson, "Notes on the Sociology of Deviance," *Social Problems* 9 (Spring 1962), pp. 307–314; John I. Kitsuse, "Societal Reactions to Deviant Behavior: Problems of Theory and Method," *Social Problems* 9 (Winter 1962), pp. 247–256. Also see Ronald L. Akers, "Problems in the Sociology of Deviance: Social Definitions and Behavior," *Social Forces* 46 (June 1968), pp. 455–465; David J. Bordua, "Recent Trends: Deviant Behavior and Social Control," *Annals of the American Academy of Political and Social Science* 369 (January 1967), pp. 149–163; Jack P. Gibbs, "Conceptions of Deviant Behavior: The Old and the New," *Pacific Sociological Review* 9 (Spring 1966), pp. 9–14; Clarence R. Jeffery, "The Structure of American Criminological Thinking," *Journal of Criminal Law, Criminology and Police Science* 46 (January–February 1956), pp. 658–672; Austin T. Turk, "Prospects for Theories of Criminal Behavior," *Journal of Criminal Law, Criminology and Police Science* 55 (December 1964), pp. 454–461.

society.[40] Furthermore, definitions of crime in a society change as the interests of the dominant segments are modified and as the positions of the segments are altered in the structure of power. In other words, those who have the ability to have their interests represented in public policy regulate the formulation of definitions of crime.[41]

The formulation of definitions of crime is one of the most obvious manifestations of *conflict* in society. The formulation of criminal law, including legislative statutes, administrative rulings, and judicial decisions, allows certain segments of society to protect and perpetuate their own interests. Definitions of crime exist, therefore, because certain segments of society are in conflict with others.[42] Through the formulation of definitions these segments are able to control the behavior

[40]See Richard C. Fuller, "Morals and the Criminal Law," *Journal of Criminal Law, Criminology and Police Science* 32 (March–April 1942), pp. 624–630; Thorsten Sellin, *Culture Conflict and Crime* (New York: Social Science Research Council, 1938), pp. 21–25; Clarence R. Jeffery, "Crime, Law and Social Structure," *Journal of Criminal Law, Criminology and Police Science* 47 (November–December 1956), pp. 423–435; John J. Honigmann, "Value Conflict and Legislation," *Social Problems* 7 (Summer 1959), pp. 34–40; George Rusche and Otto Kirchheimer, *Punishment and Social Structure* (New York: Columbia University Press, 1939).

[41]The interest approach to criminal law used here is in the general tradition of sociological jurisprudence as suggested by Roscoe Pound. See the following works by Pound: *An Introduction to the Philosophy of Law* (New Haven: Yale University Press, 1922); *Outline of Lectures on Jurisprudence* (Cambridge: Harvard University Press, 1928); "A Survey of Social Interests," *Harvard Law Review* 57 (October 1943), pp. 1–39. However, the concept of interest as used in the theory of criminal process departs from Pound's approach by assuming that definitions of crime *result from a conflict* in interests, rather than assuming that the definitions (the criminal law) *function for the control* of basic societal interests. The social order may require certain teleological functions (Pound's social interests) for its maintenance and survival, but such functions cannot be considered as being inherent in the particular interests that are involved in the formulation and administration of the criminal law.

[42]I am obviously indebted to the conflict formulation of George B. Vold, *Theoretical Criminology* (New York: Oxford University Press, 1958), esp. pp. 203–242. A recent conflict approach to crime is found in Austin T. Turk, "Conflict and Criminality," *American Sociological Review* 31 (June 1966), pp. 338–352.

of persons in other segments. It follows that the greater the conflict in interests between segments of a society, the greater the probability that the power segments will formulate definitions of crime.

The interests of the power segments of society are reflected not only in the content of the definitions of crime and the kinds of penal sanctions attached to the definitions, but also in the *legal policies* regarding the handling of those defined as criminals. Hence, procedural rules are created for the enforcement and administration of the criminal law. Policies are also established in respect to programs for the treatment and punishment of the criminally defined and programs for the control and prevention of crime. In all cases, whether in regard to the initial definitions of crime or the subsequent procedures, correctional and penal programs, or policies of crime control and prevention, those segments of society that have power and particular interests to protect are instrumental in regulating the behavior of those who have less power and with whom they have conflicting interests.[43]

Finally, since law is formulated within the context of the interest structure of politically organized society, it follows that law changes with modifications in the interest structure. New and shifting demands require new laws. When the interests that underlie a criminal law are no longer relevant to groups in power, the law will be reinterpreted or altered in order to incorporate the dominant interests. Hence, the prob-

[43]Considerable support for this proposition is found, among other places, in the following studies: William J. Chambliss, "A Sociological Analysis of the Law of Vagrancy," *Social Problems* 12 (Summer 1964), pp. 66–77; Kai T. Erikson, *Wayward Puritans* (New York: John Wiley & Sons, 1966); Jerome Hall, *Theft, Law and Society,* 2nd ed. (Indianapolis: Bobbs-Merrill, 1952); Clarence R. Jeffery, "The Development of Crime in Early England," *Journal of Criminal Law, Criminology and Police Science* 47 (March–April 1957), pp. 647–666; Alfred R. Lindesmith, *The Addict and the Law* (Bloomington: Indiana University Press, 1965); Rusche and Kirchheimer, *Punishment and Social Structure;* Andrew Sinclair, *Era of Excess: A Social History of the Prohibition Movement* (New York: Harper & Row, 1964); Edwin H. Sutherland, "The Sexual Psychopath Laws," *Journal of Criminal Law, Criminology and Police Science* 40 (January–February 1950), pp. 543–554.

ability that definitions of crime will be formulated is increased by such factors as (1) changing social conditions, (2) emerging interests, (3) increasing concern with the protection of political, economic, and religious interests, and (4) changing conceptions of the public interest. The social history of law can thus be written in terms of changes in the interest structure of society.

PROPOSITION 3 (The Application of Definitions of Crime): *Definitions of crime are applied by those segments of society that have the power to shape the enforcement and administration of criminal law.*

The interests of the power segments of society intervene in all the stages in which definitions of crime are created. Since interests cannot be effectively protected through the mere formulation of criminal law, there must be enforcement and administration of the law. The interests of the powerful, therefore, also operate in the *application* of the definitions of crime. Consequently, as Vold has argued, crime is "political behavior and the criminal becomes in fact a member of a 'minority group' without sufficient public support to dominate the control of the police power of the state."[44] Those whose interests conflict with the interests represented in the law must either change their behavior or possibly find it defined as criminal.

The probability that definitions of crime will be applied varies according to the extent to which the behaviors of the powerless conflict with the interests of power segments. Law-enforcement efforts and judicial activity are likely to be increased when the interests of the powerful are being threatened. Fluctuations and variations in applying definitions of crime reflect shifts in the relations of the different segments in the power structure of society.

Obviously, the criminal law is not applied directly by the segments that incorporate their interests into the formulation

[44]Vold, *Theoretical Criminology*, p. 202. Also see Irving Louis Horowitz and Martin Liebowitz, "Social Deviance and Political Marginality: Toward a Redefinition of the Relation Between Sociology and Politics," *Social Problems* 15 (Winter 1968), pp. 280–296.

and application of the definitions of crime. Rather, the actual enforcement and administration of the law are delegated to authorized *legal agents*. These authorities, nevertheless, represent the interests of the power segments. In fact, the legal agents' security of office is dependent upon their ability to represent the dominant interests of the society.

Because of the physical separation of the interest groups responsible for the creation of the definitions of crime from the groups delegated the authority to enforce and administer law, local conditions affect the actual application of definitions.[45] In particular, communities vary from one another in their expectations of law enforcement and the administration of justice. The application of definitions is also influenced by the visibility of offenses in a community and by the norms in respect to the reporting of possible violations by the public. And especially important in the enforcement and administration of the criminal law are the occupational organization and ideology of the legal agents.[46] Thus, the probability that definitions of crime will be

---

[45]See Michael Banton, *The Policeman and the Community* (London: Tavistock, 1964); Egon Bittner, "The Police on Skid-Row: A Study of Peace Keeping," *American Sociological Review* 32 (October 1967), pp. 699–715; John P. Clark, "Isolation of the Police: A Comparison of the British and American Situations," *Journal of Criminal Law, Criminology and Police Science* 56 (September 1965), pp. 307–319; Nathan Goldman, *The Differential Selection of Juvenile Offenders for Court Appearance* (New York: National Council on Crime and Delinquency, 1963); James Q. Wilson, *Varieties of Police Behavior: The Management of Law and Order in Eight Communities* (Cambridge: Harvard University Press, 1968).

[46]Abraham S. Blumberg, *Criminal Justice* (Chicago: Quadrangle Books, 1967); David J. Bordua and Albert J. Reiss, Jr., "Command, Control and Charisma: Reflections on Police Bureaucracy," *American Journal of Sociology* 72 (July 1966), pp. 68–76; Aaron V. Cicourel, *The Social Organization of Juvenile Justice* (New York: John Wiley & Sons, 1968); Arthur Niederhoffer, *Behind the Shield: The Police in Urban Society* (Garden City, N.Y.: Doubleday, 1967); Jerome H. Skolnick, *Justice Without Trial* (New York: John Wiley & Sons, 1966); Arthur L. Stinchcombe, "Institutions of Privacy in the Determination of Police Administrative Practice," *American Journal of Sociology* 69 (September 1963), pp. 150–160; David Sudnow, "Normal Crimes: Sociological Features of the Penal Code in a Public Defender Office," *Social Problems* 12 (Winter 1965), pp. 255–276; William A. Westley, "Violence and the Police," *American Journal of Sociology* 59 (July 1953), pp. 34–41; Arthur Lewis Wood, *Criminal Lawyer* (New Haven: College & University Press, 1967).

applied is influenced by such community and organizational factors as (1) community expectations of law enforcement and administration, (2) the visibility and public reporting of offenses, and (3) the occupational organization, ideology, and actions of the legal agents delegated the authority to enforce and administer criminal law. On the basis of such factors, the dominant interests of society are implemented in the application of definitions of crime.

The probability that these definitions will be applied in specific situations is dependent upon the actions of the legal agents who have been given the authority to enforce and administer the law. In the final analysis, the application of a definition of crime is a matter of evaluation on the part of persons charged with the authority to enforce and administer the law. As Turk has argued, in the course of "criminalization," a criminal label may be affixed to persons because of real or fancied attributes: "Indeed, a person is evaluated, either favorably or unfavorably, not because he *does* something, or even because he *is* something, but because others react to their perceptions of him as offensive or inoffensive."[47] Evaluation by the definers is affected by the way in which the suspect handles the situation, but ultimately the evaluations and subsequent decisions of the legal agents are the crucial factors in determining the criminality of human acts. Hence, the more legal agents evaluate behaviors and persons as worthy of definitions of crime, the greater the probability that definitions of crime will be applied.

PROPOSITION 4 (The Development of Behavior Patterns in Relation to the Definitions of Crime): *Behavior patterns are structured in segmentally organized society in relation to definitions of crime, and within this context persons engage in actions that have relative probabilities of being defined as criminal.*

[47]Turk, "Conflict and Criminality," p. 340. For research on the evaluation of suspects by policemen, see Irving Piliavin and Scott Briar, "Police Encounters with Juveniles," *American Journal of Sociology* 70 (September 1964), pp. 206–214.

Although the substance of behavior varies, all behaviors are similar in that they represent the behavior patterns of a particular segment of society. Therefore, all persons—whether they create definitions of crime or are the objects of these definitions—act in reference to *normative systems* learned in relative social and cultural settings.[48] Since it is not the quality of the behavior but the action taken against the behavior that gives it the character of criminality, that which is defined as criminal in any society is relative to the behavior patterns of the power segments that formulate and apply definitions. Consequently, persons in the segments of society whose behavior patterns are not represented in the formulation and application of the definitions of crime are more likely to act in ways that will be defined as criminal than those in the segments that formulate and apply the definitions.

Once behavior patterns become established with some degree of regularity within the different segments of society, individuals are provided with a framework for the creation of *personal action patterns*. These action patterns continually develop for each person as he moves from one life experience to another. It is the development of certain action patterns that gives the behavior of persons an individual substance in relation to the definitions of crime.

Man constructs his own patterns of action in participating with others. It follows, then, that the probability that persons will develop action patterns that have a high potential of being defined as criminal is dependent upon the relative substance of (1) structured opportunities, (2) learning experiences, (3) interpersonal associations and identifications, and (4) self-conceptions. Throughout the course of his experiences, each person creates a conception of himself as a human social

[48]Assumed within the theory of the social reality of crime is Sutherland's theory of differential association. See Edwin H. Sutherland, *Principles of Criminology*, 4th ed. (Philadelphia: J. B. Lippincott, 1947). An analysis of the differential association theory is found in Melvin L. De Fleur and Richard Quinney, "A Reformulation of Sutherland's Differential Association Theory and a Strategy for Empirical Verification," *Journal of Research in Crime and Delinquency* 3 (January 1966), pp. 1–22.

being. Thus prepared, persons behave rationally in terms of the anticipated consequences of their actions.[49]

In the course of the shared experiences of the definers of crime and the criminally defined, personal-action patterns develop among the latter as a consequence of being so defined. After such persons have had continued experience in being defined as criminal, they learn to manipulate the application of criminal definitions.[50]

Furthermore, those who have been defined as criminal begin to conceive of themselves as criminal. As they adjust to the definitions imposed upon them, they learn to play the role of the criminal.[51] As a result of the reactions of others, therefore, persons may develop personal-action patterns that increase the likelihood of their being defined as criminal in the future. That is, increased experience with definitions of crime increases the probability of the development of actions that may be subsequently defined as criminal.

Thus, both the definers of crime and the criminally defined are involved in reciprocal action patterns. The personal-action patterns of both the definers and the defined are shaped by the interrelation of their common, continued, and interrelated experiences. The fate of each is bound to that of the other.

PROPOSITION 5 (The Construction of Conceptions of Crime): *Conceptions of crime are constructed and diffused in the segments of society by means of communication.*

[49]On the operant nature of criminally defined behavior, see Robert L. Burgess and Ronald L. Akers, "A Differential Association-Reinforcement Theory of Criminal Behavior," *Social Problems* 14 (Fall 1966), pp. 128–147; Clarence R. Jeffery, "Criminal Behavior and Learning Theory," *Journal of Criminal Law, Criminology and Police Science* 56 (September 1965), pp. 294–300.

[50]A discussion of the part the person plays in manipulating the deviant–defining situation is found in Judith Lorber, "Deviance as Performance: The Case of Illness," *Social Problems* 14 (Winter 1967), pp. 302–310.

[51]Edwin M. Lemert, *Human Deviance, Social Problems, and Social Control* (Englewood Cliffs, N.J.: Prentice-Hall, 1964), pp. 40–64; idem, *Social Pathology* (New York: McGraw-Hill, 1951), pp. 3–98. A related and earlier discussion is in Frank Tannenbaum, *Crime and the Community* (New York: Columbia University Press, 1938), pp. 3–81.

The "real world" is a social construction: man with the help of others creates the world in which he lives. Social reality is thus the world that a group of people create and believe in as their own. The construction of this reality is related to the kind of knowledge they develop, the ideas they are exposed to, the manner in which they select information to fit the world they are in the process of shaping, and the manner in which they interpret these conceptions.[52] Man behaves in reference to the *social meanings* he attaches to his experiences.

Among the conceptions that develop in a society are those relating to what man regards as crime. Whenever the concept of crime exists, conceptions of the nature of crime also exist. Images develop concerning the relevance of crime, the characteristics of the offender, the appropriate reaction to crime, and the relation of crime to the social order.[53] These conceptions are constructed through the process of communication. In fact, the construction of conceptions of crime is dependent upon the portrayal of crime in all personal and mass communication. Through such means, conceptions of what is criminal are diffused throughout a society.

One of the most concrete ways in which conceptions of crime are formed and transmitted is through official investigations of crime. The President's Commission on Law Enforce-

[52]See Berger and Luckmann, *The Social Construction of Reality*. Relevant research on the dissemination of information is discussed in Everett M. Rogers, *Diffusion of Innovations* (New York: The Free Press, 1962).

[53]Research on public conceptions of crime is only beginning. See Alexander L. Clark and Jack P. Gibbs, "Social Control: A Reformulation," *Social Problems* 12 (Spring 1965), pp. 398–415; Thomas E. Dow, Jr., "The Role of Identification in Conditioning Public Attitude Toward the Offender," *Journal of Criminal Law, Criminology and Police Science* 58 (March 1967), pp. 75–79; William P. Lentz, "Social Status and Attitudes Toward Delinquency Control," *Journal of Research in Crime and Delinquency* 3 (July 1966), pp. 147–154; Jennie McIntyre, "Public Attitudes Toward Crime and Law Enforcement," *Annals of the American Academy of Political and Social Science* 374 (November 1967), pp. 34–46; Anastassios D. Mylonas and Walter C. Reckless, "Prisoners' Attitudes Toward Law and Legal Institutions," *Journal of Criminal Law, Criminology and Police Science* 54 (December 1963), pp. 479–484; Elizabeth A. Rooney and Don C. Gibbons, "Social Reactions to 'Crimes Without Victims,'" *Social Problems* 13 (Spring 1966), pp. 400–410.

ment and Administration of Justice is the best contemporary example of the role of government in shaping conceptions of crime.[54] Not only do we as citizens have a greater awareness of crime today because of the activities of the President's commission, but official policy regarding crime has been established in a crime bill (the Omnibus Crime Control and Safe Streets Act of 1968). The crime bill, which itself was a reaction to the growing fears of conflict in American society, creates an image of the severity of the crime problem and, in the course of so doing, negates some of our basic constitutional guarantees in the name of crime control. Our current social reality of crime has thus been shaped by the communication of the ideas and fears of those in positions of power.

Consequently, the conceptions that are most critical in the actual formulation and application of the definitions of crime are those held by the power segments of society. These are the conceptions of crime that are certain to become incorporated into the social reality of crime. Furthermore, the more the power segments of society are concerned about crime, the greater the probability that definitions of crime will be created and that behavior patterns will develop in opposition to the definitions. The formulation of definitions of crime, the application of the definitions, and the development of behavior patterns in relation to the definitions are thus joined in full circle by the construction of conceptions of crime.

PROPOSITION 6 (Construction of the Social Reality of Crime): *The social reality of crime is constructed by the formulation and application of definitions of crime, the development of behavior patterns in relation to these definitions, and the construction of conceptions of crime.*

The first five propositions can be collected into a final composite proposition. The theory of the social reality of crime, accordingly, postulates the creation of a series of phenomena

[54]President's Commission on Law Enforcement and Administration of Justice, *The Challenge of Crime in a Free Society* (Washington, D.C.: United States Government Printing Office, 1967).

that increase the probability of crime in society. The result, in holistic terms, is the construction of the social reality of crime.

Since the first proposition of the theory is a definition and the sixth proposition is a composite, the body of the theory consists of the four middle propositions. These propositions form a model of the social reality of crime. The model, as diagramed in Figure 1, relates the proposition units into a theoretical system. Each proposition unit is related to the others. The theory is thus in the form of a system of interacting developmental propositions. The phenomena denoted in the propositions and their interrelations culminate in what is regarded as the amount and character of crime in a society at any given time—that is, in the social reality of crime.

CONCLUSION

The theory of the social reality of crime as I have formulated it has been inspired by a change that is occurring in our view of the world. This change, which is pervading all levels of society, pertains to the world that we all construct and, at the same time, pretend to separate ourselves from in our human experiences. Among sociologists, an apprehension of the relativism of existence has marked the beginning of a revision in theoretical orientation, as well as a revision in the methods and subjects of investigation.

For the study of crime, a revision in thought has directed attention to the process by which definitions of crime are formulated and applied. In the theory of the social reality of crime, I have attempted to show how a theory of crime can be consistent with certain revisionist assumptions about theoretical explanation and about man and society. The theory is cumulative in that it incorporates the diverse findings of criminology.

The synthesis has been brought about by conceiving of crime as a process and by constructing a theory in terms of a system of propositions. The theory is integrative; all relevant phenomena contribute to the process of creating definitions of crime, the development of the behaviors of those who are in-

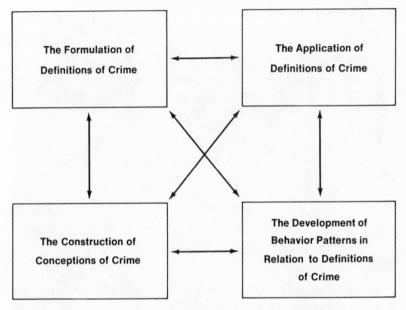

Figure 1
Model of the Social Reality of Crime.

volved in criminal-defining situations, and the construction of conceptions of crime. The result is the social reality of crime that is constantly being constructed in society.

Finally, the theory of the criminal process provides *one* way of understanding crime. Since the sociologist constructs his own world of meaning based upon his own experiences, including research, the theory of the social reality of crime is only as useful as it contributes to the kinds of questions that we currently comprehend.

PART III

Law,
Law Enforcement,
and Crime Control

The Police:
Mandate, Strategies,
and Appearances

PETER K. MANNING

I. INTRODUCTION

All societies have their share of persistent, chronic problems—
problems of life, of death, problems of property and security,
problems of man's relationship to what he consecrates. And
because societies have their quota of troubles, they have developed ways in which to distribute responsibility for dealing
with them. The division of labor that results is not only an allocation of functions and rewards, it is a moral division as well.
In exchange for money, goods, or services, these groups—such
as lawyers or barbers or clergymen or pharmacists—have a
license to carry out certain activities that others may not. This
license is a legally defined right, and no other group or groups
may encroach upon it.[1]
   The right to perform an occupation may entail the per-
mission to pick up garbage or to cut open human bodies and
transfer organs from one to another. What it always involves,
however, is a series of tasks and associated attitudes and val-

*I would like to thank Howard S. Becker, Jerome H. Skolnick, and Jack D.
Douglas for helpful comments and criticism on this essay.*

[1]See Everett C. Hughes, *Men and Their Work* (New York: The Free Press,
1958), chap. 6; idem, "The Study of Occupations," in *Sociology Today,* ed.
R. K. Merton, Leonard Broom, and L. S. Cottrell (New York: Basic Books, 1959),
pp. 442–458.

ues that set apart a specialized occupational group from all the others. Further, the licensed right to perform an occupation may include a claim to the right to define the proper conduct of others toward matters concerned with the work. The claim, if granted, is the occupation's *mandate.* The mandate may vary from a right to live dangerously to the right to define the conditions of work and functions of related personnel.

The professional mandate is not easily won, of course, for clients are often unwilling to accept the professional definition of their problem. Professions claim a body of theory and practice to justify their right to discover, define, and deal with problems. The medical profession, for example, is usually considered the model of a vocation with a secure license and mandate. Yet even in medicine the client may refuse to accept the diagnosis; he may change physicians or fail to follow doctor's orders or insist upon defining his troubles as the product of a malady best cured by hot lemonade or prayer. The contraction and expansion of an occupation's mandate reflects the concerns society has with the services it provides, with its organization, and with its effectiveness. In times of crisis, it is the professions that are questioned first.[2]

Some occupations are not as fortunate as others in their ability to delimit a societal "trouble" and deal with it systematically. The more power and authority a profession has, the better able it is to gain and maintain control over the symbolic meanings with which it is associated in the public's mind. As we have become less concerned with devils and witches as causes of mental illness, clergymen have lost ground to psychiatrists who have laid claim to a secular cure for madness; in this sense, mental illness is a product of the definitions supplied by psychiatry. A profession, therefore, must not only compete with its clientele's definitions, it must also defend itself against the definitions of competing groups. Is a backache better treated by a Christian Scientist, an osteopath, a chiropractor, a masseuse, or an M.D.? Professional groups whose tools are less well-developed, whose theory is jerry-built or unproved, and

[2]Hughes, *Men and Their Work.*

who are unable to produce results in our consumer-oriented society will be beset with public doubt, concern, and agitation. In other words, these are the groups that have been unable to define their mandate for solving social "troubles" in such a way that it can be accomplished with ease and to the satisfaction of those they intend to serve.

The police have trouble. Among the many occupations now in crisis, they best symbolize the shifts and strains in our changing socio-political order. They have been assigned the task of crime prevention, crime detection, and the apprehension of criminals. Based on their legal monopoly of violence, they have staked out a mandate that claims to include the efficient, apolitical, and professional enforcement of the law. It is the contention of this essay that the police have staked out a vast and unmanageable social domain. And what has happened as a result of their inability to accomplish their self-proclaimed mandate is that the police have resorted to the manipulation of *appearances*.

We shall attempt to outline the nature of the police mandate, or their definition of social trouble, their methods of coping with this trouble, and the consequences of their efforts. After developing a sociological analysis of the paradoxes of police work and discussing the heroic attempts—*strategies*—by police to untangle these paradoxes, we shall also consider the recommendations of the President's crime commission[3] and assess their value as a means of altering and improving the practical art of managing public order.

To turn for the moment to "practical matters," the same matters to which we shall return before concluding, the troubles of the police, the problems and paradoxes of their mandate in modern society, have become more and more intense. Police today may be more efficient in handling their problems than were the first bobbies who began to patrol London in 1829.

[3]The President's Commission on Law Enforcement and Administration of Justice (hereafter cited as President's Commission), *The Challenge of Crime in a Free Society* (Washington, D.C.: United States Government Printing Office, 1967); and idem, *Task Force Report: The Police* (Washington, D.C.: United States Government Printing Office, 1967).

Or they may not be. There may or may not be more crime. Individual rights may or may not be greatly threatened by crime or crime-fighters, and the enforcement of law in view of recent Supreme Court decisions may or may not be a critical issue in crime control. The police may or may not have enough resources to do their job, and they may or may not be allocating them properly. Peace-keeping rather than law enforcement may or may not be the prime need in black communities, and the police may or may not need greater discretionary powers in making an arrest. But however these troubles are regarded, they exist. They are rooted deeply in the mandate of the police.

SOME SOCIOLOGICAL ASSUMPTIONS

This essay makes several assumptions about occupations, about people as they execute occupational roles, about organizations as loci or structures for occupational activities, and about the nature of society. Not all activity taking place "on the job" can be construed as "work"; goldbricking is not unknown in American society and some professionals have even been known to use their places of work to conduct business somewhat outside the mandate of their organization. An individual's "organizational" behavior varies with what the organization is said to require or permit, with his particular place in the organizational hierarchy, and with the degree of congruence between the individual's personal definition of his role and the organization's definition of his role. In a given situation, then, organizational rules and regulations may be important sources of meanings ("He's working hard"), or other criteria may provide more relevant meanings of behavior ("He can't be expected to work. His wife just had a baby"). The ways in which people explain or account for their own organizational activities and those of others are problematic. How do people refer to their organizational roles and activities? How do they construct their moral obligations to the organization? What do they think they owe the organization? How does this sense of obligation and commitment pattern or constrain them in another role—the role of golfer or father or politician?

People as they perform their roles are actors. They are

alert to the small cues that indicate meaning and intention—the wink, the scowl, the raised eyebrow. Those who attend to these behavioral clues are the audience. All actors try to maximize the positive impression they make on others, and both experience and socialization provide them with a repertoire of devices to manage their appearance.

People as actors in roles must also make assumptions about their audience. The politician, for example, must make certain assumptions about his constituency, the lawyer certain assumptions about clients. Assumptions are an important part of urban life. Some actors with white faces, for instance, may make certain assumptions about others with black faces, that they will be ill-mannered or badly educated and that any request for directions is a prelude to a holdup. Assumptions are not simply individual in nature; they are shared, patterned, and passed on from one social group to the next.

One of the most important aspects of assumptions, however, is that they are the basis for strategies.[4] Strategies arise from the need of organizations and individuals to cope with persistent social problems about which assumptions have been made. Strategies are often a means of survival in a competitive environment; they can be inferred from the allocation of resources or from the behavior and pronouncements of an organization. In short, strategies assist any organization within the society in managing its appearance and in controlling the behavior of its audience.

All organizations and individuals, we assume, are bent on maximizing their impressions in order to gain control over an audience.[5] The audience for the police is diverse; it should be considered many audiences. For the police must convince the politicians that they have used their allocated resources efficiently; they must persuade the criminals that they are effective crime-fighters; they must assure the broader public that they are controlling crime. Rather than a single rhetoric—the "use

[4]The important, sociological notions of "strategy" and "tactics" come from military theory and game theory. See, for example, Erving Goffman, *The Presentation of Self in Everyday Life* (Garden City, N.Y.: Doubleday, 1956).
[5]Ibid.

of words to form attitudes or induce actions in other human agents"[6]—directed toward convincing one audience, the police must develop many rhetorics. Linguistic strategies to control audiences are only one of many ploys used by the police organization to manage its impression. Not all the results of the use of rhetorics are intended; the consequence of the rhetorical "war on crime" in Detroit in the fall of 1969, to cite one example, was a continued advance in the city's downtown crime rate. Moreover, rhetoric can take on different meanings even within the organizational hierarchy. To patrolmen, the term "professionalism" means control over hours and salary and protection from arbitrary punishment from "upstairs"; to the chief and the higher administrators, it relates to the public-administration notions of efficiency, technological expertise, and standards of excellence in recruitment and training.

Tactics are the means by which a strategy is implemented. If the strategy is to mount a war on crime, then one tactic might be to flood the downtown area with scooter-mounted patrolmen. Tactics, in other words, are the ways in which one group of people deals with others in face-to-face encounters. How does the policeman handle a family quarrel in which the wife has the butcher knife and the husband already knows how sharp it is? Strategies pertain to general forms of action or rhetoric while tactics refer to the specific action or the specific words used to best meet a specific, problematic situation.[7] The tactic of flattery may be far more effective—and safer—in wresting the butcher knife than a leap over the kitchen table.

All occupations possess strategies and tactics, by means of which they attempt to control their most significant audiences. However, our analysis must do more than describe the existence of such means of creating impressions. So far as the police are concerned, impression management, or the construction of appearances, cannot substitute for significant con-

[6]Kenneth Burke, *A Grammar of Motives and a Rhetoric of Motives* (New York: Meridian Books, 1962), p. 565.

[7]D. W. Ball makes this distinction between rhetoric and what he terms "situated vocabularies" in "The Problematics of Respectability" in *Deviance and Respectability,* ed. Jack D. Douglas (New York: Basic Books, 1970).

trol of crime. To maintain the dramaturgic metaphor, we suggest that there are significant flaws and contradictions in the performance of the police that cast a serious doubt on the credibility of their occupational mandate.

The mandate of the police is fraught with difficulties, many of them, we shall argue, self-created. They have defined their task in such a way that they cannot, because of the nature of American social organization, hope to honor it to the satisfaction of the public. We will argue that the appearances that the police create—that they control crime and that they attain a high level of efficiency—are transparent on close examination, that they may, in fact, be created as a sop to satisfy the public's impossible expectations for police performance. By utilizing the rhetoric of crime control, the police claim the responsibility for the social processes that beget the illegal acts. They cannot control these social processes that are embedded in American values, norms, and cultural traditions. Creating the appearance of controlling them is only a temporizing policy; it is not the basis for a sound, honorable mandate.

The police mandate and the problems it creates in American society are our central concern. We will rely on the concepts of actor, organization, and audience, of mandate, and of strategy and appearances. We will show that the police mandate, as presently defined, is full of contradictions. We will further demonstrate that the strategies and tactics of the American police are failing in a serious way to meet the need of controlling crime.

THE OCCUPATIONAL CULTURE OF THE POLICE

Before beginning an analysis of the police mandate, a brief comment is necessary about the occupational culture of our law enforcers. The American police act in accord with their assumptions about the nature of social life, and their most important assumptions originate with their need to maintain control over both their mandate and their self-esteem. The policeman's self is an amalgam of evaluations made by the many audiences before whom he, as social actor, must perform: his peers, his family, his immediate superiors and the higher administrators, his friends on and off duty. His most meaningful standards of performance are the ideals of his *occupational culture.* The policeman judges himself against the ideal policeman as described in police occupational lore and imagery. What a "good policeman" does is an omnipresent standard. The occupational culture, however, contains more than the definition of a good policeman. It contains the typical values, norms, attitudes, and material paraphernalia of an occupational group.

An occupational culture also prompts the *assumptions* about everyday life that become the basis for organizational strategies and tactics. Recent studies of the occupational culture of the police allow the formulation of the following postulates or assumptions, all of which are the basis for police strategies to be discussed later:

1.   People cannot be trusted; they are dangerous.
2.   Experience is better than abstract rules.
3.   You must make people respect you.
4.   Everyone hates a cop.
5.   The legal system is untrustworthy; policemen make the best decisions about guilt or innocence.
6.   People who are not controlled will break laws.
7.   Policemen must appear respectable and be efficient.
8.   Policemen can most accurately identify crime and criminals.
9.   The major jobs of the policeman are to prevent crime and to enforce the laws.
10. Stronger punishment will deter criminals from repeating their errors.[8]

[8]These postulates have been drawn from the work of Michael Banton, *The Policeman in the Community* (New York: Basic Books, 1965); the articles in *The Police: Six Sociological Essays,* ed. David Bordua (New York: John Wiley & Sons, 1967), esp. those by Albert J. Reiss and David Bordua, and John H. McNamara; Arthur Niederhoffer, *Behind the Shield* (Garden City, N.Y.: Doubleday, 1967); Jerome Skolnick, *Justice Without Trial* (New York: John Wiley & Sons, 1966); and William A. Westley, "Violence and the Police," *American Journal of Sociology* 59 (July 1953), pp. 34–41; idem, "Secrecy and the

Some qualifications about
apply primarily to the Am
man. They are less applica
departments and to memł
departments. Nor do they
and federal policemen.

 We shall now descr
date, the strategies of th
and some of the finding
dent's crime commissio
the police to make a ru

(overlapping torn fragment, partially legible, rotated:) 158 organized force tha / policeman himse / dangerous and / watchful pre / ative sanct / encourag / vented / lines / wh

II. THE "IMPOSSIBLE" MANDATE

The police in modern society are in agreement with their audiences—which include their professional interpreters, the American family, criminals, and politicians—in at least one respect:
they have an "impossible" task. Certainly, all professionals
have impossible tasks insofar as they try to surmount the problems of collective life that resist easy solutions. The most "successful" occupations, however, have managed to construct a
mandate in terms of their own vision of the world. The policeman's mandate, on the other hand, is defined largely by his
publics—not, at least at the formal level, in his own terms.

 Several rather serious consequences result from the public's image of the police. The public is aware of the dramatic
nature of a small portion of police work, but it ascribes the element of excitement to all police activities. To much of the public, the police are seen as alertly ready to respond to citizen
demands, as crime-fighters, as an efficient, bureaucratic, highly

Police," *Social Forces* 34 (March 1956), pp. 254–257; idem, "The Police: Law,
Custom and Morality," in *The Study of Society*, ed. Peter I. Rose (New York:
Random House, 1967). See also James Q. Wilson, *Varieties of Police Behavior:
The Management of Law and Order in Eight Communities* (Cambridge: Harvard
University Press, 1968); idem, "The Police and Their Problems: A Theory,"
Public Policy 12 (1963), pp. 189–216; idem, "Generational and Ethnic Differ-
ences Among Police Officers," *American Journal of Sociology* 69 (March
1964), pp. 522–528.

Peter K. Manning

keeps society from falling into chaos. The
considers the essence of his role to be the
heroic enterprise of crook-catching and the
ention of crimes.[9] The system of positive and neg-
ions from the public and within the department
es this heroic conception. The public wants crime pre-
and controlled; that is, it wants criminals caught. Head-
herald the accomplishments of G-Men and F.B.I. agents
o often do catch dangerous men, and the reputation of these
ederal authorities not infrequently rubs off on local policemen
who are much less adept at catching criminals.

In an effort to gain the public's confidence in their ability,
and to insure thereby the solidity of their mandate, the police
have encouraged the public to continue thinking of them and
their work in idealized terms, terms, that is, which grossly ex-
aggerate the actual work done by police. They do engage in
chases, in gunfights, in careful sleuthing. But these are rare
events. Most police work resembles any other kind of work: it
is boring, tiresome, sometimes dirty, sometimes technically demanding, but it is rarely dangerous. Yet the occasional chase,
the occasional shoot-out, the occasional triumph of some extraordinary detective work have been seized upon by the police
and played up to the public. The public's response has been to
demand even more dramatic crook-catching and crime prevention, and this demand for arrests has been converted into an
index for measuring how well the police accomplish their mandate. The public's definitions have been converted by the police
organization into distorted criteria for promotion, success, and

[9]Although the imagery of the police and their own self-definition coin-
cide on the dangers of being a policeman, at least one study has found that
many other occupations are more dangerous. Policemen kill six times as
many people as policemen are killed in the line of duty. In 1955, Robin found
that the rate of police fatalities on duty, including accidents, was 33 per
100,000, less than the rate for mining (94), agriculture (55), construction (76),
and transportation (44). Between 1950 and 1960, an average of 240 persons
were killed each year by policemen—approximately six times the number of
policemen killed by criminals. Gerald D. Robin, "Justifiable Homicide by Police
Officers," *Journal of Criminal Law, Criminology and Police Science* 54 (1963),
pp. 225–231.

security. Most police departments promote men from patrol to detective work, a generally more desirable duty, for "good pinches"—arrests that are most likely to result in convictions.[10] The protection of the public welfare, however, including personal and property safety, the prevention of crime, and the preservation of individual civil rights, is hardly achieved by a high pinch rate. On the contrary, it might well be argued that protection of the public welfare could best be indexed by a low arrest rate. Because their mandate automatically entails mutually contradictory ends—protecting both public order and individual rights—the police resort to managing their public image and the indexes of their accomplishment. And the ways in which the police manage their appearance are consistent with the assumptions of their occupational culture, with the public's view of the police as a social-control agency, and with the ambiguous nature of our criminal law.

THE PROBLEMATIC NATURE OF LAW AND ORDER

The criminal law is one among many instrumentalities of social control. It is an explicit set of rules created by political authority; it contains provisions for punishment by officials designated with the responsibility to interpret and enforce the rules which should be uniformly applied to all persons within a politically defined territory.[11] This section discusses the relationships between the laws and the mores of a society, the effect of the growth of civilized society on law enforcement, and the problematic nature of crime in an advanced society. The differential nature of enforcement will be considered as an aspect of peace-keeping, and will lead to the discussion of the police in the larger political system.

A society's laws, it is often said, reflect its customs; it can also be said that the growth of the criminal law is proportionate

[10]Niederhoffer, *Behind the Shield,* p. 221.

[11]See Richard Quinney, "Is Criminal Behavior Deviant Behavior?" *British Journal of Criminology* 5 (April 1965), p. 133. The following two pages draw heavily from Quinney. See also R. C. Fuller, "Morals and the Criminal Law," *Journal of Criminal Law, Criminology and Police Science* 32 (March–April 1942), pp. 624–630.

to the decline in the consistency and binding nature of these mores. In simpler societies, where the codes and rules of behavior were well known and homogeneous, sanctions were enforced with much greater uniformity and predictability. Social control was isomorphic with one's obligations to family, clan, and age group, and the political system of the tribe. In a modern, differentiated society, a minimal number of values and norms are shared. And because the fundamental, taken-for-granted consensus on what is proper and respectable has been blurred or shattered, or, indeed, never existed, criminal law becomes a basis of social control. As Quinney writes, "Where correct conduct cannot be agreed upon, the criminal law serves to control the behavior of all persons within a political jurisdiction."[12]

Social control through the criminal law predominates in a society only when other means of control have failed. When it does predominate, it no longer reflects the mores of the society. It more accurately reflects the interests of shifting power groups within the society. As a result, the police, as the designated enforcers of a system of criminal laws, are undercut by circumstances that accentuate the growing differences between the moral order and the legal order.

One of these complicating circumstances is simply the matter of social changes, which further stretch the bond between the moral and the legal. The law frequently lags behind the changes in what society deems acceptable and unacceptable practice. At other times, it induces changes, such as those pertaining to civil rights, thereby anticipating acceptable practice. The definition of crime, then, is a product of the relationship between social structure and the law. Crime, to put it another way, is not a homogeneous entity.

The perspective of the patrolman as he goes about his daily rounds is a legalistic one. The law and the administrative actions of his department provide him with a frame of reference for exercising the mandate of the police. The citizen, on the

[12]Quinney, "Criminal Behavior," p. 133.

other hand, does not live his life in accordance with a legalistic framework; he defines his acts in accordance with a moral or ethical code provided him by his family, his religion, his social class. For the most part, he sees law enforcement as an intervention in his private affairs.

No matter what the basis for actions of private citizens may be, however, the patrolman's job is one of practical decision-making within a legalistic pattern. His decisions are expected to include an understanding of the law as a system of formal rules, the enforcement practices emphasized by his department, and a knowledge of the specific facts of an allegedly illegal situation. The law includes little formal recognition of the variation in the private arrangement of lives. Even so, the policeman is expected to take these into account also. No policeman can ever be provided with a handbook that could tell him, at a moment's notice, just what standards to apply in enforcing the law and in maintaining order. Wilson summarizes the difficulty inherent in law enforcement as follows:

Most criminal laws define *acts* (murder, rape, speeding, possessing narcotics), which are held to be illegal; people may disagree as to whether the act should be illegal, as they do with respect to narcotics, for example, but there is little disagreement as to what the behavior in question consists of. Laws regarding disorderly conduct and the like assert, usually by implication, that there is a condition ("public order") that can be diminished by various actions. The difficulty, of course, is that public order is nowhere defined and can never be defined unambiguously because what constitutes order is a matter of opinion and convention, not a state of nature. (An unmurdered person, an unraped woman, and an unpossessed narcotic can be defined so as to be recognizable to any reasonable person.) An additional difficulty, a corollary of the first, is the impossibility of specifying, except in the extreme case, what degree of disorder is intolerable and who is to be held culpable for that degree. A suburban street is quiet and pleasant; a big city street is noisy and (to some) offensive; what degree of noise and offense, and produced by whom, constitutes "disorderly conduct"?[13]

[13]Wilson, *Varieties of Police Behavior,* pp. 21–22.

The complexity of law enforcement stems from both the problem of police "discretion" and the inherent tensions between the maintenance of order and individual rights. The law contains rules on how to maintain order; it contains substantive definitions of crime, penalties for violations, and the conditions under which the commission of a crime is said to have been intended.[14] Further, the law contains procedures for the administration of justice and for the protection of the individual. The complexities of law enforcement notwithstanding, however, the modern policeman is frequently faced with the instant problem of defining an action as either legal or illegal, of deciding, in other words, whether to intervene and, if so, what tactic to use. He moves in a dense web of social action and social meanings, burdened by a problematic, complex array of ever-changing laws. Sometimes the policeman must quickly decide very abstract matters. Though a practitioner of the legal arts, his tools at hand are largely obscure, ill-developed, and crude. With little formal training, the rookie must learn his role by absorbing the theories, traditions, and personal whims of experienced patrolmen.

POLICE WORK AS PEACE-KEEPING[15]

The thesis of two recent major works on the police, Wilson's *The Varieties of Police Behavior* and Skolnick's *Justice Without Trial,* can be paraphrased as follows: the policeman must exercise discretion in matters involving life and death, honor and dishonor, and he must do so in an environment that he perceives as threatening, dangerous, hostile, and volatile. He sees his efficiency constrained by the law and by the police organi-

[14]Skolnick, *Justice Without Trial,* pp. 7–8, 9.

[15]This perspective on police work is emphasized by Wilson, *Varieties of Police Behavior;* Banton, *The Policeman in the Community;* and Skolnick, *Justice Without Trial.* In addition, see the more legalistically oriented work of Wayne R. LaFave, *Arrest,* ed. F. J. Remington (Boston: Little, Brown, 1965); Joseph Goldstein, "Police Discretion Not to Invoke the Legal Process: Low-Visibility Decisions in the Administration of Justice," *Yale Law Journal* 69 (1960), pp. 543–594; and Herman Goldstein, "Police Discretion: The Ideal Versus the Real," *Public Administration Review* 23 (September 1963), pp. 140–148.

zation. Yet, he must effectively manage "disorder" in a variety of unspecified ways, through methods usually learned and practiced on the job. As a result of these conditions, the policeman, in enforcing his conception of order, often violates the rights of citizens.

Many observers of police work regard the primary function of a policeman as that of a *peace-keeper,* not a *law enforcer.* According to this view, police spend most of their time attending to order-maintaining functions, such as finding lost children, substituting as ambulance drivers, or interceding in quarrels of one sort or another. To these observers, the police spend as little as 10 to 15 per cent of their time on law enforcement—responding to burglary calls or trying to find stolen cars. The large-scale riots and disorders of recent years accounted for few police man-hours. Wilson illustrates the peace-keeping (order maintenance) and law-enforcement distinction this way:

The difference between order maintenance and law enforcement is not simply the difference between "little stuff" and "real crime" or between misdemeanors and felonies. The distinction is fundamental to the police role, for the two functions involve quite dissimilar police actions and judgments. Order maintenance arises out of a dispute among citizens who accuse each other of being at fault; law enforcement arises out of the victimization of an innocent party by a person whose guilt must be proved. Handling a disorderly situation requires the officer to make a judgment about what constitutes an appropriate standard of behavior; law enforcement requires him only to compare a person's behavior with a clear legal standard. Murder or theft is defined, unambiguously, by statutes; public peace is not. Order maintenance rarely leads to an arrest; law enforcement (if the suspect can be found) typically does. Citizens quarreling usually want the officer to "do something," but they rarely want him to make an arrest (after all, the disputants are usually known or related to each other). Furthermore, whatever law is broken in a quarrel is usually a misdemeanor, and in most states, an officer cannot make a misdemeanor arrest unless one party or the other will swear out a formal complaint (which is even rarer).[16]

[16]James Q. Wilson, "What Makes a Better Policeman?" *Atlantic* 223 (March 1969), p. 131.

The complexity of the law and the difficulty in obtaining a complainant combine to tend to make the policeman underenforce the law—to overlook, ignore, dismiss, or otherwise erase the existence of many enforceable breaches of the law.

Some researchers and legalists have begun to piece together a pattern of the conditions under which policemen have a tendency not to enforce the law. From a study of police in three Midwestern states, LaFave has concluded that two considerations characterize a decision not to arrest. The first is that the crime is unlikely to reach public attention—for example, that it is of a private nature or of low visibility—and the second is that underenforcement is unlikely to be detected or challenged.[17] Generally, the conditions under which policemen are less likely to enforce the law are those in which they perceive little public consensus on the law, or in which the law is ambiguous. LaFave found that policemen are not apt to enforce rigorously laws that are viewed by the public as dated, or that are used on the rare occasions when the public order is being threatened.

There is a certain Benthamic calculus involved in all arrests, a calculus that is based on pragmatic considerations such as those enumerated by LaFave. Sex, age, class, and race might also enter into the calculus of whether the law should be enforced. In a case study of the policeman assigned to skid row, Bittner illustrates the great degree of discretion exercised by the policeman. Yet the law, often reified by the policeman, is rarely a clear guide to action—despite the number of routine actions that might be termed "typical situations that policemen perceive as *demand conditions* for action without arrest."[18]

In the exercise of discretion, in the decision to enforce the law or to underenforce, the protection of individual rights is often at stake. But individual rights are frequently in opposition to the preservation of order, as a totalitarian state exemplifies in the extreme. The police try to manage these two contradictory

[17]LaFave, *Arrest.*
[18]Egon Bittner, "The Police on Skid-Row: A Study of Peace-Keeping," *American Sociological Review* 32 (October 1967), pp. 699–715.

demands by emphasizing their peace-keeping functions. This emphasis succeeds only when a consensus exists on the nature of the order (peace) to be preserved. The greater the difference in viewpoint between the police and the public on the degree and kind of order to be preserved, the greater will be antagonism between the two; the inevitable result of this hostility will be "law breaking."

The resolution of the contradictions and complexities inherent in the police mandate, including the problems of police discretion, of individual rights, of law enforcement and peacekeeping, is not helped, however, by the involvement of police in politics. Politics only further complicates the police mandate. The law itself is a political phenomenon, and at the practical level of enforcing it, the local political system is yet another source of confusion.

THE POLICE IN THE POLITICAL SYSTEM

In theory, the American police are apolitical. Their own political values and political aims are supposed to be secondary to the institutional objective of law enforcement. In practice, however, police organizations function in a political context; they operate in a public political arena and their mandate is defined politically. They may develop strategies to create and maintain the appearance of being apolitical in order to protect their organizational autonomy, but they are nonetheless a component of American political machinery. There are three reasons why the police are inextricably involved in the political system, the first and most obvious being that the vast majority of the police in this nation are locally controlled.

[Among the 40,000 law-enforcement agencies in the United States], there are only 50 . . . on the federal level . . . 200 on the state level. The remaining 39,750 agencies are dispersed throughout the many counties, cities, towns, and villages that form our local governments. . . . Only 3,050 agencies are located in counties and 3,700 in cities. The great majority of the police forces—33,000—are distributed throughout boroughs, towns, and villages.[19]

[19]President's Commission, *Task Force Report: The Police,* pp. 7, 8–9.

In 1966 there were 420,000 full- and part-time law-enforcement officers and civilians employed by police agencies in the United States. Most of them—371,000—were full-time employees; about 11 per cent—46,000—were civilians. Of the full-timers, 23,000 served at the federal level of government, 40,000 at the state level, and the remaining 308,000, or 83 per cent of the total, were divided between county and local political jurisdictions. Of the 308,000, somewhat more than 197,000 were employees of counties, cities under 250,000, townships, boroughs, and villages; the balance of 110,500 served in the 55 American cities with populations of more than 250,000. The number of police personnel in any one type of political division varied widely, of course. For example, on the county level of government, the roster of the 3,050 sheriff's offices in the United States ranged from a one-man force in Putnam County, Georgia, to a 5,515-man force in Los Angeles County.

What all these figures indicate is the massive dispersal of police authority—and political authority—throughout the nation. What these figures also indicate is the existence of overlapping laws governing law enforcement. Further, they show that the responsibility for maintaining public order in America is decentralized, and that law-enforcement officers are largely under the immediate control of local political authorities.

The second reason why the police are an integral part of the political system is this: law is a political entity, and the administration of criminal law unavoidably encompasses political values and political ends. The police are directly related to a political system that develops and defines the law, itself a product of interpretations of what is right and proper from the perspective of different politically powerful segments within the community.

The third reason why the police are tied to the political system emanates from the second: the police must administer the law. Many factors pattern this enforcement, but they all reflect the political organization of society. The distribution of power and authority, for example, rather than the striving for justice, or equal treatment under the law, can have a direct bearing on enforcement.

Because law enforcement is for the most part locally controlled, sensitivity to local political trends remains an important element in police practice. Since the police are legally prohibited from being publicly political, they often appeal to different community groups, and participate sub rosa in others, in order to influence the determination of public policy. Community policy, whether made by the town council or the mayor or the city manager, affects pay scales, operating budgets, personnel, administrative decisions, and, to some extent, organizational structure. The police administrator must, therefore, be responsive to these controls, and he must deal with them in an understanding way. He must be sensitive to the demands of the local politicians—even while maintaining the loyalty of the lower ranks through a defense of their interests.

There are several direct effects of the political nature of the police mandate. One is that many policemen become alienated; they lose interest in their role as enforcers and in the law as a believable criterion. The pressures of politics also erode loyalty to the police organization and not infrequently lead to collusion with criminals and organized crime.

The policeman's exposure to danger, his social background, low pay, low morale, his vulnerability in a repressive bureaucracy all conspire to make him susceptible to the lures of the underhanded and the appeals of the political. Studies summarized by Skolnick[20] reveal a political profile of the policeman as a conservative, perhaps reactionary, person of lower-class or lower-middle-class origin, often a supporter of radical right causes, often prejudiced and repressive, often extremely ambivalent about the rights of others. The postulates or assumptions of the police culture, the suspiciousness, fear, low self-esteem, and distrust of others are almost diametrically opposed to the usual conception of the desirable democratic man.

Thus, the enforcement of some laws is personally distasteful. Civil-rights legislation, for example, can be anathema. Or

[20]Jerome Skolnick, ed., *The Politics of Protest* (New York: Simon & Schuster, 1969), pp. 252–253.

truculence can be the reaction to an order relaxing controls in ghettos during the summer months. It is the ambivalence of policemen toward certain laws and toward certain local policies that fragments loyalty within a department and causes alienation.

There is another consequence of the political nature of the police mandate: the police are tempted. They are tempted not to enforce the law by organized crime, by the operators of illegal businesses such as prostitution, and by fine "law-abiding," illegally parked citizens. All too frequently, the police submit to temptations, becoming in the process exemplars of the corruption typical of modern society, where the demand for "criminal services" goes on at the station house.[21]

Police and politics within the community are tightly interlocked. The sensitivity of the police to their political audiences, their operation within the political system of criminal justice, and their own personal political attitudes undermine their efforts to fulfill their contradictory mandate and to appear politically neutral.

THE EFFICIENT, SYMPTOM-ORIENTED ORGANIZATION

The Wickersham report, the Hoover administration's report on crime and law enforcement in the United States, was published in 1931. This precursor of the Johnson administration's *The Challenge of Crime in a Free Society* became a rallying point for advocates of police reform. One of its central themes was the lack of "professionalism" among the police of the time— their lack of special training, their corruption, their brutality, and their use of illegal procedures in law enforcement. And one of its results was that the police, partly in order to demonstrate their concern with scientific data gathering on crime and partly to indicate their capacity to "control" crime itself, began to stress crime statistics as a major component of professional police work.

---

[21]There are several popular treatments of police corruption, none of them very good. Ralph L. Smith, *The Tarnished Badge* (New York: Thomas Y. Crowell, 1965); Ed Cray, *The Big Blue Line* (New York: Coward-McCann, 1967).

Crime statistics, therefore—and let this point be emphasized—became a police construction. The actual amount of crime committed in a society is unknown—and probably unknowable, given the private nature of most crime. The *crime rate,* consequently, is simply a construction of police activities. That is, the crime rate pertains only to "crimes known to the police," crimes that have been reported to or observed by the police and for which adequate grounds exist for assuming that a violation of the law has, in fact, taken place. (The difference between the *actual* and *known crimes* is often called the "dark figure of crime.") Of course, the construction of a crime rate placed the police in a logically weak position in which they still find themselves. If the crime rate is rising, they argue that more police support is needed to fight the war against crime; if the crime rate is stable or declining, they argue that they have successfully combated the crime menace—a heads-I-win-tails-you-lose proposition.

In spite of their inability to control the commission of illegal acts (roughly, the actual rate), since they do not know about all crime, the police have claimed responsibility for crime control, using the crime rate as an index of their success. This use of the crime rate to measure success is somewhat analogous to their use of a patrolman's arrest rate as an indication of his personal success in law enforcement. Questions about the actual amount of crime and the degree of control exercised are thus bypassed in favor of an index that offers great potential for organizational or bureaucratic control. Instead of grappling with the difficult issue of defining the ends of police work and an operational means for accomplishing them, the police have opted for "efficient" law-enforcement defined in terms of fluctuations of the crime rate. They have transformed concern with undefined ends into concern with available means. Their inability to cope with the causes of crime—which might offer them a basis for defining their ends—shifts their "organizational focus" into symptomatic concerns, that is, into a preoccupation with the rate of crime, not its reasons.

This preoccupation with the symptoms of a problem rather than with the problem itself is typical of all bureaucracies. For one characteristic of a bureaucracy is goal-displacement. Bureaucratic organizations tend to lose track of their goals and engage in ritual behavior, substituting means for ends. As a whole, bureaucracies become so engrossed in pursuing, defending, reacting to, and, even, in creating immediate problems that their objective is forgotten. This tendency to displace goals is accelerated by the one value dear to all bureaucracies—efficiency. Efficiency is the be-all and end-all of bureaucratic organizations. Thus, they can expend great effort without any genuine accomplishment.

The police are burdened with the "efficiency problem." They claim to be an efficient bureaucratic organization, but they are unable to define for themselves and others precisely what it is they are being efficient about. In this respect, they do not differ from other paper-shuffling organizations. The police's problem is that the nature of their work is uncertain and negatively defined. It is uncertain in the absence of a consensus not only between the police and the public but also among themselves as to what the goals of a police department should be. It is defined in the negative because the organization punishes its members—patrolmen—for violating departmental procedures but offers no specifications on what they should do or how they should do it.

What do the police do about the problematic nature of law, about the problems arising from their involvement with politics, about their preoccupation with the symptoms of crime rather than the causes? Do they selectively adopt some strategies at the expense of others? Do they vacillate? Are the roles of the organization's members blurred? Before answering these questions, let us examine how the police, through various strategies, manage their appearance before the public. The questions will then be easier to answer.

III. MAJOR STRATEGIES OF THE POLICE

The responsibilities of the police lead them to pursue contradictory and unattainable ends. They share with all organizations and occupations, however, the ability to avoid solving their problems. Instead, they concentrate on managing them through strategies. Rather than resolving their dilemmas, the police have manipulated them with a professional eye on just how well the public accepts their dexterity. Thus, law enforcement becomes a self-justifying system. It becomes more responsive to its own needs, goals, and procedures than to serving society. In this section, we will show the ways in which the police have followed the course of most other bureaucratic institutions in society, responding to their problems by merely giving the appearance of facing them while simultaneously promoting the trained incapacity to do otherwise.

The two primary aims of most bureaucracies, the police included, are the maintenance of their organizational autonomy and the security of their members. To accomplish these aims, they adopt a pattern of institutional action that can best be described as "professionalism." This word, with its many connotations and definitions, cloaks all the many kinds of actions carried out by the police.

The guise of professionalism embodied in a bureaucratic organization is the most important strategy employed by the police to defend their mandate and thereby to build self-esteem, organizational autonomy, and occupational solidarity or cohesiveness. The professionalization drives of the police are no more suspect than the campaigns of other striving, upwardly mobile occupational groups. However, since the police have a monopoly on legal violence, since they are the active enforcers of the public will, serving theoretically in the best interests of the public, the consequences of their yearnings for prestige and power are imbued with far greater social ramifications than the relatively harmless attempts of florists, funeral directors, and accountants to attain public stature. Disinterested law enforcement through bureaucratic means is an essential in our society and in any democracy, and the American police are certainly closer to attaining this ideal than they were in 1931 at the time of the Wickersham report. Professionalism qua professionalism is unquestionably desirable in the police. But if in striving for the heights of prestige they fail to serve the altruistic values of professionalism, if their professionalism means that a faulty portrait of the social reality of crime is being painted, if their professionalism conceals more than it reveals about the true nature of their operations, then a close analysis of police professionalism is in order.

Police professionalism cannot be easily separated in practice from the bureaucratic ideal epitomized in modern police practice. The bureaucratic ideal is established as a means of obtaining a commitment from personnel to organizational and occupational norms. This bureaucratic commitment is designed to supersede commitments to competing norms, such as obligations to friends or kin or members of the same racial or ethnic group. Unlike medicine and law, professions that developed outside the context of bureaucracies, policing has always been carried out, if done on a full-time basis, as a bureaucratic function.

Modern police bureaucracy and modern police professionalism are highly articulated, although they contain some inherent stresses that are not our present concern. The strategies employed by the police to manage their public appearance develop from their adaptation of the bureaucratic ideal. These strategies incorporate the utilization of *technology* and *official statistics* in law enforcement, of *styles of patrol* that attempt to accommodate the community's desire for public order with the police department's preoccupation with bureaucratic procedures, of *secrecy* as a means of controlling the public's response to their operations, of *collaboration* with criminal elements to foster the appearance of a smoothly run, law-abiding community, and of a *symbiotic relationship* with the criminal justice system that minimizes public knowledge of the flaws within this largely privately operated system.

PROFESSIONALISM

To say that a type of work can only be carried out by professionals is to make both it and them immediately acceptable. The need of the police to proclaim themselves professionals arises out of their need to control both the public and their own organization. Externally, professionalism functions to define the nature of the client, to maintain social distance with the clientele, and to define the purposes, the conventions, and the motivations of the practitioners; internally, it functions to unify the diverse interests and elements that exist within any occupational or organizational group. This view sees professionalism as an ideology. Habenstein has described it as follows:

> Certain groups, claiming special functions, have been able to arrogate to themselves, or command increased power over, the conditions of members' livelihood. . . . "Profession" is, basically, an ideology, a set of rationalizations about the worth and necessity of certain areas of work, which, when internalized, gives the practitioners a moral justification for privilege, if not license. . . .[22]

Efforts toward the professionalization of any occupation are, above all, efforts to achieve power and authority. In police work, professionalization serves the self-esteem of all practitioners, from patrolman to commissioner, by gilding the entire enterprise with the symbols, prerequisites, tradition, power, and authority of the most respected occupations in American society.

THE BUREAUCRATIC IDEAL

The organizational *ideal* of the "professional" police department is a rational, efficient, scientifically organized, technologically sophisticated bureaucracy. This is the way Niederhoffer depicts a modern police organization:

> Large urban police departments are bureaucracies. Members of the force sometimes lose their bearings in the labyrinth of hierarchy, specialization, competitive examinations, red tape, promotion based on seniority, impersonality, rationality, rules and regulations, channels of communication, and massive files.[23]

They are bureaucracies because the bureaucratic organization is perceived by the police as the best way to solve their prob-

---

[22]Robert W. Habenstein, "Critique of 'Profession' as a Sociological Category," *Sociological Quarterly* 4 (November 1963), p. 297. This notion follows H. S. Becker's in "The Nature of a Profession," in *Yearbook of the National Society for the Study of Education* (Chicago: National Society for the Study of Education, 1961).

[23]Niederhoffer, *Behind the Shield*, p. 11.

lems. To them, a bureaucracy is the best device for managing appearances and the best method of working out a running adjustment to the pressing nature of their problems. And bureaucratic rhetoric, with its reverence for science and professionalism, is accurately assessed as the most powerful source of legitimation in American society. All modern bureaucratic organizations claim to be efficient and all strive in varying degrees to become more efficient. Understandably, they inevitably fail because the organizational rules under which the bureaucrats work are never able to cover all contingencies.

TECHNOLOGY

One of the strategies employed by the police to appear professional and bureaucratically efficient is the use of technology. Again quoting from Niederhoffer:

The modern police specialist requires a wide range of technical and scientific skills. Experts are needed to operate radar, photographic equipment, electronic listening devices, instruments for analysis of evidence, computers, complex office machines, radio, television, airplanes, and helicopters. The scientific devices used in detective investigations have created a corps of specialists, quasi-scientists, [and] technicians. . . .[24]

All these devices illustrate the technological strategy and are related to the police assumptions that if they have more information more quickly, more visibility, more policemen, more firepower, and better allocation of resources, all organized around technology, they will be able to efficiently prevent and deter crime. These assumptions are also manifested in the President's crime commission report. The police have brought a scientific perspective to crime prevention, elaborating on the means of obtaining more information more quickly, and on methods of more efficiently allocating men, material, and more potent weapons. Technology, of course, does not deal with the great difficulties in obtaining information.

[24]Ibid., pp. 17–18.

OFFICIAL STATISTICS

Another strategy used by police to convey the appearance of efficiency is their pursuit of "official statistics." Nothing sells easier than a statistic, no matter what it says, and the police use them not only for self-justification and organizational survival but for enhancement of community relations. All bureaucracies ply the official-statistics strategy, and insofar as the police are concerned, they "very often corrupt the statistics," as Jack Douglas has pointed out.[25]

The police construct and utilize official statistics, such as the clearance rate and the crime index, to manage the impression of efficiency. The clearance rate, so popular among professionalized police departments, is a measure of a patrolman's or a detective's efficiency. Offenses categorized as "solved" become part of the clearance rate. The police ignore all unreported crimes and all crimes without victims where no complainant is required; these crimes, therefore, are never "cleared"—they never become part of the clearance rate. As for the index of crime being an index of efficiency, no mandatory, centralized crime-reporting system exists, although many police departments have adopted and report on the basis of the F.B.I. index of crimes: murder, aggravated assault, rape, burglary, robbery, larceny over $50, and auto theft. Needless to say, the more the police enforce the laws, the higher the crime rate. Because there has been very little in the way of standard reporting and investigation practices, the police have been able to control the crime rate to a large degree by controlling aspects of enforcement.

The use of technology and official statistics as strategies, in the context of professionalism, is related to patrol strategies adapted by departments in their efforts to resolve the "problematic nature of the law." Styles of patrol, or modes of law enforcement by patrolmen, characterize departments as a whole.

[25]Jack D. Douglas, "Deviance and Order in a Pluralistic Society," in *Theoretical Sociology: Perspectives and Development,* ed. Edward A. Tiryakian and John C. McKinney (New York: Appleton-Century-Crofts, 1970).

They represent a means of integrating community norms and expectations with the legal and procedural rules of the community and the police department.

STYLES OF PATROL

Patrol strategies, to the police at least, are an aspect of bureaucratic efficiency. They are closely related to the differential enforcement of the law. Enforcement must be differential because if it were not, "we would all," in Dodson's often quoted remark, "be in jail before the end of the first day. The laws which are selected for enforcement are those which the power structure of the community wants enforced."[26]

The tasks absorbed by the police have burgeoned in recent years—along with the demands for their services. The police have tried to answer these demands of their environment by three distinct types of patrol—what Wilson describes as the *watchman, legalistic,* and *service* styles.[27] The watchman style is the classic mode of policing urban areas and is still used in some degree in most cities. It is a style of patrol that emphasizes maintenance of public order rather than enforcement of the law. The policeman is instructed to be sensitive to the interests of groups within his beat and to overlook many of the minor offenses connected with juvenile infractions, traffic violations, vice, and gambling. A legalistic style, on the other hand, rests heavily upon enforcement of the law to control the routine situations encountered by the patrolman. The police using this style of patrol are instructed to act as if a single level of order was desirable in all settings and for all groups, and to enforce the law to that end. The service style, Wilson's third type of patrol, is "market-oriented," that is, it is designed to meet the fairly well-articulated demand of "homogeneous middle-class communities." The police respond to and take seriously all calls for police action (unlike the watchman style which ignores certain kinds of demands for intervention), but (unlike the legalistic style which it more closely resembles) the police seldom

---

[26]Daniel Dodson, as quoted in Niederhoffer, *Behind the Shield,* p. 12.
[27]Wilson, *Varieties of Police Behavior,* pp. 140–141.

use the law to control the situation. They prefer informal action to law enforcement.

The value of these varied styles to the police is the survival potential they provide. They allow the police administrator a certain leeway in trying to control his men in line with the demands of the most powerful interests in the community and to mitigate the strain between preserving individual liberty and protecting the collective social enterprise.

SECRECY AND PUBLIC COMPLAINTS

No matter what the level of operation of a police force, it will generate citizen complaints. It will generate complaints because the role of the policeman is to restrain and control, not to advise and remedy. While advice and solutions are usually welcome, restraint is not. For a substantial proportion of the population, the policeman is an adversary; he issues summonses, makes arrests, conducts inquiries, searches homes and people, stops cars, testifies in court, and keeps a jail. For the police, threats from outside, such as citizens' complaints and political moves to control police policy, are efforts to destroy their organization. One strategy used by police to withstand these threats is to keep all information they obtain secret.

The shared secrets possessed by the police assist them in creating internal cohesion. Information is concealed for the additional reason that the police fear and dislike their clients—the various segments of the public. Westley, one of the first and most profound sociological analysts of the police culture, here describes the occupational perspective of the policeman and the centrality of secrecy:

The policeman finds his most pressing problems in his relationships to the public. His is a service occupation but of an incongruous kind, since he must discipline those whom he serves. He is regarded as corrupt and inefficient by, and meets with hostility and criticism from, the public. He regards the public as his enemy, feels his occupation to be in conflict with the community, and regards himself to be a pariah. The experience and the feeling give rise to a collective emphasis on secrecy, an attempt to coerce respect from the public, and a belief that almost any means are legitimate in completing an important arrest.

These are for the policeman basic occupational values. They arise from his experience, take precedence over his legal responsibilities, [and] are central to an understanding of his conduct. . . .[28]

Most observers of the police have noted their penchant for secrecy as a strategy used for their own protection. Secrecy helps keep the public at arm's length; further, it helps the police to maintain their power. Indeed, its very existence suggests power. One aspect of the strategy of secrecy is that it deliberately mystifies, and mystification has always been a means of sustaining respect and awe. As a strategy, then, secrecy is one of the most effective sources of power that the police have over their audiences.

One aspect of the secrecy strategy is that it constrains many citizens from making complaints about police misconduct. No adequate records are kept on police malfeasance. While the misconduct of the citizen—his law-breaking activities—are closely monitored and recorded, little attempt is made by most departments to maintain publicly available records of police wrongdoing. Certainly, few cities have bureaus that make systematic examinations of police activities for public assessment. Many efforts by citizens to set up public files on police services or to create civilian review boards have failed. The police have in every instance opposed moves to establish evaluational mechanisms; they have continued to prefer losing most citizens' complaints in an endless tangle of red tape. The battle with crime thus goes on largely unmonitored by the public at large.

COLLABORATION, THE STRATEGY OF CORRUPTION

In dealing with the demands of certain segments of their criminal audience, some police departments find that the most expedient policy is simply to acquiesce. This is a strategy adopted by corrupt departments. It is a strategy that reduces the pressures of organized crime against the department and that minimizes the chances of organized crime deliberately and

[28]Westley, "Violence and the Police," p. 35.

publicly embarrassing the police in order to control police activities. As a strategy, it is the least common used by police to manage their appearance of efficient crime-fighters. What it amounts to is that the police collaborate with the criminal element by taking the line of least resistance: they enter into the vice, gambling, and protection rackets themselves or in concert with organized crime. Because the police have resorted to secrecy and the fractionalization of public demands, they have at times been free enough from the constraints of justice to engage in full-scale lawlessness. This strategy, although relatively infrequent for entire departments, involves selective enforcement of the law together with the encouragement of a lack of consensus on enforcing certain laws, particularly those pertaining to gambling, prostitution, homosexuality, and abortion. Of course, an alliance with organized crime for the purpose of receiving payoffs is involved, too. Complicity with the criminal element is sometimes also necessary in order to obtain information that can be used against those who are not in league with the police and their allies. The corruption strategy is ultimately a self-defeating strategy, but to those in our police forces who are corrupt, this is a relatively unimportant matter.

SYMBIOSIS AND JUSTICE

The relationship between the police and our system of criminal justice is symbiotic—each is dependent upon the other for support. One of the reasons why the professionalized police department is so concerned with its public image originates with its inability to control the conviction process. Because the courts control the process, the police are eager to make the "good pinch," the one that will result in a conviction. To the police, failure to obtain a conviction is a failure of their mandate.

The symbiotic relationship between law enforcement and our system of criminal justice is largely sustained through the abrogation of the right of due process. This is accomplished through the simple expedient of what has been termed "bargain justice." Under the bargain-justice system, accused persons are persuaded to plead guilty to a lesser offense than the one with which they are charged, thereby forgoing their right to a trial by jury. But the complicity of the police in this system allows them to maintain their rate of good pinches. At the same time, it permits the prosecutor's office to preserve its conviction rates and it allows the courts to meet production quotas.

The system works on the assumption that all accused persons are guilty and that almost all of them, whether they are or not, will plead guilty. As Skolnick and Blumberg have shown, the assumption of guilt is the oil that lubricates an otherwise outdated, overworked, inadequate system of justice.[29]

Complicity in bargain justice is one more strategy employed by our police departments in their efforts to manage a troublesome mandate. In the second part of this essay the major problems of the police were outlined under the general themes of the problematic nature of the law and law enforcement, the political context of police work, and the symptomatic quality of their occupational tasks. In the preceding section, we focused on the major strategies the police have used to manage their troublesome mandate. In the following section, we will assess the relative efficacy of police strategies in battling crime in American society.

IV. THE EFFECTIVENESS OF POLICE STRATEGIES

The police have developed and utilized the strategies outlined above for the purpose of creating, as we have said, the appearance of managing their troublesome mandate. To a large extent, they are facilitated in the use of these strategies, in being able to project a favorable impression, by a public that has always been apathetic about police activity. Moreover, what activity the public does observe is filtered through the media with its own special devices for creating a version of reality. The public's meaning of police action is rarely gathered from first-hand experience, but from the constructed imagery of the media—which, in turn, rely upon official police sources for

[29]Skolnick, *Justice Without Trial,* and Abraham Blumberg, *Criminal Justice* (Chicago: Quadrangle Press, 1967).

their presentation of the news. The police for their part, understandably, manipulate public appearances as much as they possibly can in order to gain and maintain public support.

The specific strategies used by the police to create a publicly suitable image were described in Section III: the guise of professionalism; the implementation of the bureaucratic ideal of organization; the use of technology, official statistics, and various styles of patrol; secrecy; collaboration with corrupt elements; and the establishment of a symbiotic relationship with the courts. This section will present evidence by which to evaluate these strategies. The term "effectiveness" is used only in the context of how well these devices accomplish the ends which the public and the police themselves publicly espouse; the recommendations and evaluations of the President's crime commission will be central in making judgments of police effectiveness. This appraisal of how well the police manipulate their appearance will also be a guideline for evaluating the recommendations of the commission's task force report on the police.

PROFESSIONALISM AND THE BUREAUCRATIC IDEAL

The assumptions of professionalism and of a bureaucratic organization include a devotion to rational principles and ends that may then be translated into specific work routines having predictable outcomes. The police are organized in a military command fashion, with rigid rules and a hierarchy governing operations. However, the patrolman, the lowest man in the hierarchy—and usually the least well-trained and educated—is in the key position of exercising the greatest amount of discretion on criminal or possibly criminal activities. Especially in his peace-keeping role and in dealing with minor infractions (misdemeanors), the patrolman has wide discretionary power concerning if, when, why, and how to intervene in private affairs.

Police work must both rely on discretion and control it. Excessive inattention and excessive attention to infractions of the law are equally damaging to a community. However, the complexity of the law, its dynamic and changing properties, the extensiveness of police department regulations, policies, and procedures, and the equivocal, relativistic nature of crime in regard to certain situations, settings, persons, and groups make it impossible to create a job description that would eliminate the almost boundless uncertainty in police patrol.

Neither professionals nor bureaucrats, however, have yet found an effective means of controlling discretion. If an organization cannot control those of its members with the greatest opportunity to exercise discretion, it flounders in its attempts to accomplish its stated purposes. Two general principles suggest why the police have not been able to control discretion. The first has to do with the general problem of control and the second with the specific nature of police work.

Men are unwilling to submit completely to the will of their organizational superiors. Men will always attempt to define and control their own work. Control means the right to set the pace, to define mistakes, to develop standards of "good" production and efficiency. But as surely as superiors seek to control the quality and the extent of work performed by their subordinates in a hierarchy, just as surely will they meet with attempts to reshape and subvert these controls.

In the specific instance of police bureaucracies, the patrolman conceives of himself as a man able to make on-the-spot decisions of guilt or innocence. He does not think of himself as a bureaucratic functionary nor as a professional. Further, since the police organization itself has become far more interested in efficiency than in purpose, since it is unable to specify its overall objectives, the patrolman finds it difficult, if not impossible, to demonstrate that necessary devotion to rational ends required of professionalism and bureaucratic organizations. Until police departments are able to control the amount and kind of discretion exercised by their members, and until the police are able, with the help of lawyers and other citizens, to develop positive means of motivation and reward in line with clear, overall policy directives, the failure of what we have called the professionalism-bureaucracy strategy is an absolute certainty.

TECHNOLOGY, STATISTICS, AND THE CRIME RATE

This section will evaluate the strategy of technology in the control and prevention of crime, the use of statistics, and the significance of the so-called crime rate. Given the sociological nature of crime, let it be said immediately that present technology deals with unimportant crime and that the F.B.I. index of crimes, by which we base judgments of police effectiveness, is biased and an unrealistic reflection of the actual crime rate.

One of the striking aspects of the President's crime commission report is the thoroughly sociological nature of the document. The discussion of the causes of crime in the first two chapters points to the growth of urbanism, anonymity, the breakdown in social control, and the increasing numbers of frustrated and dissatisfied youth who have always constituted the majority of known lawbreakers. There are no labels such as "evil people," "emotionally disturbed," "mentally ill," or "criminally insane." The first set of recommendations under prevention in the summary pages of the report are "sociological": strengthen the family, improve slum schools, provide employment, reduce segregation, construct housing. All these matters are patently and by definition out of the control of the police.

There is every evidence that the police themselves subscribe to a thoroughly social, if not sociological, definition of the causes of crime—that is, that crime is the manifestation of long-established social patterns and structures which ensnare and implicate the police and the criminals as well as the general public. And they are doubtless correct.

Surveys done by the President's crime commission revealed that there are always contingencies in the information police receive about a crime even before they are able to investigate it. These contingencies involve such matters as the nature of the relationship between the victim and the offender and whether or not the victim believes the police are competent to investigate and solve the crime. Computer technology depends on informational "input." On that point, the police seem both unable to define what sort of information would be useful and unable to obtain, and probably never can obtain in a democratic society, information that would make them better able to enforce the law.

The facts in the problem of "crime prevention" overwhelmingly doom the present professionally based notion that the application of science and technology will begin to ease the distress the police feel as they face the escalating demands of their audiences. Also, it would be easier to assess the value of the technology strategy if we were able to define exactly to what end the technology would be applied and in what ways it could be expected to work.

STYLES OF PATROL

Police strategy is subject to many contingencies. It is a basic principle of public administration that policy made at the higher echelons of an organization will be effective only if each successively lower level of the organization complies with that policy and is capable of carrying it out. It is also a truism that participants at the lowest level in the hierarchy are the most "difficult" to mobilize and integrate into the organization. A style of patrol is basically the manner in which an administrative police policy is executed. The policy may prescribe that the patrolman overlook certain types of illegal acts; it may order that he minimally enforce particular laws or be sensitive to and strictly enforce others. If the administrative order setting a patrol style does not win the cooperation of the patrolman it is certain to fail. Thus, the success of any high-echelon policy that involves the performance of the patrolman is contingent upon his compliance with that policy. If the administrator's orders are not binding on the patrolman, no distinctive style of patrol will result; all that will be demonstrated will be the responses of the patrolman to other aspects of his social environment, especially, how his fellow patrolmen perform.

The success of this strategy is dependent upon the capacity of the administrator to create loyalty to his internal policies. With the rise of police unions, the discontent of the black patrolman, low pay, and relatively less security for the policeman, organizational control is a major problem in all the large police departments of the country—with Los Angeles possibly the single exception.

The effectiveness of the watchman, legalistic, and service styles of patrol will also depend on the degree of political consensus among the community groups patrolled, the clarity of the boundaries of community neighborhoods, competition between the police and self-help or vigilante groups, and the relative importance of nonoccupational norms in enforcement practices—that is, the importance of racial or ethnic similarities between the patrolman and the people in his neighborhood. If a clear social consensus on the meaning of the law and what is expected of the police can be established within a community, a well-directed policy of control over police patrol is the most logical and rational approach to police work. In some communities, largely suburban and middle-class, the police can carry out what their public demands and a degree of harmony exists. This consensus is absent in our inner cities.

SECRECY AND COLLABORATION

The use of secrecy by the police is, as we have pointed out, a strategy employed not only to assist them in maintaining the appearance of political neutrality but to protect themselves against public complaints. Secrecy also helps to forestall public efforts to achieve better police service and to secure political accountability for police policy. Police collaboration with criminal elements—corruption, in other words—has much the same effect since it decreases the pressure to enforce "unenforceable" laws against certain segments of the police's clientele.

These two strategies were among the major concerns of the President's crime commission task force on police. The task force's report devoted major attention to the fact that political forces influence police actions and policies. The report affirmed the political nature of police work; what concerned the writers of the report was the nature and type of political influence on police actions. Their recommendations, furthermore, were based on their recognition of the fact that the police have been fairly successful in managing the appearance of being apolitical.

There are several reasons why the police strategies of secrecy and collaboration will continue in force: (1) as long as the client—the public—is seen as the enemy, the police will treasure their secrecy and use it to engineer public consent to their policies and practices; (2) as long as a new political consensus is not formed on the nature and type of police control necessary in society as a whole, the organized, self-serving survival aims of police organizations will emerge victorious. Any well-organized consensual, secretive organization can resist the efforts of an unorganized public, managed by rhetoric and appearances, to reform it; (3) as long as there remains a lack of consensus on the enforcement of many of our "moralistic" laws, police corruption and selective law enforcement will continue. Collaboration to reduce adversary relationships with the criminal segment of society will always be an effective strategy —providing a sudden upsurge in public morality doesn't temporarily subject the police to a full-scale "housecleaning." Replacements would, of course, be subject to the same pressures and would, in all likelihood, eventually take the same line of least resistance.

One solution to corruption is said to be better educated, more professional policemen. By recruiting better educated men, the more professionalized police departments also seek to diminish the expression of political attitudes on the job and the tendency of policemen to form political power groups based on their occupation. These are also assumptions made by the crime commission's task force on police. There is, however, no evidence that college-educated or better-paid policemen are "better policemen"; nor is there any evidence that "better men" alone will solve the essentially structural problems of the occupation.

We can tentatively conclude from this review that corruption will remain with us as long as laws remain which stipulate punishments for actions on which a low public consensus exists. It will remain when there is likely to be a low visibility of police performance, and it will remain while there is a high public demand for illegal services—gambling, prostitution, abortion—and the concomitant need of the police for information on these services from the practitioners themselves.

SYMBIOSIS AND JUSTICE

Although the police have the principal discretion in the field with reference to the detection, surveillance, and appraisal of alleged offenders, the final disposition of a criminal case must be made in the courts. The police are thus dependent on the courts in a very special way for their successes. The ideal model of the criminal-justice system makes the police essentially the fact gatherers and apprehenders, while the courts are to be the decision-makers.

The police attempt to appear efficient has led them, as we have noted before, to seek the good pinch, the arrest that will stand up in court. With victimless crimes, such as those involving gambling or drugs or prostitution, the police control the situation since they alone decide whether an offense has been committed and whether they have a legal case against the offender. To control the success rate in these cases, the police create a gaggle of informants, many of whom are compelled to give the police evidence in order to stay free of a potential charge against themselves for a violation similar to the one they are providing information about. In the case of more serious crimes, the problems are more complex; in these cases the police must rely on other informants, and their discretion on arrests and charges are more often exercised by administrators and prosecuting attorneys.

In the prosecution stage, the bureaucratic demands of the court system are paramount. Abraham Blumberg describes these demands and the tension between efficiency and "due process":

The dilemma is frequently resolved through bureaucratically ordained shortcuts, deviations and outright rule violations by the members of the courts, from judges to stenographers, in order to meet production norms. Because they fear criticism on ethical as well as legal grounds, all the significant participants in the court's social structure are bound into an organized system of complicity. Patterned, covert, informal breaches, and evasions of "due process" are accepted as routine—they are institutionalized—but are nevertheless denied to exist.[30]

The net effect of this strain within the court system is to produce a higher rate of convictions by means of encouraging

[30]Blumberg, *Criminal Justice*, p. 69.

a plea of guilty to a lesser charge. As far as the police are concerned, then, the strategy of symbiosis is sound.

There are several undesirable effects of this symbiosis. First, it encourages corruption by permitting the police to make decisions about the freedom of their informants; it gives them an illegal hold and power over them, and thus it undercuts the rule of law. Second, many offenders with long criminal records are either granted their freedom as informants or allowed to plead guilty to lesser charges in return for the dismissal of a more serious charge. Skolnick calls this the "reversal of the hierarchy of penalties," because the more serious crimes of habitual criminals are prosecuted less zealously than the minor violations of first offenders. Third, it helps blur the distinction between the apprehension and prosecution aspects of our criminal-justice system.

V. CONCLUSIONS AND PROPOSED REFORMS

The allocation of rewards in a society represents both its division of labor and its configuration of problems. Ironically, the allocation of rewards is also the allocation of societal trouble. Societal trouble in a differentiated society is occupational trouble. The ebb and flow of rewards emanating from the division of labor becomes structured into persistent patterns that are sustained by continuous transactions among organizations and occupational groups. Occupational structures reflect societal structures, but they reflect them in ways that have been negotiated over time. The negotiation is based upon the universal human proclivity to differentiate roles, organizations, and occupations. The more dependent an organization is upon its environment for rewards, the more likely it is to rely on the management and presentation of strategies to establish the appearance of autonomy.

Organizations without a high degree of autonomy in the environments in which they operate are greatly constrained by the internal pressure of competing aims and roles of members. The agreement on problems, goals, values, and self-concepts that emerges from occupational socialization and functioning is a strong basis for influencing organizational direction. The occupational standards in this case subvert the rule of law as a system of norms outside the informal norms of the occupation. The policeman's view of his role and his occupational culture are very influential in determining the nature of policing. The basic source of police trouble is the inability of the police to define a mandate that will minimize the inconsistent nature of their self-expectations and the expectations of those they serve.

The problems derived from a contradictory mandate remain unaffected by the efforts of the institution to solve them; they do, however, take the shape into which they have been cast by institutional functionaries. Cooley long ago discussed the process of institutional ossification, the process by which institutions stray from serving the needs of their members and their publics, thereby losing the loyalty of those within and the support of those without. The consequences of institutional ossification as related to the police are twofold. First, the police begin to search for a so-called higher order of legitimacy; they make appeals to morality, to patriotism, to "Americanism," and to "law and order" to shore up eroded institutional charters and to accelerate their attempts to control and manipulate their members and clients. Second, the police, as they develop a far greater potential for controlling those they serve through their presentational strategies, come to serve themselves better than ever before.

The problem of the police is, essentially, the problem of the democratic society, and until the central values and social structures of our society are modified (and I think we are seeing such a modification), there can be no real change in the operation of social control. The needed changes are, by and large, not those dealt with in the crime commission report. And this is telling. For an eminently sociological document, it did not focus on the heart of the problem: our anachronistic, moralistic laws, with which the police are burdened, and our dated political system, which is unable to bring political units into a state of civil accountability. The focus of the report and recommendations was predictably on symptoms of crime, not on causes of crime. The "managerial focus" of the report, or its public-administration bias, outlined needed reforms, but not ways in which to implement them, and the problem of efficiency was never really faced.

Not surprisingly for a political document having a variety of public functions, the report has little to say about the nature of the present criminal laws. It dwells, like the police themselves, on means, not ends. As Isidore Silver points out in a critique of the report, more than one-half the crimes committed do not harm anyone: more than one-third are for drunkenness, and a small but important portion are for other "crimes without victims." Most crimes are committed by juveniles who inexplicably "grow out" of their criminality. In 1965, 50 per cent of the known burglaries and larcenies were committed by youths under 18.[31] The report does note what was a central point of our discussion of the political nature of crime, that police corruption is, in almost every instance, a consequence of trying to enforce admittedly unenforceable laws. The demand for services provided by homosexuals, by gamblers, prostitutes, and abortionists is high, and the supply is legally made unavailable to anyone who wants to remain in the so-called "law-abiding" category. The laws, in effect, create the crime and the criminals.

Changes in laws to reduce their absolutistic element and to free people who deviate with little harm to others from the onus of criminalization cannot be accomplished without a parallel change in the nature of police accountability. As we have seen, the strategies of secrecy and rhetoric used by the police play on the fears of society and provide a basis for police control. The managerial reforms contained in the task force report —more public debate on and greater internal and external control over police actions—are needed. Even more urgently required are specific ways in which the cities can control the police and make them strictly accountable for their actions— methods, that is, which go a good deal further than merely disposing of the chief or convening a judicial review board. To

[31] Isidore Silver, "Introduction" to The Challenge of Crime in a Free Society (New York: Avon Books, 1968), p. 25. The President's Commission, Task Force Report: The Courts, discusses substantive criminal law, however, and does make some suggestions for legal change.

give city governments this kind of control over the police, however, entails the reorganization of police departments themselves so that their goals are clear and defined and so that the occupational rewards within the police organization are aligned with public goals.

Three interrelated organizational changes must be made to insure that police attend to the job of maintaining public order. One is to reorganize police departments along functional lines aimed at peace-keeping rather than law enforcement; the second is to allocate rewards for keeping the peace rather than for enforcing the law; the third is to decentralize police functions to reflect community control without the diffusion of responsibility and accountability to a central headquarters.

Present police departments are organized in a military fashion; orders move down the line from the chief to departmental sections assigned law-enforcement functions. These sections usually include such divisions as traffic, patrol, records, detective, juvenile, intelligence, crime-lab, and communications. The principal basis for the assignment of functions, however, is law enforcement;[32] what is needed is a new set of organizational premises so that the basis for the assignment of functions is not law enforcement but the maintenance of order. As Wilson explains:

If order were the central mission of the department, there might be a "family disturbance squad," a "drunk and derelict squad," a "riot control squad," and a "juvenile squad"; law enforcement matters would be left to a "felony squad." Instead, there is a detective division organized, in the larger departments, into units specializing in homicide, burglary, auto theft, narcotics, vice, robbery, and the like. The undifferentiated patrol division gets everything else. Only juveniles tend to be treated by specialized units under both schemes, partly because the law requires or encourages such specialization. The law enforcement orientation of most departments means that new specialized units are created for every offense about which the public expresses concern or for which some special technology is required.[33]

[32]President's Commission, *Task Force Report: The Police,* charts on pp. 46–47.
[33]Wilson, *Varieties of Police Behavior,* p. 69.

What is called for, then, is a new organizational pattern that will provide a domestic unit (as is now being tried in New York City), a juvenile unit, and a drunk unit with a detoxification center, all with a peace-keeping orientation and peace-keeping functions. Only a felony squad and perhaps a riot squad should be used to enforce the law.

One of the obvious ways in which to improve the morale of the patrolman is to let him do a greater amount of investigative work and to take on the responsibility for "solving" some of the crimes originating with his patrol. Rewards could then be allocated in accord with the more limited ends of peace-keeping— for instance, in rewarding a patrolman for a decline in the number of drunks who reappear in court. Since no comprehensive policy can be imagined to guide order maintenance, limited ends for various departments must be developed and subjected to public review. The key is to allow the policeman to develop judgment about the motives and future intentions of people with whom he comes in contact, and to reward him for peace-keeping, not "good pinches" alone.

This reappraisal of the allocation of rewards means, of course, that there must be greater coordination of police and other agencies within the criminal-justice system in order to increase the benefits to the client (the offender or the criminal) and break down the isolation of the police.[34] To allow the policeman to assume greater peace-keeping responsibilities would allow him to play a functional role parallel to that of the better general practitioner of medicine: the referral specialist, the coordinator of family health, the source of records and information, and the family friend and counselor. Such an organizational change in the policeman's function would, naturally enough, make community control of the police a greater possibility. It would begin to bridge the chasm between the police and many hostile segments within the public, a process that

[34]See John P. Clark, "The Isolation of the Police: A Comparison of the British and American Situations," in *Readings in Social Problems,* ed. John Scanzoni (Boston: Allyn and Bacon, 1967), pp. 384–410. See also David Bordua, "Comments on Police-Community Relations," mimeographed (Urbana: University of Illinois, n.d.).

could be facilitated by the creation of a community-relations division within police departments.

The third needed modification of the present structure of police work is the development of decentralized operations. One of the major social trends of the last ten years has been the increase in the lack of attachment people have for their major institutions. Police today suffer from a crisis of legitimacy, and this crisis is heightened by their failure to promote a sense of commitment to their operations by the citizens they serve. One way in which to introduce commitment and a sense of control over the police by members of a community is to make the police more accessible. St. Louis, for example, has experimented with "storefront" police stations, staffed by a few men who are available as advisers, counselors, protectors, and friends of the people in the immediate neighborhood. If the police should begin to differentiate the role of the patrolman to include the functions of a peace-keeping community agent, the control of these agents should reside in the community. Thus, public participation in the decision-making processes of the police would begin at the precinct or neighborhood level; it would not be simply in the form of a punitive civilian review board or a token citizen board at headquarters.

We began with the notion of trouble, police trouble, the troublesome mandate of the policeman. There will be little succor for him as long as our social structure remains fraught with contradictory value premises, with fragmented political power and the consequent inadequate control of the police, with the transformation of public trusts into institutional rights. There will be little succor for him as long as our political agencies resist moving to de-moralize our criminal laws. As it is, we can expect that the management of crime through police strategies and appearances will continue to be a disruptive element in American society.

Drugs and Drug Control

TROY DUSTER

There is something amusing about a people who regard themselves as advanced, postindustrial, and technologically developed demanding greater public control of the smoke from marijuana than of the exhaust fumes from their automobiles. Using the current drug laws as a standard, if controls upon physically debilitating and destructive substances were based upon contemporary empirical evidence, the production and distribution of smog and the sale of ordinary cigarettes would be crimes punishable by death in the electric chair. We may not do a rain dance to produce rain, but then the Indians did not engage in the "primitive," "childlike," or "savage" practice of caging, degrading, brutalizing, subjecting to enforced homosexuality, and otherwise psychically destroying those among them whom they wanted to return to the fold.

Any commission appointed to attack a problem, like a monkey in an experimenter's cage, inevitably assumes a posture. Sometimes that posture is a passive acceptance of the appearances—namely, the banana is out of reach! Or controls on drugs should be even tighter! Sometimes the monkey, or the commission, cocks its head in a new way, achieves some new and different insight, and succeeds in developing a fresh approach to the problem that shifts the whole perspective. While the report of the President's Commission on Law Enforcement and Administration of Justice is neither passively receptive to appearances nor refreshingly innovative, it clearly rests more on the side of the uncritical acceptance of appearances.

Perhaps, there is also something amusing about a people who appoint a commission that submits a report entitled *The Challenge of Crime in a Free Society,* a report in which there is no discussion in the section on the uses and abuses of drugs of one of the most fundamental issues in a "free" society: the degree of personal or individual choice. Here was an appropriate forum for a serious debate on the delicate and complex question of when and where the state should intervene in the private choices of private citizens. Unfortunately, the commission paid no attention to the nature of free, private choices. Such a discussion would necessarily be keyed to the gray areas of borderline drugs—such as alcohol and marijuana. Unquestionably, the issue of free choice should be foreclosed in the case of some drugs, such as thalidomide which caused deformed babies; in these instances, the state should not only inform its citizenry about the consequences of using such drugs but should also prevent their production and distribution.

What are the criteria that should be used by public policymakers in prohibiting or permitting the consumption of a drug that temporarily alters the condition of the mind, does not stimulate aggression, and causes no known permanent physical or psychic damage? The commission refused to address the question of why, in a "free" society, *certain kinds* of drug use should be prohibited as crimes while others are permitted. It refused, further, to discuss why the consumption of one particular drug, one that, demonstrably, eventually destroys body cells in the kidneys and liver, one that is a dangerous, mind-altering substance that kills people and not just on the highways—alcohol—is permissible.

A remarkable degree of confusion and some mythology exist about how segments of the political spectrum view the role of government. The myth states that the right wants less government intervention, the left more. The myth has a limited validity—depending entirely upon which aspect of social life is to be affected by the intervention. It is true that on matters pertaining to the public arena, pertaining, say, to the accumulation of wealth in the marketplace, the myth is generally applicable. The left would prefer that the state redistribute wealth on a more equitable basis, while the right abhors such intervention, arguing that redistribution destroys individual incentive and, thus, excellence. But the left and right reverse themselves in the private arena. Here it is the right that vociferously asks for government intervention into the private lives of citizens who choose to indulge in voluntary acts of "vice"; here it is the left that abhors intervention on such matters of personal taste as reading material, the growth of facial hair (prohibited by most schools, almost all police departments, and many postal stations), wearing apparel (so frequently determined by school administrators), and smoking, be it tobacco or marijuana.

The full measure of a "free" society is not, of course, the free or uncontrolled distribution of drugs. Rather, we would come closer to the conception of "free" if we freely allowed and supported debate on various alternatives to issues in which people have strong investments—emotional, financial, and moral. In sidestepping a full discussion on the crucial issue of personal choice in a "free" society, the commission proved very much a failure.

Despite this lamentable omission, the President's crime commission did make a contribution in its report on drugs: it recognized and distinguished the differences between them. Its greatest shortcoming was its inability or unwillingness to pursue some of these differences to their logical conclusion, namely, different controls on production, distribution, and use. If we admit that heroin and the barbiturates are utterly different, then we should be willing to make strong public-policy recommendations that relate to these differences. But in the climate of mass hysteria that now pervades this nation on the drug question, the commission members were either caught up in it themselves or afraid to speak out against the mindless prosecution of marijuana and heroin possession as felonies.

Regrettably, the commission accepted many traditional assumptions about the nature of drug use, and displayed almost total timidity in questioning the basis for some of these assumptions. For example, it simply acknowledged that possession of

marijuana is a criminal act. It left unexamined the political implications of a law that, applicable to hundreds of thousands of
people, can be and is used selectively and politically.

The first point to be made about the "drug problem," as
the report correctly notes, is that it is not one but several different problems, each of which must be distinguished from the
others. The most far-reaching questions about drug use and
control are tied to these distinctions. The control of heroin
should be different from the control of LSD and marijuana; the
control of these drugs should in turn differ from the state control of the amphetamines and barbiturates. Moreover, to make
distinctions is also to raise the question of whether controls on
certain drugs ought to exist at all, or if so, what kind and to
what degree. That is basically a moral question, and social
scientists have generally regarded it as their professional imperative, or prerogative, to avoid a public squabble over the
moral character of a social issue, leaving that matter to philos-
ophers of ethics or politicians.

Even the white-coated social scientists, however, agree
that it is appropriate to the sociological enterprise to call attention to the social basis of moral judgment. In the use of heroin
and marijuana, that social basis has shifted dramatically and
paradoxically in the last few decades. Heroin, once any man's
household pain-killer for just a few pennies a day, has become
the most dreaded and evil of all drugs, purchasable only
through a black market, and costing $30 to $40 for a day's supply.[1] With marijuana, the social basis of moral judgment has
shifted almost as drastically. Thirty years ago it was described
as the stimulus for rape and murder;[2] today it has become a
mild diversion for many college students and American soldiers
in Vietnam.

Although the physiological effects of these drugs differ
with the individual and the situation, the variance cannot ac-

---

[1]Troy Duster, *The Legislation of Morality* (New York: The Free Press,
1970).

[2]Alfred R. Lindesmith, *The Addict and the Law* (Bloomington: Indiana
University Press, 1965), pp. 228–229.

count for the shifts in public reaction to their use. The changes have been too systematic. Instead, if we are to understand why we have reversed ourselves in our views of heroin and marijuana, we must look at the social meanings that provide the context for their use and control. And, rather than take each of the many drugs that constitute the drug problem and trace the changes in its social meanings and social uses, it will be far more helpful to trace the changes in use and public attitudes of just two—heroin and marijuana.

Partly because of its widespread use as a pain-killer for soldiers wounded during the Civil War and partly because there was no governmental control on its production and distribution, morphine use and addiction was a rather common occurrence in the United States between 1860 and 1900.[3] The best estimate that can be made from numerous sources is that from two to four per cent of the population of the country was addicted, and that another six to ten per cent used morphine in various diluted forms as a household "remedy."[4] This was the period when the drug could be purchased from the corner pharmacist without prescription; it was also the period in which the government did not regulate the labeling of contents. Unknown to the purchaser, many soothing syrups contained morphine.

Heroin, a derivative of morphine, was discovered in 1898. For sixteen years it ranked with morphine as a popular pain-killer that physicians recommended to their patients.[5] The two essential points to be made about the use of morphine and heroin during this period are only indirectly related to its popularity. The first relates to the kinds of persons who used the drugs. The most authoritative sources on the problem indicate that the middle class had a far greater tendency to use these drugs than the working or lower classes, that the middle-aged were more likely to use them than youth, females more apt to

[3]Charles E. Terry and Mildred Pellens, *The Opium Problem* (New York: Bureau of Social Hygiene, 1928).
[4]Ibid.
[5]Ibid.

take them than males, and that whites were far more likely to be morphine and heroin users than members of racial minorities.[6]

The second point is connected with the first in a way that is of paramount interest to the sociology of law and morality: during this entire forty-year period, no evidence exists that a moral stigma was attached to addiction or use.[7] Those who were addicted were seen in the same way as those who now take insulin for diabetes—as men and women who had the misfortune to be *medically* dependent upon a medicinal product.

The patterned behavior of persons in the middle class, being at the "moral center" of society, is basically immune from moral censure. As Gusfield illustrates in his work on Prohibition and the temperance movement, the middle class not only sets the standards of morality, it imposes and enforces them.[8] So long as heroin and morphine use were primarily middle-class habits, it was "an unfortunate dependency." When it became associated in the public mind with a habit of the lower or working class, it then became vulnerable to the charge that it was a vice, that it was sinful, willful, and irresponsible.

In 1922, when public clinics supplying morphine to addicts had been closed down, after a brief three-year period of operation, the addict was cut off from a legal supply of the drug. The addict of some financial means got morphine from his doctor. He disappeared from the statistics and the public eye. The addict of no means turned to the underground and the black market. He became "visible." And as he became more visible, Americans developed their present moralistic attitudes about the use of heroin and morphine. What kind of person would use heroin? The answer "immoral" was almost automatic because the visible addict's social class made him defenseless. This legacy of moral censure is still with us, and it influenced the underlying but unstated assumptions of the President's crime commission.

[6]Duster, *Legislation of Morality*, chap. 1.
[7]Ibid.
[8]Joseph Gusfield, *Symbolic Crusade* (Urbana: University of Illinois Press, 1963).

The course of public opinion about the social meanings and social uses of marijuana has run in the opposite direction, although here, too, moral censure has been related to the visibility of the vulnerable. In the great drug-scare campaigns of the 1930's, the federal narcotics bureau's commissioner painted a picture of marijuana as a drug that stimulated its users to rape and murder.[9] In those years, marijuana was associated in the public mind with lower- and working-class youth; smoking it was dramatized as an activity in which only the evil and immoral engaged. For twenty years this was an effective device in preventing the smoking of marijuana beyond a limited circle. But in the early 1960's, white, middle-class college students began "turning on" to "pot" in large numbers. With the middle class at the moral center, we are, understandably, witnessing a critical reassessment of the moral meaning of marijuana. To smoke pot is no longer simple proof of the sinful, willful, licentious behavior of the under classes; it has come to have two different meanings, depending upon the point of view. Either it is, as some say, an "indication that something is basically wrong with the culture" or it is regarded as an individualistic expression of free choice, to be affirmed as a positive and virtuous development in American society.

What has been outlined in the sketchiest terms is an argument, with empirical support, that says we must look to the social meanings of drug use, and how these meanings vary over time, if we are to understand just how great is the social basis of moral judgment. We shall now turn to the problem of how knowledge—and ignorance—of the physical effects of drugs have an almost equally telling effect upon the judgments men make about their use and control.

THE EFFECTS AND USES OF "NARCOTICS" AND MORAL JUDGMENT

This nation is becoming increasingly enlightened about drugs, but it still has a long way to go before it can claim to be truly

[9]Lindesmith, *Addict and the Law.*

knowledgeable. Ten to fifteen years ago, laymen lumped together "narcotics" in the most simpleminded fashion, making
no distinction between heroin, marijuana, and the amphetamines; now there is a general acceptance of the fact that these
three drugs are considerably different. Further, we are slowly
beginning to accept the idea that there are very different social
categories of persons who use them. This is partly to be explained by the emergence of LSD and marijuana as "middle-
class drugs," or drugs used increasingly by the middle classes.
As indicated previously, so long as "the drug problem" was
associated in the minds of mid-century, white, middle-class
Americans with ghetto blacks, the lower class, and the criminal
element, they could afford the luxury of being ignorant about
drugs. Who cares whether "they" use Methedrine or heroin or
marijuana? But when the drug problem tripped over the middle-
class doorsill, when the police "busted" the son of the president of an Ivy League university, the son of the house speaker
of one of our most important states, and the son of a wealthy
San Francisco socialite, those controlling the mass media decided it was time to start making distinctions.

A knowledge of the physiological effects of drugs is important to an understanding of the principal social and moral
issues involved in the drug problem. For example, if a person
believes that heroin is a dangerous drug because it transforms
the individual into an aggressive, hostile, and uninhibited mo-
ron, his moral stand will be different from a person who considers heroin either destructive to health, soothing to the
nerves, or responsible for sleepless nights. Indeed, a good
many of the intensely moralistic arguments about narcotics are
based upon conceptions of the physiological consequences of
the drugs. Many of these notions are erroneous, especially the
widespread current myths about the opiates. Knowledge of the
fact that sustained use of alcohol has far more deleterious consequences to cell life in the body than sustained use of heroin
undermines many moralistic pronouncements.

If people took the trouble to be a little better informed
about the physical aspects of barbiturates and marijuana, they

would probably reverse their social and moral concerns about them. This is not to argue that knowledge of the physiological effects is the only determinant for social attitudes. It isn't. If an adolescent is sneaking behind the garage to take secobarbital or Dexedrine or marijuana, concern, irrespective of pharmacological knowledge, can be anticipated. Acts have social meanings apart from their physical ones. Thus, even when it is pointed out that alcohol is more physically debilitating than marijuana, centrifugal social forces are often strong enough to overwhelm this mere fact, and the parent is capable of saying, "Ah, but the meaning of his smoking marijuana is defiance, rebellion, insolence, pillar-shaking, etcetera, etcetera."

Many legitimate moral questions, issues, and arguments have a bearing on the sanctionable uses of drugs. Only persons reasonably informed about the physical basis of narcotics, however, can argue convincingly about their use and their control.

The term "narcotics" is used today as a blanket description of some extremely diverse drugs. In contemporary parlance, it confuses and obscures as much as it clarifies. A narcotic is something that dulls the senses or induces sleep; it is a word from the Greek *narkōtikos*—benumbing. A narcotic is a kind of drug; the term "drug" *should* be used generically and the term "narcotic" *should* be used specifically. Yet many laymen use the terms interchangeably. A drug can be natural (opium poppy) or synthetic (Demerol). Its effect on the central nervous system can be that of a stimulant (cocaine) or a depressant (morphine). Further, it may be highly addictive (heroin) or not in the least productive of physical dependence (marijuana).

In the United States, between 1920 and 1963, reference to the drug problem was usually a reference to opium and its derivatives, especially morphine and heroin. Opiates have two things in common: they are depressants and they are also addictive. Opiates depress the nerve centers that register pain; they are among the most effective analgesics (pain-killers) known. Morphine is commonly used for medical purposes in the United States, and heroin is used medicinally in other countries.

Barbiturates—including phenobarbital, secobarbital, and pentobarbital—are also depressants, but they are synthetics used as sedatives. Physicians use barbiturates in prescriptions to bring about relaxation and sleep. Effective amounts often make the user drowsy, and, to many, the aftereffects of sluggishness and heaviness are noticeable and annoying. Taken in sufficiently large quantities, the barbiturates are also highly addictive.

Stimulants, too, come in both natural and synthetic form. The most popular are the amphetamines, popularly called "pep pills" or "bennies." Drivers sometimes use them to stay awake at night, and students have been known to take them on the eve of examinations. Quite the opposite of the depressants, the amphetamines can cause heightened alertness, great nervousness, and sometimes distorted perception and hallucinations when taken in large enough quantities. What constitutes "large enough" is as much a matter of the individual physiology of the user as it is of the actual quantity used.

The term "narcotic," then, has little meaning when used alone—or used interchangeably (and imprecisely) with the term "drug." Men hold very positive views and express fervent opinions about a vast array of drugs. Where opinions are so adamant, many of us would expect them to be supported by at least a moderate knowledge of the legal and therapeutic issues involved. But that is an erroneous assumption. Because drugs do alter the physical condition of man in a significant way, a firm knowledge of these effects should be the basis of all subsequent commentaries on the social and cultural issues involved in their use. I will now turn to a discussion of some of the more widely used drugs in this country.

MORPHINE

In the United States, morphine is one of the most popular and effective analgesics used on the hospital operating table. A moderate dose, instead of producing sleep directly, evokes a kind of euphoria that is an integral part of the *absence* of pain. The same person taking morphine under normal conditions may feel more fear and anxiety from what is happening to his body than euphoria. This fact should be kept in mind when we turn to the social uses of morphine and related drugs.

In addition to killing pain, morphine in moderate dosage often produces drowsiness, apathy, detachment, and the inability to concentrate. Yet though it is primarily a depressant, it also has some ability to act simultaneously as a stimulant. The degree to which this is true depends upon the person, although women tend to react more to the stimulating effects of morphine than do men.

Normally the drug takes effect in about fifteen minutes. Peak effectiveness is reached in about twenty-five to thirty minutes and may continue for three to six hours. For some, the effects can last as long as twelve hours. For most, the body returns to equilibrium in about fourteen to sixteen hours. If the person is addicted, it is at this point that withdrawal sets in.

In moderate dosage, morphine may produce itching in the nose and a general feeling of heaviness in the arms and legs. The mouth feels dry, the pupils constrict, breathing is slower, and hunger muted. After several hours, the individual falls asleep, often to the accompaniment of pleasant dreams.

A full dose, however, has faster, more dramatic effects. Euphoria may be experienced for a very short time, followed by sluggishness and deep, dreamless sleep. An overdose of morphine produces a coma and can cause death from respiratory failure. Although morphine's pain-killing effectiveness lasts somewhat longer than that of heroin, it produces less euphoria, and actually has more undesirable side effects.

Tolerance for morphine usually develops after fifteen to twenty days of continued use at the same dosage. That is, the body begins not to respond to nearly the degree it did during the initial experiences. After becoming tolerant of morphine, the user must take increasingly powerful dosages in order to achieve the same pain-killing results.

The physical effects of morphine addiction are generally

the same as those of heroin. An addicted individual may remain in good health and be productive in his work if he remains on the drug.[10] However, addiction may cause serious physiological consequences that lead to other kinds of problems. The dulling of pain may effectively obscure important danger signals indicating that something is physically wrong. Also, there are sufficient reports to indicate that the sexual appetite of morphine and heroin users decreases, and an addict married to a non-addict may face a sexual problem. Once off the drug, the level of sexual desire reportedly returns to normal.

Traffic in morphine rarely moves into the black market. Physicians and nurses with legitimate access to the drug may administer it to patients, close relatives, or themselves to diminish pain. A tolerance may develop, and for a number of reasons, the decision may be reached to continue administration. Morphine addicts apprehended by the law are very likely to report that their primary reason for continuing to use the drug was to maintain themselves at a level which would prevent withdrawal; this reason is in contrast with the excuse of the heroin addict who often reports the yearning for euphoria as the primary motivation.[11]

The morphine addict is, therefore, likely to be an individual who was addicted in the course of medical treatment. Among morphine addicts, physicians and nurses are probably the most frequently represented occupational groups. Most morphine addiction is found among the middle class, primarily because medical practitioners and the patients they treat with morphine are likely to be from this strata of society.

HEROIN

A semisynthetic derivative of morphine, heroin is far more potent and causes far greater euphoria. The basic effects of the two drugs are the same, and the preceding discussion of the physiological effects of morphine applies generally to heroin—

[10]Louis S. Goodman and Alfred Gilman, *The Pharmacological Basis of Therapeutics,* 2nd ed. (New York: Macmillan, 1960), p. 222.
[11]Duster, *Legislation of Morality,* chaps. 6 and 7.

with a few important differences. Heroin has more of a depressant effect upon the respiratory system, and its action is considerably faster. After only twenty minutes, the drug reaches its peak as an analgesic. Relief from withdrawal is almost immediate. As has been noted, there are few undesirable physical side effects from heroin, something addicts who have tried both are quick to point out.

Heroin has medical uses as an analgesic in several countries, including Great Britain, but it has been banned in the United States since 1924. As Eldridge notes, the association of the drug with the underworld produced a scare in this country that resulted in the medical profession's abandonment of the addict.[12] After the Harrison Act required registration of and prescriptions for heroin, it became a choice commodity on the underworld market. It is easily transported and distributed in bulk and in a form that requires only minimal preparation before being used. The user simply makes some minor alterations with readily accessible additives, and the heroin is ready for injection. Morphine is more difficult to handle, especially for one who may want immediate relief from the debilitating problems in early withdrawal.

Winick finds no evidence that sustained use of heroin or morphine produces any toxic effects, nor that either causes damage of any kind to the central nervous system.[13] As many others have pointed out, the physiological problems that heroin users face result from *withdrawing* from the drug once physically dependent upon it.[14] As long as the individual remains on the drug, he can, and often did up until the first few years of this century, live a healthy and productive life.[15]

[12]William B. Eldridge, *Narcotics and the Law* (New York: New York University Press for the American Bar Foundation, 1962), pp. 6–7.
[13]Charles Winick, "Narcotics Addiction and Its Treatment," *Law and Contemporary Problems* 22 (Winter 1957), pp. 9–33.
[14]See especially the excellent discussion of this point by Marie Nyswander, *The Drug Addict as a Patient* (New York and London: Grune and Stratton, 1956).
[15]Duster, *Legislation of Morality*, chap. 1. See also Terry and Pellens, *The Opium Problem*.

AMPHETAMINES

The amphetamine drugs stimulate the central nervous system, but the responses they evoke depend largely upon the mental state and personality of the individual. The two most popular forms are generally known to college students as Benzedrine and Dexedrine, a popularity that stems from their ability to keep students awake for long periods of study. When taken initially or infrequently in moderate dosages, amphetamines generally produce alertness, increased initiative for otherwise boring or dreaded tasks, and a greater ability to concentrate. Frequently, the individual also becomes more talkative and physically active, giving the appearance of being nervous or agitated.

Larger doses or sustained usage has some unpleasant results ranging from headaches, palpitation, and dizziness to delirium and mental depression. Clinically, amphetamine drugs do have an analgesic action, and when used in combination with morphine, prolong the latter's pain-killing powers.

Addiction can occur, but it is very uncommon. Some heroin addicts use amphetamines to accelerate the action of heroin and to achieve a "stimulated euphoria" that is a different kind of "kick." One of the more frequently cited precautions to sustained use of amphetamines is that they mask fatigue, which can delude the user into assuming that his body can take the physical and mental exertion that is being abnormally pursued.

A good deal of controversy surrounds the therapeutic ability of amphetamines in psychogenic disorders. They have been satisfactorily employed to elevate persons out of mental depressions and certain psychoneuroses, and some reports show that certain forms of epilepsy are aided by their administration. They have even been used effectively to help chronically overweight persons reduce. However, their use in each of these instances has also been accompanied by failures to accomplish desired ends, and the varying effects of amphetamine drugs on different personalities have been sufficient to elicit urgent warnings from medical researchers that they should not be self-administered as a possible solution to these problems.

METHEDRINE (METHAMPHETAMINE HYDROCHLORIDE)

Methamphetamine is closely related in its chemical construction and some of its physiological effects to amphetamine. It has one important difference that makes it of special interest: although it is more powerful as a stimulant to the central nervous system, its effect on the cardiovascular system is weaker. In this fact lie some significant consequences of its nonmedical and illegal use. The drug is marketed under almost a dozen different trade names, the best known of which is Methedrine. It is used clinically for the same purposes as amphetamine, such as sustaining blood pressure during spinal anesthesia.

Methedrine is taken by some because of its ability to stimulate the mind without greatly affecting other parts of the body. Illegal users tend to have artistic or intellectual propensities, and as a class they are much more self-consciously concerned about creativity and individual expression than are, say, heroin users. As has been noted, opiates depress the nervous system, and the user floats away from this world and its considerations; Methedrine, on the contrary, heightens perceptivity and responsiveness to selected aspects of the environment, and the user is apparently stimulated to relate to the world rather than to withdraw from it.

Methedrine users are a small percentage of drug users, and they have some of the trappings of a cult. They are disdainful of heroin addicts, and hold many of the same attitudes toward them as does society in general.

THE BARBITURATES

Barbital, the first discovered of the barbiturates, was used at the turn of the century. Phenobarbital was introduced in 1912. Since that time, more than 2,500 barbiturates have been developed, and more than 50 have been cleared and marketed for clinical use. These acids are widely prescribed by physicians and are commonly used to induce sleep for countless reasons. They are addictive and can be quite dangerous in dosages that exceed a minimum; in combination with alcohol, they have proved unpredictably fatal.

The barbiturates are depressants to the central nervous system, and are used clinically as sedatives and hypnotics. The inducement of sleep is the most frequent reason for their use. They differ from the opiates in analgesia because they are unable to produce sleep in the presence of even moderate pain. Barbiturates do not raise the threshold of pain significantly enough to be called true analgesics.

Despite the publicity given to heroin and morphine addiction, barbiturate addiction is a far more serious physiological matter than addiction to either of the opiates. A 1950 research report relates how some volunteers at the Lexington, Kentucky, federal hospital for drug addicts were given barbiturates for an extended period:

. . . when the drugs were withdrawn after three to five months, four of five subjects developed convulsions and four of five became psychotic. This experimental demonstration of addiction, later amplified with additional cases, did much to inform the American medical profession that primary barbiturate addiction does occur and that the abstinence syndrome is characteristic and dangerous. [Compared with morphine] barbiturate addiction is a more serious public health and medical problem because it produces greater mental, emotional, and neurological impairment and because withdrawal entails real hazards.[16]

The barbiturate addict is more sluggish in physical mobility and thought. His speech is slow, his memory poor, and his comprehension narrowed. Typical patterns also reveal exaggeration of selected personality traits, moroseness, and irritability.

Withdrawal from barbiturates for an addict can be serious for his psychic equilibrium. The trauma varies with the individual, but hallucinations are frequent. In the early stages of withdrawal, these hallucinations are recognized by the subject for what they are, but as they continue he loses his facility to dis-

[16]Goodman and Gilman, *Pharmacological Basis of Therapeutics*, p. 150.

tinguish between his own unique perceptions and those consonant with reality, a primary characteristic of schizophrenia. The withdrawal psychosis may clear after a few days, but there have been cases in which hallucinations have persisted for more than a month. Barbiturate addiction withdrawal is a difficult problem to treat because the various physical symptoms are hard to distinguish from those of more traditionally known illnesses, such as delirium tremens, epilepsy, and encephalitis, to name but a few. Extensive investigation is required to rule out these other sources of the manifested symptoms.

A standard reference work on therapeutics states that while the incidence of barbiturate addiction cannot be known, it is not only "common, but appears to be on the increase."[17] In view of the greater physical seriousness of barbiturate addiction, it is indeed odd that morphine and heroin addiction should receive so much more attention. The media make very little of barbiturate addiction because it is not perceived in the same moralistic light that heroin or morphine addiction is.

In recent years, barbiturates have been used increasingly without medical and clinical recommendation—in other words, illegally. When heroin or morphine is not readily available to a person addicted to either one, he may turn to a short-acting barbiturate—secobarbital or pentobarbital, known among addicts as "goofballs" in honor of their effects. It is possible to develop a simultaneous addiction to the opiates and the barbiturates, and in order to stave off withdrawal, an addict who has a double addiction must take both heroin and secobarb.

Most heroin addicts, because of the unpleasant sluggishness attending the use of a barbiturate, dislike the drug and will use it only as a last resort. They can achieve either euphoria or physiological equilibrium with heroin, and in either state they do not feel burdened by the drug. With secobarbital, on the other hand, they feel restrained in their ability to manage the world.

Despite the public's greater preoccupation with opiate addiction, it is beginning to register alarm over barbiturate use

[17]Ibid.

and addiction. And this increased concern has paralleled an increase in the illegal traffic of barbiturates. The present status of barbiturates is similar to that of morphine in 1912: predominant usage by persons for medical purposes with few taints and few charges of sensual gratification explaining addiction. The lower classes, young male adults, and ethnic minorities now seldom take barbiturates, not only because prescriptions are required but because the subjective desire for sedation rather than euphoria seems to be more of a middle-class phenomenon. If a new federal law outlawed barbiturate use, except for medical reasons, and if physicians were imprisoned for simply prescribing without close attention, barbiturate addicts would suddenly be prime candidates for a black-market traffic and the cost of the drug would go up substantially. The middle-class addicts would fade out of the statistics, partly because they could get barbiturates from their family physicians and partly because law-enforcement agencies systematically differentiate between classes in the application of the law.[18] Those in social categories further and further removed from the "moral center" would appear with greater and greater frequency in criminal citations, and barbiturate use would be transformed in the mind of the public into a vicious, evil habit in which only the willfully immoral engage. One reason why this hypothetical situation has not occurred has been because barbiturate use has not been associated with the pursuit of sensual gratification. Morphine and heroin use did not come in for strident moral censure until the interpretation and enforcement of the Harrison Act and sensational stories in yellow journals combined to instill in the public the idea that the pursuit of opiates was the pursuit of sensual pleasure—and, therefore, was evil. Until recently, barbiturate users were almost entirely in the social categories that do not lend themselves to moralistic denigration.[19]

[18]Aaron Cicourel, The Social Organization of Juvenile Justice (New York: John Wiley & Sons, 1968).

[19]Joseph Gusfield, "Social Structure and Moral Reform: A Study of the WCTU," American Journal of Sociology 61 (November 1955), pp. 221–232.

COCAINE

Cocaine is the drug most responsible for the erroneous public image of the narcotic addict as a "dope fiend"—one who takes a drug and becomes an aggressive maniac dangerous to himself and others. Cocaine is obtained from the leaves of the *Erythroxlyon coca* shrubs of Peru and Bolivia. The drug acts first as a powerful stimulant, producing pleasurable hallucinations, great excitement, and often an exaggeration of one's own powers. It elicits a feeling of tremendous mental and physical strength, and, indeed, there is some evidence that it increases the mental faculties. Because cocaine acts to lessen the perception of fatigue, greater physical exertion is possible.

The tendency to feel stronger and more insightful than usual has been known to produce paranoia in the cocaine user, one reason being because he comes to attribute his relative ineffectiveness to a conspiracy. Suffering from feelings of persecution, cocaine users may become physically aggressive toward "hostile" individuals in their immediate environment. Visual, auditory, and tactile hallucinations are reported, especially the feeling of something crawling on the skin, a perception that gives further impetus to the paranoia.

Cocaine usage is rare in the United States, and cocaine addiction even rarer. Physical dependence on the drug is not nearly so apparent as it is with opium narcotics, and withdrawal from it is not nearly so difficult. A tolerance for the drug can be acquired, so that increased dosages are necessary to produce the same effect, but little is known about the physiological mechanisms of cocaine tolerance.

Although cocaine is not a problem of any dimension or urgency, the sensational newspaper accounts of its use during the 1920's and '30's have lent it an unwarranted significance that still persists whenever narcotics are discussed by laymen. Unfortunately, many people associate the effects of cocaine with the opiates, and this common misconception seriously impedes a calm discussion of the narcotics problem.

MARIJUANA

"Marijuana" is the term used in the United States to refer to those parts of the hemp plant, or any of its extracts, that produce psychic changes when chewed, smoked, or ingested. The technical name for the drug is *Cannabis,* and it was known to the Chinese five centuries before Christ. Because of the relative paucity of research on marijuana, we do not know whether it is primarily a stimulant or a depressant. It affects the system in both ways. It was used as an anesthetic in surgery 2,000 years ago, but has long since been replaced by more powerful and dependable analgesics, such as the opiates. Marijuana now has almost no medical use in Western societies, and is not used clinically in the United States.

Marijuana has both stimulant and depressant effects upon the central nervous system, and it is impossible to say which effect is the more important, or predominant. It varies, as Becker clearly points out, with the individual, with his psychic condition at the time of exposure, and with the kind of social environment in which it is used.[20] In experiments on animals, no strong evidence has ever demonstrated that marijuana significantly affects or alters the nervous system as either a sedative or hypnotic agent.[21]

The primary reason for smoking marijuana seems to be to achieve a "high"—an exhilaration or euphoria that gives one the feeling of being disconnected from mundane life. Vivid and pleasing hallucinations are often part of a high, plus the loss of time and space perceptions. A marijuana user once described to me his experience of driving an automobile while under the influence of the drug: "I kept saying to myself, 'Slow down, slow down. You're going too fast, way too fast.' I was sure that I must have been doing 60 to 70 in a 25-mile-an-hour zone. And while I had this feeling, some guy comes zooming past me on a bicycle."

[20]Howard S. Becker, *Outsiders: Studies in the Sociology of Deviance* (New York: The Free Press, 1963), pp. 41–78.
[21]Goodman and Gilman, *Pharmacological Basis of Therapeutics,* pp. 171–172.

There are reports that suggest a sexual quality to some of the more pleasant experiences in smoking marijuana, but the drug is evidently not an aphrodisiac. The unfounded scare information disseminated in the late 1930's by the federal Bureau of Narcotics linked marijuana with rape and murder and culminated in the passage in 1937 of federal legislation on its sale.[22] The bureau assailed the results of an empirical study of marijuana published in 1945 which disputed its contention that the drug was associated with murder and rape. Just ten years later, the bureau changed its position: its new argument against marijuana was that it led to heroin.[23] This has remained the predominant argument against marijuana ever since, a subject to be addressed momentarily.

With continued use, a small degree of tolerance for the drug may develop, but it is minimal and disappears when the subject stops smoking marijuana for even a short period. There is no physical dependence upon marijuana, and therefore the drug is not addictive. As for the psychological issue of habitutation, a primary reference on the pharmacological effects states:

> . . . psychic dependence is not as prominent or compelling as in the case of morphine, alcohol, or perhaps even tobacco habituation. Marijuana habitués often voluntarily stop smoking for a time and do not necessarily experience undue disturbance or craving from deprivation. Organic (physiological) dependence, as evidenced by characteristic withdrawal symptoms, apparently does not develop.[24]

Despite the furor and clamor about it, marijuana is less physically harmful than alcohol. Research on its physiological effects has determined that many of its side effects can be attributed to the general excitation associated with the drug's use.[25] Nausea and diarrhea may result, as may frequent urina-

---

[22]Lindesmith, *Addict and the Law,* pp. 228–231.
[23]Ibid., pp. 222–242.
[24]Goodman and Gilman, *Pharmacological Basis of Therapeutics,* p. 174.
[25]Samuel Allentuck, "Medical Aspects," *The Marihuana Problem in the City of New York* (Lancaster, Pa.; The Jacques Cattell Press, 1944).

tion, but they are hardly predictable. An excellent comparison between the effects of marijuana and alcohol, to which this discussion is indebted, is contained in Alfred Lindesmith's most recent work on addiction.[26] Sustained use of alcohol is destructive to cell life in the body. Further, it has been known to produce psychosis, and it clearly alters the mind with only moderate intake. Some men lose time perceptions, others are slowed in reaction time, and dexterity is drastically curtailed. Just as with alcohol, marijuana is capable of altering time perception, evoking a euphoria, and releasing inhibitions. Just as with alcohol, rare cases of psychotic episodes do result from its use. When it comes to addiction, however, the parallels end; alcohol is addictive, marijuana is not.

The strongest case against marijuana now being made by the narcotics bureau is that marijuana leads to heroin. In order to "prove" the point, the bureau argues that heroin addicts smoked marijuana before turning to heroin. Any freshman in an introductory course in logic can see the foolishness of this "proof." We know almost nothing about the population of marijuana users who do not go on to heroin; they aren't talking, and law-enforcement agents and social scientists have little access to them.

To illustrate the fallacy of the bureau's contention, suppose a team of physicians discovered that a large percentage of persons with cancer drink alcohol regularly. Physicians know they could not make any statement about a relationship between the two until they found out whether others who drink alcohol regularly develop cancer; that is, in order to assert a relationship, they would have to look at a larger population of alcohol consumers than simply those in hospitals with cancer.[27] Yet it is precisely this kind of illogical relationship that people are touting when they say that marijuana leads to heroin; they are dealing only with a population of heroin users, not with the critical population of marijuana consumers. A physician would be ridiculed both within his profession and outside it if he pro-

[26]Lindesmith, Addict and the Law.

[27]Total abstainers would also have to be the subjects of an intensive study in order to make reliable statements about a probable relationship.

posed to make some connection between alcohol and cancer on the basis of looking only at cancerous patients. Yet men are constantly making outrageous claims about the relationship of marijuana to heroin by looking only at heroin users.

A more empirical example of the bureau's foolishness is available. Juvenile gangs in urban areas are commonly considered as supportive of narcotics use. Yet findings by Isador Chein and his associates after an intensive study of juveniles in New York City show that adolescent gangs are strong forces *against* narcotics usage.[28] Among several hundred gangs, few will use narcotics as part of their activities—and get their names on the police blotter and in the press. The basic fact is that gangs typically act as a bulwark against drug use; they have their own systems of internal sanctions even in the high-heroin slum neighborhoods of New York.

The essential point is that if all we know about juvenile gangs—through the press and the law-enforcement agencies—relates to those that use narcotics, then our ignorance expands into an unfounded generalization about narcotics and gangs. If all we know about heroin addicts is that they once smoked marijuana, then our ignorance expands into an unfounded generalization about marijuana and heroin addiction. Obviously, even a tentative, exploratory statement on any possible relationship is dependent upon a great deal of knowledge about the population of marijuana smokers, not simply those known as heroin addicts.

Were the consequences not so grave, it might be almost amusing to observe the illogic and inconsistency of the current argument that marijuana leads to heroin. For example, the narcotics bureau has acknowledged that marijuana is widely used on college campuses without leading to heroin use:

Collegians on practically every major college campus in the country have used marijuana or other drugs—often with the approval of educators—the nation's narcotics chief has warned Congressmen. Commissioner of Narcotics Henry L. Giordano noted with alarm: "We have had a problem in just about every one of the major universities

[28]Isador Chein et al., *The Road to H* (New York: Basic Books, 1964).

in the country with marijuana. Fortunately, you will not run into heroin. It is amphetamines, hallucinogenic drugs, tranquilizers and drugs of that sort."[29]

The precise nature of the traffic in marijuana is unknown, but there is good reason to believe that Giordano is right in saying that marijuana is widely used on the campus. Any young man, or woman, attending college on an urban campus in the United States can obtain and experiment with marijuana simply by saying often enough that he wants to. Between 30 to 40 per cent of American college students are estimated to have experienced marijuana. If marijuana leads to heroin, with even the most moderate frequency, droves of heroin addicts would be enrolled in American colleges. The fact that there are almost none is glibly and somewhat erroneously "explained" on the ground that heroin is not readily available. True enough, there is no heroin market on the college campus. But the largest percentage of undergraduate marijuana smokers are on campuses located in or around New York City, Chicago, San Francisco, and Los Angeles—metropolitan areas where the traffic in heroin is greatest. It is entirely reasonable to assume that any enterprising college student (and students who smoke marijuana are likely to be enterprising) could make his way into the appropriate section of town, make "contact," and return with his heroin packet, physically expending himself no more than he would by going, say, to the right jazz night spot.

LSD (LYSERGIC ACID DIETHYLAMIDE)

Unlike several other drugs we have discussed, LSD is rarely if ever mislabeled a narcotic. Depending upon personal biases, it is either a psychedelic drug or an hallucinogen. If a person is favorably disposed toward the effects of the drug, or is sympathetic to the goals of its users—is a cultist, in other words, or a "believer"—then the chances are he will call LSD a "psychedelic" drug.[30] The reason for the term is that the effects pro-

[29]The San Francisco Chronicle, March 31, 1966, p. 1.
[30]The writings of Timothy Leary and his followers almost never refer to LSD as a hallucinogen; the Bureau of Narcotics does not call it a psychedelic either.

voked are seen as mind-enriching experiences that expand the horizons of the sensory perceptions and offer new dimensions to thought and imagination. If, on the contrary, a person is skeptical, hostile, or reserved about LSD, the chances are he will term it an "hallucinogen." The drug sometimes elicits fantastic imagery and auditory and tactile perceptions that to "nonbelievers" are like hallucinations because they are beyond the working social consensus of what is "really" out there, of what reality is.

The effects of LSD differ greatly with the temperament of the subject, his attitude toward the impending experience, his social milieu, and the amount of the drug used. Nonetheless, some patterns in the effect of the drug have emerged. At slight to moderate dosages, between 50 to 100 milligrams, LSD tends to produce minor changes in sensory perception; some report no effect, however, while others have experiences that parallel those who have taken larger doses.

With a dosage of 100 to 200 milligrams, a feeling of heaviness pervades the extremities and the user tends to fix his attention on a single object for long periods of time. Aldous Huxley reports that he could look at his trouser leg for half an hour, fascinated by the intricate weave and the interplay of colors that otherwise escaped his notice.[31] Others report how they can look at a vase, a painting, or a leaf for extended periods, marveling for the first time at certain internal relationships. (One might speculate that the ability of the catatonic to "stare" for long periods could be related to just such a heightened sensory fixation; there is already disputed evidence concerning the alleged similarity of the blood chemistry of those who habitually hallucinate to changes in the blood of those who have used LSD.)

It is also common for the subject to see new patterns and movement in ceilings and walls. Whether colors appear brighter and more sensational because the ability to concentrate is increased or because the receptors are transformed has not been definitely determined; it is known, however, that the pupils

[31]Aldous Huxley, *The Doors of Perception* (New York: Harper & Row, 1954).

dilate considerably, and the LSD user finds bright lights annoying. Auditory receptors are not themselves noticeably affected, but some report that a familiar piece of music takes on completely new meanings.

One effect of LSD is that it mutes or destroys the "normalizing" ability of the mind.[32] For example, we know that the size of the feet of our adult friend remains constant; his feet do not grow or shrink. When we look at his feet propped on a table facing us, therefore, we know that although they *appear* much larger than his head they are not. This conception of the perceived object as a constant object is achieved by "normalizing." We know that the size of our friend's feet remains normal despite the incongruity; we know that we cannot rely solely upon what strikes the retina. LSD affects this normalizing process. It has led some to conclude that the drug allows the world to be seen as it *really* is—without the constraints of normalizing, which, it is argued, are a consequence partly of man's recall of sensory experience and partly of his *a priori* learning relationships. Those who argue against this position do so by asserting that LSD simply produces unreal perceptions or hallucinations—an argument that seems to be at the core of the discussion as to whether it is an hallucinogen or a psychedelic.

These two orientations toward LSD also reflect the schism between an underlying fear and an underlying optimism about explorations into the psychic unknown, since precisely what LSD does to the mind has not been determined.[33] Tolerance for the drug is minimal, receding after a few days' abstinence, and there is no physical dependence to worry about. Psychotic episodes occur with large doses of alcohol or barbiturates, but whether these episodes are more common with alcohol and barbiturates than with LSD is an empirical matter about which we currently have no empirical evidence.

Nonetheless, in 1966 LSD took its place alongside mari-

[32]Egon Brunswik, *Perception and the Representative Design of Psychological Experiments,* 2nd ed. (Berkeley and Los Angeles: University of California Press, 1956).

[33]Sidney Cohen, *The Beyond Within: The LSD Story* (New York: Atheneum, 1965).

juana as an officially labeled "dangerous drug." As with marijuana, a stormy controversy swirls over its distribution and use.
Lindesmith correctly points to the civil and political issues in
marijuana consumption, issues that involve the relationship between individual autonomy and public control.[34] These same
issues are relevant to a discussion of LSD. The argument that
"we don't know enough" about the physical effects of the drug
—or that uncertainties exist about its psychotherapeutic value
—is an interesting one. There are hundreds of drugs distributed
every year that "we don't know *enough*" about, drugs that have
had serious and unfortunate effects on body tissues, spleens,
livers, kidneys, and other organs. So many thousands of variables are present in prescribing an appropriate drug that no
drug company could hope to control them all. It may be that
certain foods combine with certain drugs in an unknown way.
Unanticipated, harmful side effects often accompany the mar-
keting of drugs, and some measure of this is unavoidable. A few
of these become sensational cases, such as chloromycetin and
thalidomide. Chloromycetin was an antibiotic advertised and
marketed for household use for minor cuts and burns; it turned
out to cause aplastic anemia, a fatal disease.[35] Thalidomide
was a sedative that when taken by pregnant women caused
deformed babies.

With LSD, however, we are dealing with the mind and
thought processes, not simply with bodily processes. Men become particularly wary when drugs start altering the working
consensus of perceptions of reality and truth. We know *some*
things about the effect of LSD upon the mind. To some observers, these are alarming. To others they reveal a remarkable
opportunity for exploration.

At the beginning of this essay, I pointed out that the moral
arguments concerning the use of drugs are based principally
upon beliefs about the physiological effects of drugs. In the
1930's, the federal Bureau of Narcotics saw "danger" in the

[34]Lindesmith, *Addict and the Law*, pp. vii–xiii and 222–242.
[35]Richard Harris, *The Real Voice* (New York: Macmillan, 1964), pp. 99–
112.

probability that marijuana would produce aggressive sex mani-
acs and murderers; when empirical research undercut that
argument, the big "danger" became the probability that the
drug would lead to heroin consumption. We have seen how the
bureau came to acknowledge that the conditions and circumstances of marijuana use determine whether it will lead to
heroin; we have also seen how the bureau got caught in an embarrassing contradiction because it now admits that marijuana
does not lead to heroin on college campuses.

This "strongest argument" that marijuana leads to heroin
is full of contradictions and is based neither on logic nor on
any research on the population in question, namely, marijuana
users. Indeed, the physiological effects of marijuana are such
that Lindesmith is correct in asserting that its use can be
treated as a morally private matter and regulated by the state
in the same way in which other private matters of consumption
are handled.

The physiological effects of heroin, however, are such that
the private consequences may be of significance in the public
sphere. Millions of citizens incapable of experiencing pain
might be regarded as a public concern. If that is the case, lawmakers may wish to implement legislation that addresses itself
to the specific public concern for its use.

Any call to "legalize" heroin or morphine would mean little
until the advocates of legalization spell out a detailed program
of distribution and consumption. This could range all the way
from a free and open market in the drug, the way aspirin is now
distributed, to a tightly controlled prescription legalization. In
the latter form, only those with specific problems or reasons
could obtain the drug; in the former, mass consumption would
be possible. Both, however, entail legalization, and for these
reasons proponents of legalization need to make more than a
simple statement about being in favor of new laws.

With heroin, keeping the above qualifications about any
future legalization in mind, it seems that the primary issues in
its legalization and availability to a mass market might better
revolve around the question of how the members of a society
feel about the artificial, external lessening of suffering, both

physical and psychic. With heroin, the added dimension is the development of a dependence upon the drug, but then many men are dependent upon other drugs without others raising a cry of moral outrage. When the question is posed about whether we ought to alleviate suffering through pill and injection, the replier is driven back to a moral position.

We would do well to distinguish between the fear of the known (alcohol) and the fear of the unknown (LSD). We know that alcohol is a "mind-transforming" substance with systematic and observable consequences to the physical well-being of the individual. LSD may prove to be a drug that is dangerous to the mind and the body, but at this point in our knowledge about it, it is hardly consistent for our society to label it a "dangerous mind-transforming drug" while millions are swallowing a "dangerous mind-transforming cocktail."

LSD may be dangerous to "society" at another level, however. A social order is capable of being maintained through an operating consensus of reality, and the real danger of LSD may prove to be that it destroys that operating consensus by provoking some to conclude that what they "really" perceive is different and unique. Of even greater significance, it may cause some to view ordinary, everyday life as so meaningless that total withdrawal and detachment from one's fellow man becomes the consequence.[36] Its advocates minimize this problem and emphasize the enriching experiences of new dimensions of thought and perception. In any event, it should be clear that whatever moral position one takes on LSD, the basis of it should be the actual physical effects of the drug.

THE PRESIDENT'S CRIME COMMISSION REPORT:
SOME ASSUMPTIONS AND CONSEQUENCES

Any commission attacking a public problem can consider it from an entirely new viewpoint—or it can merely accept the terms of the problem as they have always appeared. The Presi-

---

[36]Alfred Schütz, *The Problem of Social Reality: Collected Papers I* (The Hague: Martinus Nijhoff, 1962).

dent's Commission on Law Enforcement and Administration of Justice opted for the latter tactic; it did not, as it might have and as I mentioned at the beginning of this essay, cock its head in a new way to achieve some fresh, new, different insight into the problem of drugs and drug control in the United States. Commission members seemed to take the established medical utility of a drug as the only possible criterion for its production or consumption. Other uses of a drug were not even momentarily entertained, much less seriously considered. Yet diversion, pleasure, escape, and sociability are valued sufficiently that arguments are made publicly in support of these purposes by those who have indulged, now legally, in the use of certain drugs (alcohol, for example, or the amphetamines). The commission report, however, not only informs us that marijuana has no medical value, it implies by its wording that marijuana, therefore, has no other valid or positive use, be that social, physical, psychological, or recreational:

> Marijuana has no established and certainly no indispensable medical use. Its effects are rather complicated, combining both stimulation and depression. Much of its effect depends on the personality of the user. The drug may induce exaltation, joyousness and hilarity, and disconnected ideas; or it may induce quietude or reveries. In the inexperienced taker it may induce panic. Or, one state may follow the other. Confused perceptions of space and time and hallucinations in sharp color may occur; the person's complex intellectual and motor functions may be impaired.[37]

The same words could be written about alcohol, and anyone might "induce panic" in an inexperienced person imbibing a martini, for instance, through simple and ordinary manipulations of the environment.

Another major shortcoming of the commission's report is its failure to discuss some of the public issues involved in the

---

[37]The President's Commission on Law Enforcement and Administration of Justice (hereafter cited as President's Commission), *Task Force Report: Narcotics and Drug Abuse* (Washington, D. C.: United States Government Printing Office, 1967), p. 3.

use of drugs. The following passage describes the increase in marijuana consumption:

[Marijuana] use apparently cuts across a larger segment of the general population than does opiate use, but again adequate studies are lacking. An impressionistic view, based on scattered reports, is that use is both frequent and increasing in depressed urban areas, academic and artistic communities, and among young professional persons. There are many reports of widespread use on campuses, but estimates that 20 percent or more of certain college populations have used the drug cannot be verified or refuted.[38]

Yet the report ignores the important social and political implications of having a law on the books that is repeatedly violated but rarely prosecuted. Further, it also ignores the fact that when arrests and prosecutions do occur, they are largely a matter of discretion on the part of the police and the court system. One result of this circumstance is that authorities can then use the law selectively for political reasons, and sanction those they want to sanction *for reasons other than the offense itself.*

Federal authorities and local police occasionally admit privately that student political activists are far more likely to be harassed and prosecuted for marijuana violations than are the apolitical. Does America want to have marijuana laws that give such remarkable discretionary powers to police and prosecuting authorities? I find it reprehensible that a presidential report on the use and control of drugs refused to take up a question of such paramount interest and consequence.

The report's discussion of the treatment of narcotics users is especially poor in its lack of analysis. It describes several programs that have tried unsuccessfully to deal with the heroin addict, and admits the almost total failure of the three forms of institutional treatment that are now public policy: *incarceration* for the commission of other crimes; *voluntary treatment* at the two federal "prison" hospitals; and *involuntary civil commitments* to rehabilitation centers. The commission report readily acknowledges a high rate of recidivism for all three methods of

[38]Ibid.

dealing with addicts and that each program, as treatment or rehabilitation, is clearly a washout.[39] Yet, rather than propose new methods or support for experimental programs, the report rests on conserving the failures. In the discussion of civil commitments, the following passage illustrates how far the commission would go to affirm the viability of existing treatment programs in the face of recidivism statistics and the embarrassing illogic of its own position on the commitment issue:

> The involuntary commitment of noncriminal addicts and the voluntary commitment of criminal addicts are controversial and raise difficult issues.
>
> The most heated debate centers on the involuntary commitment of the addict who is not accused of crime. Its proponents compare it to the practices of involuntarily committing the mentally ill, or isolating persons with serious contagious diseases; they argue that the addict is both a health risk to himself and a crime risk to others; they point to the evidence that addiction is spread by social contact with addicts rather than by the recruiting efforts of peddlers. These premises, buttressed by the right of a State to protect the general health and welfare of its citizens, lead them to the conclusion that commitment for treatment offers the maximum benefit to the individual and the minimum risk to society. Its opponents dispute both the premises and the conclusions. They contend that at the very least there should be a specific finding that the person to be committed is reasonably likely to commit dangerous acts; that mere proof of addiction is not a sufficient showing that a person is dangerous to himself or others; and that, in any event, the commitment is a subterfuge—it holds out the promise of a known method of treatment, or a reasonable prospect of cure, which does not exist.
>
> These questions are not easily resolved. However, the Commission believes that involuntary civil commitment offers sufficient promise to warrant a fair test. But it must not become the civil equivalent of imprisonment. The programs must offer the best possible treatment, including new techniques as they become available, and the duration of the commitment, either within or outside an institution, must be no longer than is reasonably necessary.[40]

[39]Ibid., pp. 14–15.
[40]Ibid., p. 17.

First of all, the report makes no mention of the content of the "promise" that involuntary civil commitment makes. To the contrary, elsewhere in the report[41] the commission cites "success" figures for such commitments that are so small they prompt the question of whether *by chance alone* 27 of 5,000 addicts might not be drug-free after three years. What is more astounding, however, is the sentence which ends, ". . . it [involuntary civil commitment] must not become the civil equivalent of imprisonment." What is the meaning of *involuntary* here if it is not imprisonment? The addict so committed has no choice; he is behind bars, and is heavily guarded. As for the prisons themselves, officials there have always claimed to "offer the best possible treatment, including new techniques as they become available." They also have always claimed that the duration of the commitment "must be no longer than is reasonably necessary."

The commission report goes on to describe the *voluntary* commitment for treatment of persons accused of other crimes, such as theft, indirectly linked with drugs:

> The claimed advantages of such a commitment are that the addict can receive immediate treatment and avoid the stigma of criminal conviction. The eligible addict is given the choice of proceeding to trial or being committed. If he elects commitment, the criminal case is suspended pending the completion of treatment.
> The objection in principle to this form of commitment is that a defendant, even though mentally competent in a legal sense, can avoid trial simply by asserting the fact of his addiction in a preliminary proceeding. Thus, so contend the critics, the ultimate issue of guilt or innocence is never reached at all.[42]

One central problem with this arrangement is not mentioned. Prosecuting attorneys frequently use civil commitment as a bargaining tool with accused addicts. Many will offer to get the addict a civil commitment to a rehabilitation center instead

---

[41]Ibid., pp. 14–15.
[42]Ibid., p. 17.

of prosecuting him for armed robbery, usually a twenty-year sentence, if the accused will just inform on his source of drugs. This device subverts one of the primary purposes of commitment for treatment: it is an affirmation of the greater concern for punishment than for rehabilitation. The significance of this bargaining is not lost on the addict, and he enters the treatment center with a cynical view of an unwritten, contracted bribe.[43] His view is that the "state" and "society" are far less concerned with his treatment and his rehabilitation than with the punishment of the supply source. In that assessment, he is correct.

The commission does mention two privately sponsored treatment projects, but their value in contrast with public-policy programs is ignored. Synanon, which has had a success with rehabilitation far greater than any other program, is described briefly,[44] but the report offers no assessment of Synanon's treatment. Considered reservation about the applicability of the Synanon approach to a large addict population is certainly in order, for it requires a level of self-deprecation that few possess or should even want to possess. Nonetheless, in a document purporting in part to explain various treatment and rehabilitation programs for the addicted, Synanon at least deserves to have its successes explained.

Treatment of the addict by administering doses of a synthetic opiate, methadone, is also described as a separate project sponsored by private sources. Here the commission is correct in drawing no conclusions, as the project is in its earliest stages. But once again, an analysis of the basic issues in the argument about ambulatory treatment deserved to be made.

There now exist a number of new private programs for addicts that offer various methods for treating withdrawal symptomatically. In many of these programs, rather than attempting gradual withdrawal from heroin or morphine with a

---

[43]Duster, *Legislation of Morality,* chaps. 6 and 8.
[44]President's Commission, *Task Force Report: Narcotics,* p. 15.

gradual lessening of the dosage, medical treatment is given for particular localized physiological problems resulting from withdrawal.

As a final comment on the commission's consideration of treatment, its failure to engage in a full debate and analysis of the feasibility of ambulatory treatment must be pointed out. We need to explore more fully the possibilities and problems of a system where addicts can obtain medical treatment not only locked behind bars but able to walk in and out of a clinic like any other ambulatory patient.

The commission report states flatly that drug addicts are "crime-prone persons," even though it recognizes the complexities of that phrase. Those who favor liberalizing the drug laws so that addicts may obtain drugs legally have countered with the following argument: to sustain an exorbitantly expensive habit, addicts must go out and commit crimes for money (unless, of course, they come from well-to-do families or have large incomes). They are then arrested for these crimes. Thus, their criminality comes *after* their addiction and is a direct result of it.

To meet the challenge of this argument, the F.B.I. and the federal Bureau of Narcotics produced statistics which showed that most heroin addicts had a criminal record *before* their first arrest for narcotics.

As of December 31, 1966, there were 4,385 persons identified as users of heroin in the FBI's "Careers in Crime Program"—a computerized record of criminal histories. This data is based on criminal fingerprint cards submitted by local and Federal agencies.

The 4,385 people who were identified as heroin users had an average criminal career (the span of years between the first and last arrest) of 12 years during which they averaged 10 arrests. Six of these arrests on an average were for offenses other than narcotics. Of the total arrests accumulated by heroin users in the property crime and violent crime categories, 26 percent were arrests for violent crimes and 74 percent were arrests for property crimes. On the other hand, all criminal offenders in the program (over 150,000) averaged 23 percent arrests for violent crimes and 77 percent for property crimes. Seventy-two percent of all heroin users had an arrest for some other criminal act prior to their first narcotic arrest.[45]

The fact that 72 per cent of all heroin users in this population had an arrest record for a crime other than narcotics prior to their arrest on drug charges seems on the surface to be evidence that drug users are criminals first, then drug users. But this is the kind of unanalytic acceptance of surface data of which the commission was generally guilty.

The fact is, of course, that the drug user takes his drugs in a private setting; he is a willing "victim" and there is no party to act as plaintiff.[46] (Theft and robbery, on the other hand, are public acts wherein, additionally, there is a victim to press for prosecution.) Thus, even if a man is addicted, the chances of his being apprehended for drug use *first* are infinitesimal. Simply by referring to its own statements on a previous page, the commission might have concluded that the addict will almost inevitably be caught first for a violation of the criminal law other than narcotics abuse.[47]

LEGAL CONTROLS AND DRUG USE

In the United States, increasing legal controls have paralleled the decrease in heroin users. This simple fact has led public policy-makers to some erroneous conclusions about heroin control in particular and drug control in general. Correlation usually implies causation, but the connections between events have to be made in more than a merely statistical fashion. It is equally true, for example, that heroin use declined as public knowledge increased about its highly addictive qualities. In such a situation, is the decline in heroin use to be explained by citing the legal controls or the increase in information about heroin, or perhaps, a combination of the two?

That question can be answered more convincingly by taking a look at what has happened typically with a host of other

[45]Ibid., p. 11.
[46]Ibid., p. 8. The same point is made in Edwin M. Schur's *Crime Without Victims* (Englewood Cliffs, N.J.: Prentice-Hall, 1965).
[47]President's Commission, *Task Force Report: Narcotics,* p. 8.

drugs. I will return to that point in a moment, but first it is important to ask whether or not a simple decline in the number and proportion of addicted persons is such a positive accomplishment. I think this question can be put in allegorical form:

Once upon a time there was a kingdom in which one man in every twenty was dependent upon a group of valuable medical drugs called "Setaipo." So long as there was a supply of these drugs available, the men who were dependent upon them led good lives. Some were bank directors, Boy Scout leaders, blacksmiths, some were physicians and lawyers, some were factory workers, some were tool-and-die makers, and many were simply nice housewives and mothers. The one basic difference between them and their fellow countrymen was their need for the drugs. They had to have them every day. One day, a very smart and a very good doctor got the idea that if doctors prescribed these drugs only when absolutely necessary and if fewer stores sold them, as the years went by there would be fewer persons dependent upon them. He did not want to take the drug away from the addicted, he just wanted to keep a lot of other people from becoming dependent, unnecessarily.

He went to the king with the problem. He persuaded him that the drugs ought to be strictly controlled. Eventually, the proportion of men and women who had to have Setaipo went down to 1 in 200. However, those who still were dependent became very very bad, robbing people on the highways, and prostituting themselves to get enough money to get around the controls. They became both the hunted and the hunter. Their prey was the unsuspecting normal citizen: the bank director, the Boy Scout leader, the blacksmith. And so the king set up a special legion to go out and hunt down and jail these evil people.

They were hunted by the king's men and, when captured, beaten and tortured in the king's prisons in order to "solve" the problem of the supplier.

When the legion failed, and when the jails failed, the king appointed a commission to find out why. No one on the whole commission thought to speculate: maybe the answer lies somewhere in the very efforts to reduce the number of men and women dependent on Setaipo. The number and the proportion addicted had dropped 100 times over, but the problem was now a million times worse.

The question before us is this: what effect does the legal repression of a drug and the distribution of information about it have on its use?

The Bureau of Narcotics and other hard-line organizations have chosen to hold up heroin use as the model for what happens "when you get tough" and severely restrict the availability of a drug. They have studiously avoided the history of marijuana, which would make the opposite case. While some statistics on heroin users are plausible, not even tentative figures are available on marijuana smokers. The best-informed guesses, however, are that the use of marijuana has risen substantially in the last three decades.[48]

The increase in the use of marijuana has paralleled the increase in legally repressive acts to stop it. Thirty years ago it was a misdemeanor to sell or use marijuana; today it is a felony. Thirty years ago only a few hundred persons a year were arrested for violating the marijuana laws; today thousands are processed through the courts.

The indications are, then, that while legal repression of both marijuana and heroin have increased dramatically in the last few decades, marijuana use has gone up and heroin use has declined. Obviously, repressive laws and their enforcement cannot be the explanation for the fluctuations in the use of drugs. A far more compelling explanation is the dissemination of information about a drug. When morphine and heroin were known simply as pain-killers, and public fear about their use was absent, hundreds of thousands purchased the drugs daily, innocent of their addictive qualities. As the dangers of addiction became increasingly known, and the fear of addiction spread, the rate of consumption fell off markedly. Conversely, as the "ravages and evils of marijuana" came to be identified with very mild "highs," the use of the drug increased even as legal controls were tightened.

It seems reasonable to assume, therefore, that people's opinion about a drug—whether it is physically or psychically harmful or whether it is not—has much more to do with the increase or decline in its consumption than do tightened controls. Consequently, young potential drug users would listen

[48]Ibid. The commission accepts the evidence of such an increase.

with respect to the narcotics bureau if they could find some correlation between what they are told and what they see and experience with drugs.

Perhaps the most serious and the most pathetic consequence of this "official lying" by drug and legal authorities is that it can lead disbelieving youngsters into using amphetamines and barbiturates. And these drugs are truly dangerous. Young people hear these authorities describe marijuana as a wicked despoiler of mind and body; they then see their normal friends turning on; they try it and find either no effect at all or some mild sensations that are less noticeable than the effects of two martinis. They may continue to turn on and learn to enjoy the sensations, but their experiences never approximate the kind of horrors they have been warned about by the "authorities."

Here the pathos begins. Because of the authoritative lies about marijuana, warnings against using barbiturates are easily dismissed as more official drivel. But barbiturates are really dangerous. We know that in a certain combination with alcohol they are fatal.

The increase in the use of amphetamines is at least partially understandable in terms of misleading information, or just plain misinformation. The long-term effects of extended Methedrine use cannot be known to the novice; he only experiences the sensations and must depend upon others to inform him of the serious consequences of his act. To whom will he turn? To someone who has told him about the great evils of marijuana? The death from cocaine of a sixteen-year-old girl in San Francisco in 1968 is as much to be blamed upon those who have cried "Wolf!" about marijuana as it is upon those who sold or gave it to her.

It is on the issue of information that the commission might have made a substantial contribution. If it had produced a document that the young could respect for its forthrightness in dealing honestly and explicitly with the consequences of drug use, it would have helped to prevent the expanding abuse of amphetamines and barbiturates.

DANGEROUS DRUGS AND DANGEROUS LIES

The most important reason why the current laws against the possession of certain drugs were passed was because legislators were advised that such a broadening of the narcotics laws was necessary to "get at the dealers." The argument was this: unless caught in the act of a sale, drug dealers were immune to prosecution; to make their task of arresting dealers easier, argued the government's narcotics officials, possession alone must constitute a felony. Many lawmakers expressed concern about the obvious abrogation of civil liberties if mere possession was to be a crime, but their fears were quieted by the assurance that the possession law would be applied only against dealers, not against users.

Whether such assurances were made in good faith or whether they were deliberate, conscious lies is of little importance. The police in every major city of the United States now selectively, arbitrarily, and sometimes politically invoke the possession statute against users. "Pot busts" have occurred on college campuses in which local police have arrested not only those smoking marijuana but those who were in the same house where marijuana was being used. Most of these students have nothing to do with selling marijuana. They are not dealers. Yet they are now marked with a criminal record. There are dangerous drugs, to be sure, but there are also many dangerous lies in our "free" society. The possession statute has evolved into another dangerous lie. Federal and state authorities have voiced the desirability and the tentative plan to stamp out political dissent on university campuses by "raiding pot parties" of militant and activist students. This is a long way from the "virtuous, maidenly, clean suggestion" that the only purpose of the possession laws was to get dealers, a long way from the "assurance" that "mere possessors" would not be bothered.

In sum, the President's crime commission never grappled with the fundamental issues of drug use and control. From the outset, the report passively accepted current assumptions about drugs and how to control their use. It recommended more agents and a larger staff in organizations trying to suppress the illegal drug traffic. It recommended "more research." But there was no serious discussion of new methods for treating the drug addict, no critical review of the viability of clinical dispensation of drugs to the addicted, no penetrating criticism or evaluation of the present practices of punitive treatment through prison and other forms of incarceration.

Finally, the President's crime commission gave almost no attention to the nonmedical uses of drugs. Here was the real challenge. For the question of when the state should intervene in the private choices of its citizens is eminently debatable. That debate embraces the issue of when an individual is a private person and when he is a public person. How these distinctions are made—and honored—determines both the force and legitimacy of the challenge of dissidents and lawbreakers in a "free" society.

Contrary Objectives:
Crime Control
and the Rehabilitation
of Criminals

LEROY C. GOULD

and

J. ZVI NAMENWIRTH

Twenty-two recommendations for America's correctional system—its jails, its prisons, and its probation and parole programs—were made recently by a presidential crime commission.[1] Of these 22 recommendations, 21 dealt with how to improve treatment and rehabilitation. Quite obviously, "treatment" and "rehabilitation" have become the watchwords of modern penology,[2] and the prestige of a prison today is measured more in terms of the number and the quality of its treatment programs than in terms of the strength of its walls. Even the county jail is now sometimes referred to as a "rehabilitation center." Indeed, the fact that the system is called "correctional" rather than "penal" attests to the new orientation in American penology. To be sure, more talk than action is still the rule when it comes to treatment and rehabilitation, and many jurisdictions offer no rehabilitation

[1] President's Commission on Law Enforcement and Administration of Justice (hereafter cited as President's Commission), *The Challenge of Crime in a Free Society* (Washington, D.C.: United States Government Printing Office, 1967), pp. 159–185.

[2] A national survey of correctional personnel has found rehabilitation cited most often as the prime objective of correctional programs. Joint Commission on Correctional Manpower and Training (hereafter cited as Joint Commission), *Corrections 1968: A Climate for Change* (Washington, D.C.: 1522 K. St., N.W., 1968), p. 14. The survey of correctional personnel was conducted by Louis Harris and Associates.

237

services at all, or only very few. Nevertheless, the pace at which these services are being introduced into the correctional system is quickening.

Beginning with probation and parole, the indeterminate sentence, and the juvenile court, programs which are now integral parts of the correctional system nationally, correctional programs have gradually come to employ a wide array of treatment services. Vocational and educational training, individual counseling and psychotherapy, honor farms and group therapy, work-release programs, halfway houses, chemotherapy—all these are correctional programs designed to treat and rehabilitate the criminal. While all these programs are not in wide use, they are becoming more prevalent and, unquestionably, the trend today is in the direction of making these programs even more readily available.[3] Because rehabilitation has become the dominant philosophy in the correctional community, and because this philosophy is beginning to receive support nationally,[4] it is time to question whether this philosophy is wise. Have the rehabilitation programs fostered by this new correctional philosophy been effective? Will their implementation on a broader scale reduce recidivism and prevent crime?

EFFECTIVENESS OF CURRENT PROGRAMS

The answer to the first question is not encouraging. A fairly large body of research reports has been produced, especially in the past ten years, on the effectiveness of most treatment

[3]A majority of workers in the field of corrections believe that rehabilitation is currently the most important goal of the correctional system, and an even larger percentage think this goal should be stressed in the future. Ibid., p. 15.

[4]Besides the endorsement given to rehabilitation by the President's Commission, a number of local jurisdictions have also begun to give greater emphasis to rehabilitation in their correctional systems. The New York Governor's Committee on Criminal Offenders, for example, has just finished a lengthy study of that state's correctional system and recommends the creation of an integrated department of rehabilitative services. *Preliminary Report of the Governor's Committee on Criminal Offenders* (New York: State of New York, 1968).

programs now in use,[5] and none of these programs have proved effective in the long-term reduction of recidivism. Some have, in fact, increased recidivism.[6] Others have shown gains, but these have never been large even though they are at times statistically significant.[7] At most, there is usually no more difference in recidivism between experimental and control groups than a few percentage points,[8] and these differences tend to diminish over time. It simply is not true, as the President's crime commission rather wistfully said, that there are "experimental programs whose results in terms of reduced recidivism [are] dramatic."[9] Even though the commission found programs that offer great promise, an optimistic prognosis is commensurate with almost all new programs. When new programs do get into full operation, however, and when they are then prop-

---

[5]The number of these reports is far too extensive to detail the references here (there are at least 200), but a good summary has been prepared by The New York Governor's Committee on Criminal Offenders.

[6]Cf. Evelyn S. Guttman, "Effects of Short Term Psychiatric Treatment on Boys in Two California Youth Authority Institutions," mimeographed (State of California Youth Authority, Research Report no. 36, December 1963); idem, "Intensive Treatment Program, Second Annual Report," mimeographed (Sacramento: California Department of Corrections, September 1958); LeMar Empey et al., "The Silverlake Experiment: A Community Study in Delinquency Rehabilitation—Progress Report No. 3," mimeographed (Los Angeles: University of Southern California, Youth Studies Center, 1966).

[7]Since statistical significance depends both on the magnitude of difference between experimental and control groups and on the number of people in these groups, a small difference between large groups of people can be "statistically" significant; whether this difference is significant in a more substantive sense is another matter.

[8]Often a difference of ten percentage points is heralded as success, and this magnitude of difference can be statistically significant if the experimental and control groups are of reasonably large size. However, a difference in percentage of ten points is analogous to a correlation of .10 and explains only about one per cent of the variance. Cf. Hubert Blalock, "A Double Standard in Measuring Degree of Association," *American Sociological Review* 28 (December 1963), pp. 988–989. In other words, if 70 per cent of the control group and 60 per cent of the experimental group were recidivists, the impact of the program would account for only one per cent of the factors leading to recidivism.

[9]President's Commission, *The Challenge of Crime,* p. 159.

erly evaluated by acceptable experimental procedures, the early success turns out to be largely spurious. "Success" has depended upon choosing only inmates with a good prognosis for the experimental program—inmates who would have done as well without the special program—or upon measuring success in terms of the subjective evaluations of those who founded and continued to support the program. The sad conclusion is that no treatment program in corrections, when evaluated by acceptable scientific procedures, has proved to make more than the slightest impact on recidivism rates. Most have either had no impact at all or have been harmful.

These findings are in accord with other, more general, observations. The rate of recidivism in the more progressive correctional jurisdictions is not significantly lower than the rate in less progressive jurisdictions. The state of California, for example, which has placed more emphasis on rehabilitation in recent years than any other state, has one of the highest crime rates in the country,[10] as well as a rate of recidivism that is among the highest nationally.[11] Furthermore, the national crime rate has been rising rapidly since the end of World War II—even though this same period has been one in which treatment innovation and correctional reform have made their most rapid advances.

These observations, although discouraging, do not prove that treatment cannot be effective, as people in correctional work are quick to point out when confronted with this failure. Most treatment programs, they explain, are new and, to a large extent, still experimental. No conclusive evaluation can be made of their effectiveness until those who administer them have had time to work out their difficulties, sharpen their procedures, train sufficient personnel to conduct them properly, and gain the broad institutional support necessary for their sustained and unencumbered operation. In addition, few ad-

[10]United States Department of Justice, Federal Bureau of Investigation, *Uniform Crime Reports* (Washington, D.C.: United States Government Printing Office), vols. 1965 through 1968.

[11]Daniel Glaser, *The Effectiveness of a Prison and Parole System* (Indianapolis: Bobbs-Merrill, 1964), p. 25.

ministrators of treatment programs have been able to control their source of clients sufficiently well to maximize the program's potential effectiveness. Depending upon a legal structure that has its own classification system for offenders, treatment personnel have been generally unable to develop the diagnostic procedures that would be relevant to their programs, and if they have developed such procedures, they have not been allowed to use them to best advantage.

Despite these rationalizations of why rehabilitation has failed, the persistence of this failure inevitably leads to a lack of confidence in the correctional system. The President's crime commission expressed this lack of confidence in "corrections" as follows ("corrections" is a commonly used shorthand term meaning "correctional system"—that is, federal, state, and local prisons, jails, and probation and parole departments): "For a great many offenders . . . corrections does not correct. Indeed, experts are increasingly coming to feel that the conditions under which many offenders are handled, particularly in institutions, are often a positive detriment to rehabilitation. . . ."[12] This note of pessimism notwithstanding, the crime commission went on to conclude that correctional programs have not failed because of anything inherently wrong with rehabilitation but because they have not provided enough treatment services. The lack of success shown by rehabilitation programs has not dampened the growing enthusiasm for rehabilitation; if anything, the enthusiasm has grown even stronger.[13]

This response seems paradoxical. If a medication does not seem to be working, one would not expect the doctor to double the dosage—unless, of course, the doctor is absolutely convinced that his diagnosis is correct and that the medication would work if only the necessary dosage were determined. Like the doctor, the crime commission seems certain that the

---

[12]President's Commission, *The Challenge of Crime*, p. 159.

[13]The national survey of correctional workers (Joint Commission, *Corrections 1968*) found that 24 per cent of those interviewed thought treatment efforts had been very successful in the past and 61 per cent thought they had been somewhat successful. Eighty-five per cent thought more emphasis should be placed on treatment in the future.

diagnosis is correct and that a heavier dose of treatment will succeed, even though it has not succeeded, in lesser amounts, in the past.

It is altogether possible, however, that the current diagnosis is incorrect and that no amount of additional treatment will reduce recidivism or lower the nation's crime rate. That is the possibility to which the remainder of this essay is addressed.

CONFLICTING GOALS
IN THE CORRECTIONAL SYSTEM

Shortly after the United States became a nation, an historic experiment began in the handling of criminals. A number of Americans, who had become unwilling to subject criminals to the pains of the whip and the public shame of the stocks, conceived the notion of sending criminals to prison. To be sure, criminals had been sent to prison before. But they had not been sent there to serve sentences for crimes. Instead, the prison, up to that time, had been only a place to hold criminals until their cases could be tried or until their debts could be paid. For the first time, people came to think that the prison might also be a place where criminals could be punished—or rehabilitated.

Considerable disagreement manifested itself, however, over whether prisons should be institutions to reform the individual or institutions to punish him.[14] One group, greatly influenced by Quaker religious philosophy, argued that the prison should be a place for penitence (thus giving rise to the name penitentiary), and they constructed their model institution—the famous Philadelphia Penitentiary—in order to accomplish this

---

[14]Excellent accounts of these early penal movements and of the Philadelphia and Auburn prison systems may be found in Gustave de Beaumont and Alexis de Tocqueville, *On the Penitentiary System in the United States and Its Application in France* (Carbondale: Southern Illinois University Press, 1964), and Kai T. Erikson, *Wayward Puritans* (New York: John Wiley & Sons, 1966), pp. 199–205.

goal. Designed with individual cells, the Philadelphia Penitentiary offered prisoners a place of solitude where introspection,
private industry, and protection from the temptations of the
world would allow personal reformation. Working under another
philosophy, Elam Lynds and a group of his supporters established a different kind of prison in New York State—the famous
Auburn Prison. Believing that the reformation of criminals was
not possible, this group of penal reformers established an institution to tame and control them. Lynds, who became warden of
the Auburn Prison (and later warden of Sing Sing), was convinced that criminals were beyond redemption. He handled his
inmates as if they were caged animals who had to be forced
into absolute obedience. While this procedure might not save
an inmate's soul, Lynds contended that it would teach him a
trade, establish habits of industriousness, and force him to
become an obedient and productive member of society.

In the course of time, the Auburn rather than the Philadelphia prison became the prototype of American prisons.[15] While
the policy of absolute silence, forced labor, and excessive corporal punishment used at Auburn was gradually abandoned,
prison employees throughout the nation remained concerned
for decades with security, order, and obedience. Not until well
into this century did reform-minded prison officials begin to
think again about rehabilitation. But by then it was too late to
fashion a prison system solely for rehabilitation, as the Quakers
of Philadelphia had tried to do. The idea of the prison was no
longer new and the institution no longer a mere set of plans.
Over the years American prisons, in both their architecture and
organization, had developed a system to accomplish goals that
had nothing to do with rehabilitation. These other goals had
become well entrenched, and large segments of society and
many correctional employees were unwilling to abandon them.

Today, the situation is only somewhat changed. While most
prison personnel are now of the opinion that rehabilitation

---

[15]Interestingly, the Philadelphia Penitentiary became the prototype of
most prisons built in Europe.

should be their primary goal, they pursue this goal within physical facilities and under criminal codes that were never designed to achieve rehabilitation. To be sure, some institutions have been built in recent years, especially institutions for juvenile offenders, that were designed for rehabilitation. But their number is still small. Smaller still is the number of criminal jurisdictions that have overhauled their penal codes to foster rehabilitation.

This situation places a great burden on reform-minded correctional personnel who are now trying to overhaul a system that remains, in many respects, antagonistic to treatment and rehabilitation. But should this overhaul even be attempted? Will it entail social costs most people do not expect? Will it jeopardize those traditional prison objectives that are incompatible with good treatment and rehabilitation practices? What are these traditional objectives? Can the correctional system afford to abandon them?

In order to answer these questions it is necessary, first, to describe the traditional objectives of America's prison system —deterrence, punishment, retribution, and protection of society —and to discuss how these objectives are incompatible with good treatment and rehabilitation programs.

DETERRENCE

The primary aim of the Auburn Prison, and of American prisons that followed its model, was deterrence. Deterrence, however, meant two things: discouraging those released from prison from committing further crimes, and discouraging the general public from becoming criminals.[16]

It has generally been assumed, although we disagree, that prisons have not been very effective with respect to the first of

[16]This aspect of deterrence is scarcely discussed in prison literature, but it was an important component of legal reform that spread across Europe and the United States in the late eighteenth and early nineteenth centuries. For a classic statement of this philosophy of deterrence, see Cesare Beccaria, *On Crimes and Punishments,* trans. Henry Paolucci (Indianapolis: Bobbs-Merrill, 1963).

these deterrent objectives.[17] Instead of becoming law-abiding after their release, most former prisoners have persisted in a life of crime. In addition, the assumption is that many first-time offenders, who did not seem bent on a criminal career, have come out of prison not only embittered but well equipped to become dedicated criminals. The prison, many people believe, is less an institution for deterrence than a school for thieves.

This belief, it seems to us, may involve more myth than reality; certainly it has not been substantiated. While case histories show that some criminals committed to a life of crime seem to have gained their commitment, their contacts, and some of their skills in prison, there is no evidence to show that this is true for all inmates, or even for a sizable number of them. Most inmates, contrary to popular assumptions, are not recidivists.[18] For them, or at least for many of them, imprisonment may have played a deterrent role. If it did, then the prison's goal of deterrence would have been partially met—just so long as the number of crimes it prevented among the nonrecidivists outnumbered those committed by its recidivists. Even here, however, the question arises as to whether the recidivists might not have committed just as many crimes, or maybe even more, if they had never been imprisoned or if they had been handled in some altogether different manner.

Nevertheless, even if imprisonment encouraged further crime among ex-convicts, this would not mean that the threat of imprisonment would not deter crime among those who have never been to prison. If the *threat* of imprisonment discouraged more crime in the general population than imprisonment itself encouraged on the part of ex-convicts, then the overall impact of prisons would be to deter crime.

Again, however, pertinent data do not exist which would allow us to say whether prisons deter crime more than they encourage it. In fact the deterrent value of prisons is almost

[17]Cf. President's Commission, *The Challenge of Crime*, p. 159.

[18]It is hard to gather accurate data on recidivism, but the rates seem to be somewhere between 30 and 50 per cent; cf. Glaser, *Effectiveness of a Prison*, pp. 13–35.

completely unknown and will remain unknown until this function of prisons is explored and evaluated more carefully. If it turns out that prisons have failed in their deterrent role, this would be good reason to question the value of imprisonment as part of the correctional system. It would not, however, be sufficient reason to ignore the question of deterrence altogether or to concentrate only on deterring the criminals who get caught and jailed. Most criminals never get caught (or, at least, most crimes never get solved), and only a small percentage of those who are caught ever come under the jurisdiction of a correctional system.[19] Most people arrested for crimes are not convicted and many of those who are convicted are not sentenced to prison. Therefore, the deterrent value of a correctional system is not restricted to those who come into direct contact with it but applies to the whole population. Whether prison, by its existence alone, is the best institution for general crime deterrence is a moot point. What is important is that society must be concerned about the general deterrence of crime. If this task is not assigned to a prison system, then it must be assigned to some other social institution.

One danger inherent in our correctional system is that an emphasis on treatment and rehabilitation may diminish the prison's capacity to serve as a general deterrent to crime. Under the popular rubric of "coddling criminals," treatment programs have a tendency to do away with the undesirable aspects of prison life or even with imprisonment altogether. The reformers' ideal of good treatment in the correctional system is little different from the ideal of good treatment for people who are not criminals. To the extent that this ideal is realized, there is little reason not to be a criminal.

This is not to say that prisons should be barbaric institutions, as many in this country have been; it is only to say that imprisonment, or whatever form of deterrence society chooses, should be undesirable. Just how undesirable remains to be determined, but it probably should be undesirable enough so

[19]Cf. Courtlandt C. Van Vechten, "Differential Criminal Case Mortality in Selected Jurisdictions," *American Sociological Review* 7 (December 1942), pp. 833–839.

that most people would avoid it, yet humane enough so that it does not unduly embitter those who must endure it.[20] To the extent that imprisonment is unpleasant, however, it will be less than an ideal environment in which to conduct treatment. To the extent that a correctional system becomes a therapeutic environment, it will be less than an ideal institution for general crime deterrence.

PUNISHMENT

Punishment is closely related to deterrence; it is the fear of punishment that is supposed to deter crime. Even so, certain aspects of punishment can be separated from the notion of deterrence, and they deserve some consideration.

Aside from its deterrent role, punishment is closely linked with the community's sense of justice. Americans, generally, believe that one who has committed a wrong should suffer some pain as a consequence. This belief, moreover, is not related to whether anyone has been seriously hurt by that wrong or whether punishment would necessarily serve to deter further wrongs of the same kind. It is simply that Americans seem to find it immoral for anyone to get by without being punished when he has violated rules that the community holds to be important.

It is often argued that punishment for the sake of punishment is out of keeping with a rational society and also out of keeping with current psychology. Nevertheless, most people are not particularly rational, nor are they usually conversant with the latest psychological theories or research. Until people are, and until the public abandons the notion that a criminal should suffer for his crime, it is unwise to ignore the function the correctional system serves as punishing agent.

It is on this particular point, however, this belief that the penalty must be properly paid, that programs of rehabilitation for criminals run into their greatest difficulty. One of the pre-

[20]This is essentially the argument set forth by Beccaria, *On Crimes and Punishments,* and other penal reformers during the Enlightenment that gave rise to the penal philosophy of "punishment to fit the crime."

requisites of a good treatment program is that it treat different kinds of offenders differently. But as a rule, little correspondence is discernible between the kind of treatment an offender may need and the kind of crime he has committed. A murderer, for example, may be a good parole risk[21] and a drunk a very poor one;[22] yet to release a murderer from prison before an alcoholic would be viewed by the public as absurd and unjust.

The lack of congruence between the demands of treatment and the demands of community justice is a serious problem. On the one hand, the community believes that a person who has committed a crime should pay for that crime and, generally, that the payment should be calculated in terms of years of imprisonment, the number of years being commensurate with the seriousness of the offense. On the other hand, good treatment practice must calculate its mission in terms of the psychological or social maladjustment of the offender, not in terms of the crime he has committed. When the maladjustment is serious, even when the crime is not, the offender must be detained for a relatively long period of time; when the maladjustment is not so serious, though the crime is, it is not necessary to spend a comparatively long time in treatment. Indeed, treatment might not be called for at all. Certainly the treatment need not call for incarceration and, in fact, might be impeded by it.[23]

This absence of congruity between the community's demands for justice and the correctional system's demands for good treatment practice has become especially apparent in the field of juvenile deliquency, where the philosophy of treatment is most advanced.[24] For many years, America's juvenile courts have operated, both philosophically and legally, differently from adult courts.[25] Juveniles, who are legally not considered to be

[21]Cf. G. I. Giardini and R. C. Farrow, "The Paroling of Capital Offenders," in *Capital Punishment*, ed. Thorston Sellin (New York: Harper & Row, 1967), pp. 169–184.

[22]Cf. David J. Pittman and C. Wayne Gordon, *Revolving Door: A Study of the Chronic Police Case Inebriate* (New York: The Free Press, 1958).

[23]Cf. President's Commission, *The Challenge of Crime*, p. 159.

[24]Cf. President's Commission, *Task Force Report: Juvenile Delinquency and Youth Crime* (Washington, D.C.: United States Government Printing Office, 1967).

[25]Ibid., chap. 1.

of an age of reason, are thereby technically not capable of committing crimes (although they are capable of committing acts that would be judged crimes had they been committed by sane adults). Therefore, the only important judgment in the case of a juvenile is whether or not he is a delinquent, not whether he is a criminal. And this judgment may depend on many factors other than whether the juvenile has committed an act that violates the criminal statutes. It may involve nothing more than general unruliness or a decision that the youngster could benefit by being removed from his family or community environment.

Handling juveniles as youths who need treatment, rather than as persons who need punishment, leads to situations that the community sometimes finds hard to understand. It sees some juveniles detained for long periods of time against their will, or the will of their parents, without ever having been convicted of a crime.[26] It sees others, who have committed serious offenses, not institutionalized at all.

To the degree, then, that the demands of treatment do not correspond to the community's demands for justice, a correctional system will find it hard either to administer effective treatment programs or to fulfill the expectations that society has for it. Although it is possible that the assumptions of Americans about a correctional system could change, there is no evidence that they have and some evidence that they have not, especially in regard to juvenile justice.[27] In any event, the problem is sufficiently serious to render good treatment practice problematic within the correctional system.

RETRIBUTION

However primitive the desire to retaliate against someone who has caused pain, suffering, or loss of property, the urge seems nonetheless to be universal. Of course, an "eye for an eye" does not restore sight or a "life for a life" bring back life, and

---

[26]Supreme Court Justice John Marshall Harlan, *In re Gault,* 387 U.S. 1, 76 (1967), noted that probably 26 to 48 per cent of the youngsters brought before juvenile courts "are not in any sense guilty of criminal misconduct."
[27]Cf. ibid.

in this sense the penchant for revenge is irrational. But rationality is not always apparent in human relations, and at times the forces of rationality and irrationality conflict.

In most nations today, the institutions of social control do not deny the desire for revenge. They do, however, try to control it. They control it, first of all, by establishing time-consuming legal procedures. Since the impulse for revenge (be it on the part of the offender or the community at large) is immediate, protracted proceedings give time for passions to subside. Presumably, this allows reason to emerge.

Secondly, modern governments control revenge by no longer allowing an offended party to be the agent who executes criminal sanctions against the offender. Modern governments, in other words, have declared a monopoly on retribution. This monopolization in turn is but one instance of the widening appropriation by public authorities of all forms of violence. In the process of civilization, and especially since the advance of industrial society, domestic violence has come to be less and less tolerable. As Max Weber noted, outbursts of violence disrupt the need for predictable human interchanges and the fulfillment of contractual obligations which are prerequisites of human conduct in a complex, yet ordered, industrial society.[28]

Although the public monopolization of retribution denies the lust for private revenge, it has a number of long-range advantages. Unbridled private revenge often leads to interminable vendettas. In a vendetta, the circle of accomplices tends to widen and the demands for vengeance often escalate. The loss of a purse, for example, will demand the mutilation of a hand which leads to the loss of an eye, the taking of a life, and total havoc, while the wider community is torn asunder.

But private revenge is not only private, it is particularistic as well. The weaker party must always lose when private conflicts are adjudicated through the exchange of revenge. In a vendetta, the larger clan, the stronger knight, or the richer entrepreneur (with more hired hands) is always at an advan-

[28]Max Weber,*The Theory of Social and Economic Organization,* ed. Talcott Parsons, trans. A. M. Henderson and Parsons (New York: The Free Press, 1964), p. 156.

tage. The weaker party, in these circumstances, will therefore seek the protection of an authority—which at first is ad hoc and contractual—to safeguard life and property. Once this contractual arrangement is institutionized, however, and once central authority gains sufficient power to enforce its position, private revenge is eliminated, or nationalized.

For the state to continue to monopolize revenge, however, the notion of equality before the law must be accepted. Even though public revenge, through public trial and public correction, is bureaucratic, time-consuming, cumbersome, and consequently less satisfactory than quick, personal revenge, it better guarantees the rights of all, especially those of the weaker party. It better guarantees the rights of the accused as well as the accuser.

Private revenge is, assuredly, always a lurking possibility, especially in times of public unrest. During these periods, the possibility is ever present that private conflicts will polarize along social, racial, religious, or moral lines and that public authority, as a result, will lose its legitimacy. On occasion, therefore, public authority must resort to a form of public retaliation that can easily deteriorate into permanent institutions of public revenge. Only processes of law seem to offer any hope of ameliorating oppressive tendencies, for public revenge can be as brutal as private revenge. Numerous examples of brutality against convicted criminals, or even against those who have only been accused, are reminders of this.

Whatever the shortcomings in public retaliation, it continues to be preferable to private revenge. At any rate, it seems reasonable to assume that one of the implicit charges of America's correctional system today is to serve as the means by which a public monopoly over retribution is maintained. Insofar as the correctional system neglects this charge, disorders inherent in a system of private revenge become all the more likely. In view of the centuries it has taken for modern states to monopolize this form of violence, its surrender would seem to be a step backward.

While it is not altogether necessary that retribution and rehabilitation be incompatible, correctional personnel usually argue that they are,[29] and it is probably reasonable to accept their word on this point. To the extent that they are right, however, expanded treatment programs can only jeopardize society's current hold on retribution.

PROTECTING SOCIETY

One task a prison performs (as well as other institutions like mental hospitals and tuberculosis sanatoriums) is that of protecting society from persons who have proved to be dangerous or otherwise objectionable. But, like the demands for punishment, the community's demands for protection do not always correspond with correctional personnel's judgments of how much danger is in fact involved; often those whom correctional workers find to be the best parole risks, the community fears the most. Conversely, correctional workers often appraise some offenders as still dangerous even though they must release them when their sentence has expired.

This absence of accord between the public's attitude on protection and the professional's estimate of danger interferes with rehabilitation. Those inmates who correctional personnel think are not dangerous, but who society does think are dangerous, often must be restricted to maximum security settings, which are the least conducive to good treatment. Those, on the other hand, who correctional personnel clearly see as a danger to society are also a danger to the correctional programs themselves; unless these people can be segregated, and often they cannot, they pose not only a security problem but a disruption to the rest of the inmate population.

Overshadowing these problems, however, is a more general issue involving the role of the correctional system as society's protective agent. Why is society today so afraid to have criminals loose in its midst? Unfortunately, the answer to this question seems all too obvious: because criminals are dangerous. But are they? And if they are, what is the danger? It has only been within the past 150 years that Western societies

[29]Cf. Joint Commission, *Corrections 1968,* and President's Commission, *Task Force Report: Corrections* (Washington, D.C.: United States Government Printing Office, 1967).

have become uneasy about allowing any except the most vicious criminals to be in their midst. Before inventing prisons as a place of banishment, societies were forced to either execute or exile those whom they feared. Since these were drastic actions, they were applied only to the truly vicious, leaving most criminals to be handled in the open community. Often the means of dealing with petty criminals involved a form of public ceremony in which they would be identified so that the public could take heed and protect itself. Sometimes this was done by public whippings or a day in the stocks; at other times it was done by disfigurement, which left the criminal well identified for life. But most criminals, certainly all the petty ones and probably most of the felons as well, were permitted to remain in the open community. Why is it different today?

Perhaps the simplest answer is that we can afford to build prisons today and people could not 150 years ago. This answer is not too convincing, however, since prison labor itself is sufficent to build and maintain a prison system.[30] A more satisfactory answer is to be found in changing Western attitudes that no longer tolerate criminals in the open community.

These changes, we maintain, are due in some part to the belief that criminals are a threat to good morals. The criminal's way of life is considered bad and its example threatens the moral order because it seduces the innocent.[31] In other words, crime is attractive and the human spirit weak. Because man is innately evil, he is apt to follow the road of least resistance—namely, the bad examples set by criminals. Or, because man, however good, is frustrated by the inevitable constraints society imposes on his appetites,[32] he is prone to forfeit social strictures once others show him the way. In either case, bad ex-

[30]Sing Sing Prison, for example, was built entirely by prison labor from Auburn.

[31]That people become criminals by associating with criminals is at the heart of one of the most influential theories of criminal behavior in America today—the theory of "differential association" developed by Edwin Sutherland. Edwin Sutherland and Donald R. Cressey, *Principles of Criminology,* 7th ed. (Philadelphia: J. B. Lippincott, 1966), pp. 77–98.

[32]Sigmund Freud, *Civilization and Its Discontents,* ed. and trans. James Strachey (New York: W. W. Norton, 1962).

amples seduce the weak, leading them into vice, thievery, and degradation. For these reasons, it is paramount that criminals be removed from the everyday scene.

The evidence supporting this notion of human frailty is not particularly strong.[33] Even so, fears of the community on this score are evident and they have hindered correctional reforms, especially those designed to integrate rehabilitative functions with those of the community. A correct understanding of the sources of the community's fears will help to accommodate rather than deny them. At present, only such accommodations will make it possible to overcome the deep-seated resistance to an overhaul of correctional institutions.

TREATMENT AND REHABILITATION

These many conflicts place the correctional community in a considerable dilemma. Correctional institutions are asked to accelerate their treatment-and-rehabilitation programs while at the same time they must maintain their traditional role as agents that deter crime, punish wrongdoers, monopolize private retribution, and protect society from presumably dangerous persons. To the degree that the newer demands diminish the ability of a correctional system to discharge its more traditional responsibilities, the system may become less, rather than more, effective as an institution for crime control. In any event, the conflicts between the demands for good treatment and rehabilitation and the demands for deterrence, punishment, retribution, and community safety seem real enough to justify considerable investigation before treatment becomes the only goal in American correctional philosophy.

Acknowledging this dilemma, however, is to overlook a very important point: many—perhaps most—offenders who come under the jurisdiction of the correctional system are in need of some treatment or rehabilitation. While these needs may have little or nothing to do with their status as criminals,

---

[33]Leroy C. Gould, "Juvenile Entrepreneurs," *American Journal of Sociology* 74 (May 1969), pp. 710–719.

it is nonetheless true that many people coming under the aegis of the correctional system do suffer from personality disorders and social maladjustments.[34] If nothing else, prisoners, as a rule, are poorly educated, poorly motivated, and have minimal occuaptional skills.

Many prisoners, therefore, would seem to warrant help. But should the correctional system give them this help? We think not. To do so implies that they are being helped because they are criminals, not because they are people who need treatment. There are, after all, many other people, not criminals, who are equally in need of treatment; it would seem paradoxical if they had to commit a crime before they could gain access to treatment facilities. More important, treatment cannot be given satisfactorily within the context of a correctional system; it should, therefore, be separated completely from correctional institutions.

Such a separation would have a number of beneficial consequences. Among others, it would allow treatment and rehabilitation to be organized within institutions that are both solely devoted to those ends and effectively organized to maximize the chances of achieving them. This, in turn, would avoid the premature judgment that criminals are criminals *because* they are psychologically or socially maladjusted—that is, people would be offered treatment because they need it, not because they are criminals. Also, removing treatment from correctional institutions would allow the correctional community to pursue its more traditional roles without the encumbrance of treatment. So organized, the success of a correctional program would no longer be judged by standards that it cannot hope to fulfill.

THE NATURE OF CRIME
AND THE RECRUITMENT OF CRIMINALS

Even if treatment could be carried out successfully within a correctional system, would it have a significant impact on the

[34]Glaser, *Effectiveness of a Prison.*

level of crime? The answer to this question *seems* obvious—it would. As the President's crime commission observed:

> On any given day, [correctional institutions in the United States are] responsible for approximately 1.3 million offenders. In the course of a year, [these institutions handle] nearly 2.5 million admissions, and [spend] over a billion dollars doing so. If [correctional systems] could restore all or even most of these people to the community as responsible citizens, America's crime rate would drop significantly. For as it is today, a substantial percentage of offenders become recidivists; they go on to commit more [crimes] and . . . often more serious crimes.[35]

With recidivism rates of between 30 and 50 per cent,[36] it would appear that a reduction in these rates would result in a significant reduction in crime. Yet closer examination of crime statistics does not support this view. Even if all recidivism could be eliminated, the impact on overall crime rates would be minimal because recidivists account for only a small percentage of all crimes committed; most people who commit crimes are never caught,[37] and only a small proportion of those who are caught ever come under the jurisdiction of a correctional program. One study in the District of Columbia, for example, found that for every 100 crimes that were known to the police in that city, only 19 persons were charged, only 7.5 prosecuted, 5.9 convicted, and 3.7 sentenced to prison.[38] We therefore strongly disagree with the crime commission's contention; with such a small proportion of criminals even getting a chance to be recidivists, reducing recidivism cannot be a cure-all for crime. Nor will reduced recidivism diminish the overall level of crime as much as many people have claimed.

We have further doubts about the importance of recidivism. Recidivism could be eliminated completely without materially affecting the crime rate if new criminals come along to

[35]President's Commission, *The Challenge of Crime,* p. 159.

[36]Glaser, *Effectiveness of a Prison,* pp. 13–35.

[37]James S. Wallerstein and Clement J. Wyle, "Our Law-abiding Law-breakers," *Federal Probation* 25 (March 1947), pp. 107–112.

[38]Van Vechten, "Differential Criminal Case Mortality," pp. 833–839.

take the place of all those who have been rehabilitated. To say that reduced recidivism would decrease the crime rate is to assume that only a small, fixed proportion of the population is available for recruitment into a life of crime. However popular this assumption may be, there is little evidence to support it. It is easier to support the notion that a sizable proportion of the population would not only commit crimes if the circumstances were right, it would also be available for a criminal career if a sufficiently attractive opportunity presented itself. A number of studies have shown, for example, that most people have committed relatively serious crimes at one time or another during their lifetimes.[39] While most of these people did not commit crimes on anything like a regular basis—nor could they, in the conventional sense, be called criminals—they nevertheless demonstrated that if the circumstances were right they were capable of committing crimes. It would seem to be a relatively short step from this kind of questionably criminal position to one in which a person would dedicate himself more completely to a criminal career. Everyone may not have a "price," but most people do. Some might demand far greater rewards at far lower risks before committing a crime, but many people are available to commit crimes for relatively low rewards and in the face of reasonably high risks. Presumably, this fact applies to persons currently engaged in crime.

The number of crimes committed at any one time, then, depends on the number of opportunities to commit crimes at a level of risk acceptable to criminals.[40] Taking active criminals out of the marketplace does nothing to reduce these opportunities; all it does is leave some of the opportunities unexploited. Since people go where the opportunities are, it seems reasonable to assume that new criminals will come in to exploit the market for crime as fast as old criminals are promoted into civil society.

More rapid promotion out of criminal careers results in more rapid turnover among criminals. This increased turnover

---

[39]Wallerstein and Wyle, "Our Law-abiding Lawbreakers."
[40]Cf. Gould, "Crime and Its Impact in an Affluent Society."

is itself a matter of concern. Would it be desirable? It would
certainly produce a larger proportion of the population that had
at one time engaged in systematic criminal activity; if the rotation of persons through criminal careers is accelerated, it can
only mean that more people will have committed crimes. While
the consequences of this result might be counterbalanced by
rehabilitation programs within the correctional system, what
might happen to the nation if a larger percentage of its population has engaged extensively in crime?

But there is another reason for concern. Should there be
a more rapid rotation of people through the ranks of criminals,
some breakdown is likely to occur in the norms that now govern
the activities of full-time, professional criminals. Although it is
not easy to condone the norms of thieves, it is nonetheless true
that these norms are advantageous to society. Professional
criminals, for example, ordinarily shy away from violence.[41]
They evidently have learned that violence usually works to their
detriment; it is certain to bring on the "heat" and the criminal
committing it is much more likely to be dealt with severely
when caught. While novices in crime could learn this same lesson, they are, at least according to professional criminals, far
more prone to violence than are the pros.[42] Without much question, therefore, the real danger is that a more rapid turnover of
criminals would increase the level of violence connected with
crime.

Thus, the connection between crime and recidivism is a
complicated matter and it cannot be assumed too quickly that
reducing recidivism will either reduce the rate of crime or be
in the best interest of society. Nonetheless, this is an assumption of both the President's crime commission and most contemporary criminologists and penologists.

THE DISEASE MODEL OF CRIME AND CORRECTIONS

Advocating treatment for criminals is based on a fairly simple
assumption—that crime is a disease, or something very much
like a disease. Just what kind of disease criminality is, however,

[41]Edwin H. Sutherland, *The Professional Thief* (Chicago: University of
Chicago Press, 1937).
[42]Ibid.

remains in dispute. Some say it is a disease of biological origin and its cure is to be found in biological or medical adjustments. Others say it is a disease caused by psychological malfunction and its cure will be found in psychiatric treatment. Still others argue that criminality results from social maladaptation and that its remedy involves either resocialization or social change. Of course, it is also argued that crime results from all these conditions or from some particular combination of them.

Although this diversity in theories might suggest that criminologists strongly disagree about what the causes of crime are and what its cures should be, they do agree on one point: that crime is pathological. Criminologists also assume not only that crime results from pathological conditions in the individual but that the presence of crime in society is a symptom of social pathology. Both these assumptions have been challenged.

THE SOCIAL PATHOLOGY OF CRIME

Concerning the social pathology of crime, Emile Durkheim observed:

> There is . . . no phenomenon that presents more indisputably all the symptoms of normality [than crime], since it appears closely connected with the conditions of all collective life. To make of crime a form of social morbidity would be to admit that morbidity is not something accidental, but, on the contrary, that in certain cases it grows out of the fundamental constitution of the living organism; it would result in wiping out all distinction between the physiological and the pathological. No doubt it is possible that crime itself will have abnormal forms, as, for example, when its rate is unusually high. This excess is indeed undoubtedly morbid in nature. What is normal, simply, is the existence of criminality, provided that it attains and does not exceed, for each social type, a certain level, which it is perhaps not impossible to fix. . . .[43]

To assert that deviance is a normal component of a healthy society seems absurd. Durkheim was not unaware of this ap-

[43]Emile Durkheim, *Rules of Sociological Method,* 8th ed., trans. Sarah Salvay and John Mueller, ed. George Catlin (New York: The Free Press, 1950), p. 60.

parent absurdity, and to make his position perfectly clear, he wrote:

> Here we are, then, in the presence of a conclusion in appearance quite paradoxical. Let us make no mistake. To classify crime among the phenomena of normal sociology is not to say merely that it is an inevitable, although regrettable, phenomenon, due to the incorrigible wickedness of men; it is to affirm that it is a factor in public health, an integral part of all healthy societies. This result is, at first glance, surprising enough to have puzzled even ourselves for a long time. Once this first surprise has been overcome, however, it is not difficult to find reasons explaining this normality. . . .[44]

Durkheim's observations concerning the place of crime in society have gone relatively unnoticed until quite recently, no doubt partly due to the fact that they were little more than a parenthetical note in a work on another subject. It is more likely, however, that these observations have been overlooked because they conflict with the basic values of Western culture and with what the public and the academic community accept as common sense. To say that crime is normal seems self-contradictory; to say that it is healthy, even a useful component of society, is to state a patent absurdity. But this is exactly what Durkheim said:

> Crime is . . . necessary; it is bound up with the fundamental conditions of all social life, and by that very fact it is useful, because these conditions of which it is a part are themselves indispensable to the normal evolution of morality and law.[45]

There are essentially three reasons, according to Durkheim, why crime is useful for social order. First, crime is necessary as an expression of the kind of individual creativity that introduces important social change. Since the heretics of one era often become the saints or scientific heroes of a later era, it is essential for the growth of a society that it produce a certain number of heretics.

[44]Ibid., p. 67.
[45]Ibid., p. 70.

Secondly, crime is useful because without it there would be no punishment, and without punishment there would be no mechanism for establishing and promulgating the norms of the community. In other words, Durkheim contends that law and morality are established and maintained, not by legislation or coercion, but by concrete examples of people being punished for transgressing what the society deems desirable. Finally, crime is important as an agent for producing social solidarity:

Crime brings together upright consciences and concentrates them. We have only to notice what happens, particularly in a small town, when some moral scandal has just been committed. [People] stop each other on the street, they visit each other, they seek to come together to talk of the event and to wax indignant in common. From all the similar impressions which are exchanged, for all the temper that gets itself expressed there emerges a unique temper . . . which is everybody's without being anybody's in particular. That is the public temper.[46]

Kai Erickson in his book, *Wayward Puritans*,[47] elaborates on the role of crime and punishment in strengthening society and reifying norms. Drawing upon historical records from the early Massachusetts Bay Colony, Erikson shows how three "crime waves" in that colony coincided with grave threats to the identity, if not the existence, of the precarious community. These so-called crime waves (The Antinomian controversy, the Quaker invasion, and the witches of Salem) served two important functions: the presence, or imagined presence, of threats to the community strengthened the bonds within the community; and the punishment of those who constituted the threat clearly marked the limits between acceptable and unacceptable behavior.

If a certain amount of crime helps to strengthen rather than weaken the social order, then society's goal must be to regulate and control crime—not to eliminate it. This position,

[46]Emile Durkheim, *The Division of Labor in Society,* trans. George Simpson (New York: The Free Press, 1960), p. 102.

[47]Kai Erikson, *Wayward Puritans* (New York: John Wiley & Sons, 1966).

however, has far-reaching implications. Again to quote from Durkheim:

> From this point of view the fundamental facts of criminality present themselves to us in an entirely new light. Contrary to current ideas, the criminal no longer seems a totally unsociable being, a sort of parasitic element, a strange and unassimilable body, introduced into the midst of society. On the contrary, he plays a definite role in social life. Crime, for its part, must no longer be conceived as an evil that cannot be too much suppressed. There is no occasion for self-congratulation when the crime rate drops noticeably below the average level, for we may be certain that this apparent progress is associated with some social disorder. Thus, the number of assault cases never falls so low as in times of want. With the drop in the crime rate, and as a reaction to it, comes a revision, or the need of a revision in the theory of punishment. If, indeed, crime is a disease, its punishment is its remedy and cannot be otherwise conceived; thus, all the discussions it arouses bear on the point of determining what the punishment must be in order to fulfill this role of remedy. If crime is not pathological at all, the object of punishment cannot be to cure it, and its true function must be sought elsewhere.[48]

THE INDIVIDUAL PATHOLOGY OF CRIME

Just as Durkheim and Erikson have questioned the notion that crime is socially pathological, so too have people questioned the view that crime is an expression of individual pathology.[49] Indeed, that crime is a symptom of individual illness is a viewpoint that has developed rather recently. During the nineteenth century, when our current penal system and criminal law were being established, the prevailing notion was, as is ours in part, that crime was a rational act and could be committed by anyone under the proper circumstances.[50] In particular, crime would be committed by people to further their own personal interests or pleasures. To prevent crime, then, society needed a

[48]Durkheim, *Rules of Sociological Method,* p. 73.

[49]See in particular David Matza, *Delinquency and Drift* (New York: John Wiley & Sons, 1964).

[50]The classic statement of this argument was made in the eighteenth century by Beccaria.

universal and impartial criminal law and a sure system of crime detection and punishment. To talk about "treating" criminals, however, would have been out of place during this period for no one assumed that criminals were sick.

It was possible, even so, to talk about reforming the institutions that prevent and control crime and many reforms were introduced during this period.[51] Criminal law, throughout the Western world, was revamped and the power of judges to fix sentences was circumscribed. Corporal punishment, banishment, and public displays were abandoned as means of punishment and capital punishment was drastically curtailed. Imprisonment became the primary method of crime control.

Today the respectable idea is that crime, like mental illness or alcoholism, is a disease. While praised as humanitarian and progressive, this view is not shared by all (including ourselves) who are intimately involved with the problem. More and more sociologists and psychologists are coming to question the usefulness of the disease model in understanding such forms of deviant behavior as mental illness and crime.[52] Behind this question is a growing awareness that society is applying the term "deviant" not to individual instances of behavior that depart from the norms (an isolated theft, a bizarre act, smoking a marijuana cigarette) but, as a means of classification, to groups of people (criminals, lunatics, dope fiends). Since many people commit acts that are deviant, but few are identified as deviants, it has become obvious that the problem of deviance goes far beyond the deviant behavior of individual persons. Specifically, the problem involves a series of social responses that select some people who commit deviant acts and define them as deviants.[53]

[51]Elmer H. Johnson, *Crime, Correction, and Society* (Homewood, Ill.: Dorsey Press, 1968), pp. 151–153.

[52]Matza, *Delinquency and Drift;* Thomas Szasz, *The Myth of Mental Illness: Foundations of a Theory of Personal Conduct* (New York: Hoeber Medical Books, 1961); Edwin M. Lemert, *Social Pathology* (New York: McGraw-Hill, 1951); Erving Goffman, *Asylums* (Garden City, N.Y.: Doubleday, 1961).

[53]Howard S. Becker, *Outsiders: Studies in the Sociology of Deviance* (New York: The Free Press, 1963), esp. chap. 1, and Erikson, *Wayward Puritans,* esp. chap. 1.

But the disease model of crime may not be merely incorrect, and thereby a faulty basis for social action and crime prevention: it can be pernicious as well. This becomes particularly clear in the case of political crimes (rather than crimes against property or the person). All crimes break legal rules, but political crimes attack the rules.

No political authority, whether authoritarian or democratic, can condone attacks on its legal rules for long, especially if these rules are essential to the more fundamental political processes—succession, interest aggregation, the resolution of conflict, allocation of collective resources, defense. Such attacks threaten the survival of the political system itself.[54] This threat, of course, is part of the nature of political crimes; they are crimes directed against the survival of the status quo and toward the demise and replacement of either rulers or rules, or both. But a lack of deviation, as Durkheim and others have noted, may also imperil society, and intellectual and social invention are often viewed as deviant. Considered as deviant, political crimes will be condemned; considered as innovative, they will be viewed as acts of supreme courage, motivated by moral outrage. To treat political crimes as if they were a disease[55] would deny the moral basis of dissent and the social creativity of occasional violence and revolution.

Treating dissent as a disease has frightening implications. True, it seems more humane to detain political criminals in sanatoriums and asylums than to starve them in concentration camps or behead them under the guillotine. Even so, direct oppression at least admits that the actions and ideas of the oppressed minorities have been taken seriously rather than passed off as mere lunacy. This ability to treat dissent as insanity is the malignant element in the disease model of crime and deviance, a true evil that makes corrections in the name of

[54]Where there is no distinction between the body politic and society, or where such distinction is not part of common conceptions, the distinction between political and other crimes does not exist; political crimes are then only the more serious types of criminal acts.

[55]To be sure, some assassins may well be lunatics; others, however, are hired hands or persons highly motivated by transcendent goals.

normality a pervading instrument of ideological manipulation in modern society.[56]

CONCLUSIONS AND RECOMMENDATIONS

We have discussed some of the contrary objectives of the correctional system in America and some of the ways in which they cause much of society's malaise about crime control and rehabilitation. To integrate our arguments, we shall briefly restate our central contentions, summarize our major conclusions, and make a few recommendations for improving America's correctional system.

First. Crime is a part of the normal social order, known to all societies, and indispensable to the maintenance of effective social organization. It is not crime, therefore, that is injurious to social order, but rapid changes in the rate of crime.

Second. To prevent dangerous changes in the rate of crime, and thus keep crime within acceptable bounds, punishment and deterrence are necessary instruments of social control. Effective punishment for crime must be certain and only painful enough to outweigh the advantages of crime. Excessive punishment will not further social control: on the contrary, it may well lead to a breakdown in respect for law and order, or the credibility of government, and thereby cause a drastic change in the crime rate.

Third. Demands for retribution are almost universal responses of victims. To leave retribution in the hands of victims, however, endangers the stability of a society.

Fourth. Many offenders who are detained in correctional institutions are in need of rehabilitative services. Without further education, training, or psychiatric help, they will find it difficult to make an honest living.

Fifth. Punishment, deterrence, retribution, and other means of crime control are usually incompatible with treatment and rehabilitation.

[56]A similar uneasiness is expressed by Kenneth Keniston, "How Community Mental Health Stamped Out Riots (1968–1978)," *Transaction* 5 (July–August 1968), pp. 21 to 29.

Sixth. The rehabilitation of offenders will not noticeably affect the overall crime rate.

It follows from these contentions that the task of a correctional system must be to control, rather than to eliminate, crime. To control crime, correctional institutions must serve as an agency of deterrence and punishment. For this reason, the correctional system should not itself attempt to engage in treatment or rehabilitation, but should serve as a referral agency for those criminals who need treatment or rehabilitation. Further, to control retribution on the part of individuals and vigilante groups, the severity of punishment for a crime must approximate the community's definition of the seriousness of the crime.

Incarceration is expensive, its effectiveness unproved, and its compatibility with rehabilitation much in doubt. Therefore, existing facilities and programs should be curtailed in favor of more sweeping changes in correctional philosophy and practice. Incarceration should be prescribed only as a means of last resort, and greater effort placed on experimenting with more diverse modes of punishment, such as the imposition of temporary restrictions on the use of government-owned, -subsidized, or -licensed facilities—banks, post offices, transportation systems. Exclusion from certain geographical regions, stores, and community functions or forced, but socially useful, labor in leisure time might be considered as other forms of punishment. Compulsory restitution to victims should also be weighed as an alternative. When incarceration is deemed advisable, sentences should be short and designed to accentuate their deterrent value. If sentences are short, hard labor and other disagreeable activities could be included as part of the punishment.

Parole, on the other hand, should not be part of punishment at all, but an avenue toward rehabilitation. Not all convicts are in need of rehabilitation, and some who need it may not profit from it. In either case, if rehabilitation is not called for, parole is not needed either. In contrast with prison sentences and other forms of punishment, parole should be flexible and its terms dictated by the needs of the convict. The term of parole should be indeterminate and should last as long as the former convict needs rehabilitative services. Whether halfway houses and similar institutions should be maintained is an open question; for the most part, however, the continued segregation of former convicts in rehabilitative institutions should be avoided.

The correctional reform we are calling for, although necessary, is beyond immediate realization for political, legal, and practical reasons. The political reasons are twofold: many people have vested professional and monetary interests in the existing system; moreover, the ideology of using correctional institutions as an instrument of rehabilitation has many fervent partisans. Existing legal philosophy and practices run counter to our recommendations for short, fixed sentences and indeterminate parole. Practically, correctional institutions, their physical structure and personnel practices, are not designed for short sentences; considerable investment in money and time would be needed to restructure the system along the lines we have proposed.

Nevertheless, as population and urbanization expand, as the crime rate mounts, and as the present institutions of crime control become increasingly overtaxed, reform becomes imperative. Further, reform, it seems to us, should begin with a set of basic conceptions and common priorities. Among these we submit the following:

First, punishment and deterrence exclude the possibility of effective rehabilitation. Second, deterrence requires fixed sentences, while rehabilitation requires indefinite and flexible parole. Third, the causes of crime are many and its control will involve more than corrections. Fourth, the reform of correctional institutions for the purpose of crime control should not be confused with reform for humanitarian reasons. In short, the correctional system should not be asked to pursue contrary objectives; deterrence, punishment, controlling retribution, and protecting society from feared criminals are objectives that are contrary to sound treatment and rehabilitation.

Systems Analysis
Confronts Crime

LINDSEY CHURCHILL

In this essay I have concentrated on systems analysis, the major method used by the presidential crime commission's task force on science and technology to generate solutions to problems caused by crime.[1] Roughly speaking, systems analysis is a technique for simulating or "modeling" the operation of an organized process for doing something, such as manufacturing cars, educating students in the public schools, or moving produce from farmer to consumer. The simulation is a model of the real system under study in the same way that a street map is a model of the actual streets in a city. It is important that we understand systems analysis because it is a powerful tool that will be used increasingly on social problems. I have tried here to display some of its advantages and limitations.

The essay consists of two parts. The first briefly summarizes the work of the task force, as reported in the commission's *The Challenge of Crime in a Free Society,* and the second part examines systems analysis as it is used in the task force's supporting document.

[1]My remarks are based on the President's Commission on Law Enforcement and Administration of Justice (hereafter cited as President's Commission), *The Challenge of Crime in a Free Society,* chap. 11, and its supporting document, *Task Force Report: Science and Technology* (Washington, D.C.: United States Government Printing Office, 1967).

BRIEF SUMMARY OF THE WORK
OF THE TASK FORCE

I was immediately struck with the enormous scope of the charge to the task force: "The task force was given the job of showing how the resources of science and technology might be used to solve the problems of crime."[2] The task force was allowed to specify the charge as it saw fit, so that specific problems about crime could be studied. The manner in which the task force interpreted its task is interesting because it reveals the values and predispositions of the task force itself. The task force is quite explicit about the way in which it specified its charge:

With a scope so broad and time and manpower severely limited, it was necessary to make an early selection of areas to be emphasized. The social and behavioral sciences were de-emphasized, largely because these were subjects already receiving treatment elsewhere in the Commission's work. The system sciences—information systems and computer applications, communications systems, and systems analysis—were given primary emphasis. In examining the applicability of technology, the emphasis was placed on identifying requirements rather than on detailed design or selection among equipment alternatives.

Among crimes, the primary focus was on the 'Index' crimes—willful homicide, forcible rape, aggravated assault, robbery, burglary, larceny of $50 and over, and auto theft—the predatory crimes which are a principal source of public concern today. Only limited attention was paid to public disorder and vice crimes, and to 'white collar crimes,' such as illegal price fixing, tax evasions, and antitrust violations.

. . . Of the methods for controlling or reducing crime, the primary focus was on the criminal justice system—the police, courts, and corrections agencies. Within the criminal justice system the greatest potential for immediate improvement by analysis and technological innovation appears to be in police operations. Hence, police problems were emphasized heavily; less attention was given the problems of

[2]President's Commission, *The Challenge of Crime*, p. 245.

courts; and still less to the inherently behavioral problems of corrections.[3]

From this perspective, the task force generated twenty
recommendations. I present them here because the work of the
task force is neatly summarized by them. The recommendations
show that the task force did what it set out to do: emphasize
systems analysis and de-emphasize social science; work within
the existing criminal-justice system; concentrate on the police.
Within this perspective, I think its recommendations are sensible and should be given careful evaluation:

1. Similar studies exploring the detailed characteristics of
    crimes, arrests, and field investigation practices should be
    undertaken in large metropolitan police departments.
2. Police call boxes should be designated "public emergency
    call boxes," should be better marked and lighted, and
    should be left unlocked.
3. Wherever practical, a single police telephone number
    should be established, at least within a metropolitan area
    and eventually over the entire United States, comparable
    to the telephone company's long-distance information
    number.
4. A versatile laboratory for continuing simulation of com-
    munications center operations, looking primarily toward
    changes in operating procedures and arrangements,
    should be established with Federal support.
5. An experimental program to develop a computer-assisted
    command-and-control system should be established with
    Federal support.
6. Frequencies should be shared through the development of
    larger and more integrated police mobile radio networks.
7. The FCC should require metropolitan areas to submit co-
    ordinated requests for additional frequencies, with the
    manner in which action on a local level is coordinated left
    to the discretion of local governments.

[3]President's Commission, *Task Force Report,* pp. 4–5.

8. Greater use should be made of multichannel radio trunks.
9. The FCC should develop plans for allocating portions of the TV spectrum to police use.
10. The Federal Government should assume the leadership in initiating portable-radio development programs and consider guaranteeing the sale of the first production lots of perhaps 20,000 units.
11. Two studies leading to the development of a semiautomatic fingerprint recognition system should be undertaken: A basic study of classification techniques and a utility study to assess the value of a latent print-searching capability.
12. Police departments should undertake data collection and experimentation programs to develop appropriate statistical procedures for manpower allocation.
13. The simulation techniques developed [by the task force] should be extended to several large urban areas as pilot studies with Federal support to determine their applicability to other court systems and to develop them in further detail.
14. Statistical aids for helping in sentencing and selection of proper treatment of individuals under correctional supervision should be developed.
15. Personal criminal-record information should be organized as follows:

   There should be a national law enforcement directory that records an individual's arrests for serious crimes, the disposition of each case, and all subsequent formal contacts with criminal justice agencies related to those arrests. Access should be limited to criminal justice agencies.

   There should be State law enforcement directories similar to the national directory, but including less serious offenses.

   States should consider criminal justice registries that could record some ancillary factual information (e.g., education and employment records, probation reports) of individuals listed in their State directories. This information must be protected even more carefully than the information in the directories, and would be accessible only to court or corrections officers.

16. A National Criminal Justice Statistics Center should be established in the Department of Justice. The Center should be responsible for the collection, analysis, and dissemination of two basic kinds of data:

Those characterizing criminal careers, derived from carefully drawn samples of anonymous offenders.

Those on crime and the system's response to it, as reported by the criminal justice agencies at all levels.

17. The Federal Government should sponsor a science and technology RDT&E [research, development, technology, and engineering] program with three primary components: systems analysis, field experimentation, and equipment-system development.

18. A Federal agency should be assigned to coordinate the establishment of standards for equipment to be used by criminal justice agencies, and to provide those agencies technical assistance.

19. The Federal Government should encourage and support the establishment of operations research staffs in large criminal justice agencies.

20. A major scientific and technological research program within a research institute should be created and supported by the Federal Government.[4]

There are a number of points that I could call attention to about the work of the task force, but I think two are fundamental and incorporate the others. One point is "bad" and the other "good," in my opinion.

The "bad" point. The primary consequence of the way in which the task force specified its charge is that it made no

[4]President's Commission, *The Challenge of Crime*, pp. 248, 250–252, 254–255, 257, 259–260, 268–271.

serious scientific study of how to solve the problems of crime. Rather, it accepted the structure of the criminal-justice system as given, and devoted its energies to the business of trying to make that system more efficient. Though the task force itself recognizes that it chose not to consider either the causes of crime or new systems for controlling it,[5] I am not sure that it realized how significant a choice this was. In effect, members of the task force chose to become handmaidens to the existing system—a dangerous position for independent scientific evaluation.

The handmaiden position became inevitable once the task force turned to experts in computer techniques and other technical fields to conduct its research—rather than to experts in the different phases of work connected with the criminal-justice system. In other words, regarding its charge the task force made several initial decisions that manifested endorsement of the present system of criminal justice. First, it decided to use the Institute for Defense Analyses for the preparation of its report. The I.D.A. is a private research institute that conducts studies for government agencies; it has done most of its work for the Department of Defense. By their own admission, the I.D.A. staff members who worked on the report were not experts in the problems of either crime or the criminal-justice system. Their expertise lay in the methods of systems analysis only.

Secondly, the de-emphasis of the social sciences meant that the task force did not fully exploit whatever experience social scientists have had with crime. Social scientists with firsthand experience in the problems of crime would, I think, be much less willing to accept uncritically our criminal-justice system than would persons, like the I.D.A. staff members, with little familiarity with that system.

Thirdly, the task force chose to not use members of the criminal-justice system—police, court personnel, and correction personnel—as anything more than informants on their own

[5]"Within the limited time, there was no attempt to address questions of the basic causes of crime, nor even to stray very far outside the criminal justice system for means of criminal control." President's Commission, *Task Force Report,* p. 5.

scenes. I find little evidence in the report that it made any attempt to exploit whatever theoretical resources might lie within these groups of persons. I would suppose that among members of our criminal-justice system, there would be some with thoughtful and original suggestions for tackling the problems of crime beyond what is being done now.

In making these decisions, the task force had to work within the existing system. It is my belief, however, that the problems of crime cannot be solved no matter how efficient we make the existing criminal-justice system. Therefore, I think the task force largely avoided its charge by the way in which it specified it.

The "good" point. The most innovative aspect of the work of the task force was its extensive use of systems analysis in studying the criminal-justice system. I think their applications of systems analysis to our system of criminal justice deserve much attention, and I have devoted the remainder of the essay to studying them.

SYSTEMS ANALYSIS

The task force report is a contribution to the growing interest in the use of systems analysis on social problems. The belief that organizations can streamline their activities through systems analysis is becoming widely accepted because systems analysis "works." In my remarks here I will try to show how it works and then discuss some of its advantages and limitations.

The task force defines systems analysis in the following way: "[Systems analysis] uses mathematical models of real-life systems to compare various ways of designing and using these systems to achieve specified objectives at minimum cost."[6] Put a little differently, an application of systems analysis consists of two parts. Part one: a *model* is created of a real-life system under study. The real-life system is likely to be a processing system, such as a wholesaler's system for purchasing eggs from farmers and delivering them to local markets or a city's

[6] Ibid., p. 3.

system for moving vehicular traffic. The model is called a "mathematical model" if it consists of mathematical equations that describe the operation of the system. However, the models that will concern us consist of a set of instructions—a *program* —for a high-speed computer. The computer is then instructed to "operate" the model in much the same way that a wholesaler would operate his egg-distribution system. The computer would pretend to buy quantities of eggs, ship them to warehouses, put them in cold storage, send them out to local markets, and so forth.

The computerized form of the model is called a *simulation.* The systems analyst keeps "tinkering" with his simulation, which, as I said before, is really a computer program, until it successfully reproduces the basic, or "base line," character-istics of the real system under study.

Part two: changes are made in the simulation correspond-ing to contemplated changes in the real system. Then the changed simulation is run on the computer, and the gain and loss in efficiency on a variable of interest is determined by com-paring the new results with the old results. For example, sup-pose that the mayor of a city recommends that certain streets be changed from two-way traffic to one-way traffic; he thinks these changes will have the beneficial effect of speeding the flow of traffic. But before experimenting with the actual traffic flow, he asks a traffic engineer to see what would happen to simulated traffic in a simulation of the real system. The engi-neer makes a simulation of the original system, and runs "traf-fic" in it to see what the average speed of cars is under the existing system. He then makes adjustments in his simulation corresponding to the traffic changes that would occur should the two-way streets become one-way streets. The changed simulation is then run on the computer, and the average speed of cars is noted again. Comparing the old results with the new results tells, theoretically, whether or not the mayor's proposal will increase or decrease the average speed of cars.

The enormous advantage of systems analysis is, obviously, that the analyst can experiment with his simulation as much as he pleases, something he cannot ordinarily do with the real-life system under study. The insights and knowledge he gains from making changes in the simulation and assessing their consequences can, perhaps, be successfully transferred to the real-life system. It is that "perhaps" that is the crux of the problem. The success of the transfer depends, clearly, on how accurately the simulation represents or "captures" the real-life system.

AN EXAMPLE

One of the problems the task force analyzed was that of undue delay in processing criminal cases in the courts. The researchers[7] chose the District of Columbia court system as their real system for analysis.

The different steps through which persons charged with felonies have to pass in this court are shown in Figure 1. The researchers tabulated the median delay in days between steps for 1,550 persons indicted for felonies in 1965 in the U.S. District Court for the District of Columbia. Those statistics, and the task force's recommendation on the number of days each step should take,[8] are also given in Figure 1.

It was not necessary for the researchers to invent a mathematical model to study time delay here. They simply adopted as their mathematical model the flow diagram of the steps through which felony defendants have to pass (more detailed than the one shown in Figure 1). They then wrote a computer-simulation program of the flow diagram. The simulation works roughly in the following manner: the first "person" goes right through the system; later "persons," however, may have to queue up at a given step because that unit—the grand jury, say, or the court —is processing previous "persons" at full capacity. "Persons" then wait their turn at that step. All this takes place as a "quick

[7]The researchers were Joseph A. Navarro and Jean G. Taylor. See their report, "Data Analyses and Simulation of Court System in the District of Columbia for the Processing of Felony Defendants," ibid., Appendix I, pp. 199–215. I wish to thank the authors for their comments on an earlier version of this section and for supplying additional information. Any remaining errors are, of course, mine.

[8]As recommended by the task force on the administration of justice. President's Commission, The Challenge of Crime, pp. 154–155.

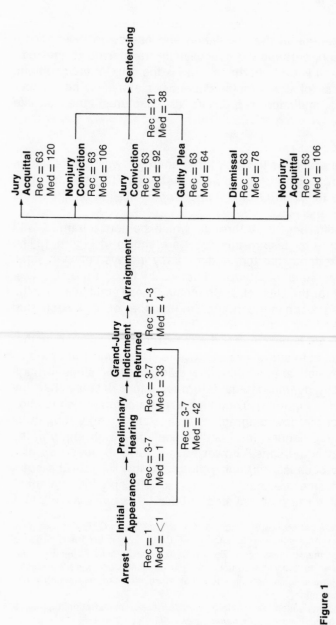

Figure 1

Median Time (in days) Between Events for the Felony Cases Filed in the District Court of Columbia in 1965. Adapted from Figure 4, *The Challenge of Crime in a Free Society*, p. 258. "Rec" is the recommended maximum number of days to be spent between two steps; "Med" is the actual median number of days spent there in the sample of defendants.

time" clock programmed for the computer is running; the computer is instructed to keep track of how long it takes each "person" to go between any two steps.

The simulated court is "empty" when the simulation starts, unlike the situation faced by the first actual defendant in 1965. Therefore, the researchers decided to start the simulation as of July 1, 1964. When the first 1965 "person" came through on January 1, 1965, he entered a system much more like the real system, with many "persons" ahead of him as well as behind him.

More insight into the nature of this simulation can be gained by looking at the different kinds of information needed by the researchers to make the simulation run. They described these needs as follows (the quotes are theirs):

1. "Resources available at each stage of the process (number of judges, prosecutors, grand juries)."[9] The average number of available personnel were obtained through interviews with court personnel.
2. "The daily and weekly work schedule of the resources (number of hours per day and days per week available for processing felony defendants)." This information was also obtained through interviews with court personnel.
3. "The time required to process a defendant at each stage (e.g., case preparation time, courtroom time for presentment, preliminary hearing, motion hearing, trial, etc.)." This information was hard to obtain because no one had ever kept a record of how long it took to process a person at each step in the District of Columbia court system. The researchers used estimates obtained from interviews with court personnel and from observation of cases in the courtroom.
4. "The workload on the court system and flow between processing units (number arrested and percentage flow be-

[9]I follow the researchers' outline here, as given in their paper, no. P–415. Jean G. Taylor, Joseph A. Navarro, and Robert H. Cohen, "Data Analyses and Simulation of the District of Columbia Trial Court System for the Processing of Felony Defendants," offset printing (Washington, D.C.: Institute for Defense Analyses, Science and Technology Division, 1968), pp. 21–32.

tween processing units from arrest to disposition)." These figures were determined by the District of Columbia Crime Commission from public records and estimates for 1965.

5. "Characteristics of defendants and cases (e.g., percentage of cases with one, two, three, etc., defendants, most serious crime charge, number of motions filed per defendant, etc.)." This information was determined from the 1,550 felony cases that were initiated in this court in 1965.

6. "Distribution of elapsed time, measured in days and weeks, between stages of the process (e.g., presentment to preliminary hearing, preliminary hearing to return of indictment, etc.)."

The first five kinds of data listed are "inputs" necessary to make the simulation run. With this information, the simulation produced as "output" the length of time it took each "person" to be processed between each pair of steps. The "fit" of the simulation was then tested by comparing the medians of the distributions of times produced by the simulation with the medians of the actual distributions, as determined in number 6 above. (See Table 1.)

One final descriptive point should be made. In running the simulation, the actual cases for 1965 weren't "rerun"; simulated cases were run. That is, the researchers not only simulated the court operation but simulated the 1965 defendants as well. I will return to this point in the next section. Because simulated defendants were used, the path that each actual defendant took in his progression through the criminal-justice system was lost. In other words, whether the defendant pleaded guilty or had his case dismissed (or any of the other four possibilities) after arraignment was lost (see Figure 1). Nevertheless, the researchers still had to get their simulated "persons" through the simulation. They therefore had them progress randomly in accordance with the relative frequencies with which the actual persons took the different alternative steps. For example, after being arrested, 93 per cent of the defendants were brought before the Court of General Sessions while the remaining 7 per cent were brought before the U.S. Commissioner (not shown in

Figure 1). The researchers used these percentages as probabilities and randomly sent about 93 per cent of the "persons"
along the first path and about 7 per cent along the second.

The simulation run using information based on the existing
structure of the court produced median time delays that were
fairly close to those found in the data. The comparison is shown
in Table 1. From this result the researchers concluded that the
simulation was a good representation of the actual court system so far as time between steps was concerned.

The simulation was then rerun under different assumptions
—one allowing for, as an example, "more help" at the grand-
jury step. It was found that if just the queue of defendants wait-
ing to have their cases brought before the grand jury was
eliminated, median time delay in the system came very close to
the recommended times between steps given in Figure 1. The
results also suggested that removing the queue at the grand-
jury step would not overload the trial step that follows it.

Table 1
Actual and Simulated Time Delay Between Selected Steps
in the District of Columbia Court System

	From initial appearance to:					
	Return of indict- ment	Arraign- ment	Guilty pleas	Dis- missal	End of motions	Ready for trial
Actual time (in median days)	40	53	107	134	148	167
Simulated time (in median days)	47	54	116	122	152	160

Adapted from Table I–8, *Task Force Report,* p. 212. Note that the values
in the first row do not correspond to the values in Figure 1 because the simulation was made of a more complicated model of the court system than the
one shown in Figure 1. Note also that the two points "End of motions" and
"Ready for trial" do not appear in Figure 1.

However, because of lack of data, the researchers were not able to carry out the second part of the method, a cost-effectiveness analysis of how much it would cost for what degree of reduction of the grand-jury queue.

COMMENTS ON THE EXAMPLE

I have five general comments on the systems analysis of the District of Columbia court system made by the task force on science and technology:

1. Some questions about delay in processing felony cases could have been handled in other ways. For instance, simply a study of the courthouse records would have discovered the inordinate delay at the grand-jury step. In fact, an examination of the data in Figure 1 shows the delay at this point.[10] Thus, a simulation is not necessary in order to answer some questions (even though it can answer those questions), and an investigator should consider whether or not he needs to "tool up" for such a complicated and expensive method of determining efficiency as systems analysis. Other questions, of course, could not have been handled in any other way, questions, for example, referring to the impact of a change in the length of one queue on the lengths of queues at other points. It would have been harder by a method other than systems analysis to discover that removal of the queue at the grand-jury step will not appreciably lengthen the queue at the trial step.

2. I don't think the researchers tested the accuracy of their simulation thoroughly enough. Their judgment that the simulation is an accurate representation of the court system is based only on the time-delay results shown in Table 1. A more thorough test of fit should be made by seeing if the simulation reproduces other statistics in the original data equally well. For

[10]Figure 1 shows that the recommended time from initial appearance to return of a grand-jury indictment is three-to-seven days while the actual median time was 42 days. (A similar discrepancy is seen at the alternative route, from the initial appearance, to a preliminary hearing, and then to return of a grand-jury indictment.) The excess of actual time over recommended time, about 800 per cent, is larger by far than any other such excess in the system and would be detected by the first examination of the data.

instance, how accurate a fit would be obtained on the averages and standard deviations of the time delays, in addition to the median delays, and on the averages and standard deviations of the daily lengths of the queues at each step? It is likely that some statistics derived from the sequence of simulated cases will fit well and others won't, just as is typical in tests of mathematical models. The ones that don't fit well suggest that the simulation is a poor representation in some perhaps unseen ways. Any lack of fit should be assessed for its effect on the dependent variable, time delay, particularly when the simulation is rerun under different assumptions.

As a matter of fact, the researchers offer no evidence that the fit shown in Table 1 is a close one. It just looks close by eye. I suppose the compelling reason is that the simulated times are sometimes below and sometimes above the actual times, in no particular pattern, and generally "close" to the actual times. But put in percentage terms, it is seen that some of the discrepancies are sizable:

| | *From initial appearance to:* | | | | | |
	Return of indict-ment	Arraign-ment	Guilty pleas	Dis-missal	End of motions	Ready for trial
Simulated minus Actual, divided by Actual	7/40	1/53	9/107	-12/134	4/148	-7/167
Per cent of discrepancy	17.5	1.9	8.4	-9.0	2.7	-4.2

In general, I find that I am at a loss to tell if the simulation is a good one or not. I have no way of knowing whether or not the fit is close.

3. It is important to note that the researchers did not reproduce the actual cases in 1965 in their simulation and to understand the reasons for that. The reader can see from the description above that the researchers were careful to get good estimates of the number of processors and average time of processing at each step. But they "invented" their defendants

from aggregate data about the real defendants in 1965. Their reasons for doing so follow.

As noted earlier, the researchers set their "initialization" period at six months and began their simulation runs as of July 1, 1964, rather than as of January 1, 1965. But they did not have the data for 1964 which pertained to actual 1965 cases and they did not have time to collect it. Therefore, they decided to "invent" the entire sequence of defendants from July 1, 1964, through December 31, 1965.

The researchers also looked ahead to the time when they would want to experiment on their simulation by changing the rate at which felony cases came into the system; the purpose here, of course, would be to see what would happen to elapsed times if the existing system should ever have to process a higher rate of felony cases per unit of time. For such an experiment, the sequence of actual cases would have to be modified, either by selection from it or addition to it, to meet the change in rate of flow. Any procedure for doing that would amount to "inventing" persons, the researchers reasoned, so why not do it right from the beginning?

Finally and most important, the researchers believed that their sequence of simulated persons was sufficiently similar to the sequence of actual persons so that time delays at different steps would not be affected. That belief should have been tested more thoroughly.

There are two consequences of "inventing" persons.

(a) Untested assumptions are added that are, ideally, unnecessary. For example, at each step that has more than one exit, the researchers had to decide which "persons" to send along which path. The researchers had to decide, that is, which "persons" to send from arraignment to dismissal, which "persons" to send from arraignment to guilty plea, and so forth. They did so by sending "persons" randomly along the alternative paths with the same relative frequency that these paths were taken by actual defendants in 1965. If the sequence of real cases had been used, each defendant would follow the path he actually did follow, and the necessity of this additional assumption about how defendants move through the system would have been precluded.

Similarly, the researchers had to decide the most serious charge against their "persons" and the sequence in which the charges were made. Using the same strategy as above, they solved both problems by randomly assigning the most serious charge to "persons" in accordance with the relative frequencies of those charges among the 1965 defendants. Using the sequence of actual cases would have eliminated both problems.

(b) If the sequence of actual cases were simulated, the time characteristics of a simulated career in the process of criminal justice could be compared with the actual progression to provide further checks on the accuracy of the simulation. I could then see, for example, if Person No. 243 in the simulated sequence appeared at each step in his court career on the day and hour when he actually did so.

My preference would be to use the set of actual cases as an "anchor." My uneasiness goes back to the fact that the flow diagram used in the simulation is not a complete description of what happens to defendants in the court system; it is a model of the court system that idealizes it—and, hence, distorts it—in a variety of ways. I do not want to make the "obvious" assumption, that the flow diagram is correct, though I certainly have no reason to doubt it; I would prefer to test it out in the process of the systems analysis. What I fear is the result of making recommendations that turn out to be unsatisfactory because the "theory" of the court, that is, the flow diagram, is inadequate. Thus, I would rather collect the data on cases back to July 1, 1964, and run the actual cases just as they occurred, even though a much greater effort must then go into data collection.

With my approach, the simulation should give virtually identical results to the actual results since I am recreating the operation of the court as accurately as possible. Then I would know two things more definitely than the researchers presently know: that the work of developing the simulation had been carried out properly; and that the flow diagram is an accurate model for solving time-delay questions. If my simulated results do not fit closely with the actual results, I will know almost immediately that something is wrong with the simulation which should be corrected before any further research is carried out.

I may appear overly cautious here, but the researchers got into one difficulty because they did not take sufficient care with their "base line" work. They generated too many "persons" in their simulation. The researchers drew a random number between 20 and 80 to represent the number of "persons" arrested and charged with a misdemeanor or felony on a given day.[11] The average of these numbers will be 50 in the long run, and preliminary estimates from knowledgeable persons suggested that the rate of 50 per day was accurate. Therefore, about $50 \times 365 = 18{,}250$ "persons" were drawn for their simulation. But the researchers discovered later that there were only about 12,600 felony and misdemeanor arrests made by the police in this jurisdiction in 1965, and, therefore, they generated about 5,650 "persons" too many. The researchers argue that this discrepancy did not affect their basic results. While the number of simulated "persons" was too high at the beginning steps of the process, they say that the number of defendants at the grand-jury step and later steps corresponds closely to the actual number of cases for 1965. The point is that they must make an argument here, when simulating the actual cases would have removed the necessity for this argument.

It is true, of course, that when I later change the conditions under which I run the simulation, I am deliberately creating an imaginary court system. How real is it to run real cases under imaginary conditions? I would still be more comfortable doing that than doing what the researchers did at this point: they ran a "new" sequence of imaginary cases under imaginary conditions. Even when the court conditions are kept the same and the case load changed, I would prefer to add or subtract cases from the actual sequence than I would to invent the whole sequence. My point is not that "inventing" cases is wrong, but that the researchers are responsible for all the theorizing that goes into the invention. And unnecessary theorizing adds unnecessary responsibility and ultimately unnecessary doubt about the fit of the simulation.

[11]Though essentially concerned with felony cases, the researchers thought they had to include misdemeanor cases at the beginning of the court system because felony and misdemeanor cases are initially processed the same way.

4. One thing that struck me about the District of Columbia court system is the great amount of time when the court is *not* in session. The judges hear cases for only a few hours on weekdays; evenings and weekends are not utilized. I do not mean to imply that judges are shirking their duties; they spend some of their time when the court is not in session writing opinions and carrying out other court-related tasks. But nevertheless, the physical facilities of the court are not utilized to the fullest extent. It would be instructive to study how to use more hours per day and more days per week to process defendants and thereby contribute to the solution of undue delay.

5. One major finding of the analysis is that reducing the queue at the grand-jury step would help to bring the actual time delays between all the steps close to the recommended time delays (as shown in Figure 1). The researchers suggest that this reduction be accomplished by providing more grand juries and supporting personnel. But there is another, more radical way to achieve a reduction here. Eliminate the grand jury. There has been some discussion of this proposal in legal circles for two reasons: (a) most members of a grand jury simply do not have the legal competence to do anything but rubber-stamp the recommendations made to them by district or prosecuting attorneys; and (b) the defendant is not represented by counsel in the presentation of his case to the grand jury, thereby giving the prosecution unfair advantage. To have considered the elimination of the grand jury, however, would have led the researchers away from the initial decision made by the task force: to work within the existing criminal-justice system.

I turn now to a discussion of the advantages and limitations of systems analysis as reflected in the work of this task force.

ADVANTAGES

1. What impresses me most about systems analysis is how little the researcher need know about the real system he is simulating in order for the analysis to be effective. As noted earlier, the task-force researchers were not experts in the criminal-justice system. Yet in a short time they were able to make specific recommendations that were sensible and original.

As an example, the task force concluded from a study of the process by which police officers are dispatched in response to telephone calls that "the police command and control center appears to be the best place to invest dollars to decrease response time."[12] The researchers did not just "guess" that this was true; they identified five elements of delay in response time and compared the relative efficiencies of the following solutions:

Element of delay	Solution
Time from detection of crime by a citizen to attempt to transmit telephone message to police	Open police call boxes to the public
Waiting time in incoming message queue at police headquarters	Add more telephone operators
Time spent processing telephone message by police headquarters	Install computer and related hardware for command and control center
Time spent by police headquarters in locating an available patrol unit in the field	Install automatic patrol-car-locator system
Time taken by patrol unit to reach scene of crime after receiving message from police headquarters	Add one-man patrol cars[13]

The system analysis showed that installing a computer and related hardware to make the command-and-control center more efficient would produce greater savings in response time per dollar expended than would any of the other four solutions. This result is incorporated in Recommendation 5 noted earlier.

When I say that systems analysis is effective, I mean that it provides specific answers to questions about the efficiency of the system. If the questioner accepts an answer and acts upon

[12]President's Commission, *Task Force Report,* p. 12.
[13]Ibid., Table 5, p. 11.

it, then the systems analyst has done his job—and future operation of the system will tell whether or not he did his job well. If the questioner disputes it with good reason, then the systems analyst may be able to translate his objections into corrections for the simulation, and thereby improve the simulation.

Two important results that stem from the ability of systems analysis to answer questions about efficiency are the following:

(a) Systems analysis can furnish answers to questions about the effects of making certain changes in real systems. A simulation is, in effect, a "little world" on which the systems analyst can experiment freely. To the degree that the simulation is an accurate representation of the real system, the systems analyst can draw more trenchant conclusions than can the sociologist who is ordinarily unable to carry out rigorous experiments.

(b) More easily than by any other method, such as the survey, a simulation allows one to ask questions about a real system that cannot be anticipated at the beginning of a study. Whatever the desired statistical quantities, they can be produced by rerunning the simulation with the necessary changes in the program. It ordinarily requires less expense to rerun the simulation than to carry out a second survey of the same system to collect data not collected the first time. In effect, a larger number of variables can be studied after the fact than in other methods of research. This "recovery" feature allows the simulation to be effectively used as a guide to intuition about new problems as well as a test for hypotheses proposed in advance.

2. A second advantage of systems analysis is the instructiveness of creating an explicit mock-up of a real system. Though the systems analyst may start "blind," the process of creating a simulation forces him to learn a great deal about the real system. All the little things that ordinarily escape notice must be built into the simulation to make it run. I think that the necessity of having to be completely familiar with details permits a deeper understanding of a real system than can be gained from other methods. The task-force researchers were "creators" of the court system because they had to create its

operation in their simulation. I think they learned more about the court's operation than they could have through any other method in the same amount of time. Systems analysis, therefore, promises to be a particularly valid means of learning about systems.

LIMITATIONS

The major limitation to systems analysis is that its proponents are too often unwilling to question the main features of the existing system itself. Systems analysts ordinarily study "little" changes, not "big" ones. In this sense the systems analyst is more like a contractor who builds a house from an architect's plans than he is like the architect. It is my impression that the systems analyst prefers to have a system to copy rather than to design a system himself and then copy it. Thus, the gain discussed above in having a "blind" technique has its cost as well. Ordinarily, the systems analyst is not prepared to make a serious appraisal of how the system under study might better achieve its goals *even if the efficiency of present procedures were maximized.*

Aside from the unwillingness to question the existing system, the technical aspects of systems analysis contribute to this limitation. At present, writing a simulation program that "works" is a tremendously time-consuming task. Systems analysts today devote the largest part of their energies to getting simulations running; they just don't have time for critical appraisals of the systems under study.

This problem may pass, much as did the technical difficulties of factor analysis when high-speed computers came in. In the future it will probably be possible to write simulations in a much shorter time because efficient solutions to computer-programming problems will be known and "packaged" for easier use than at present. However, I do not assume that merely making time available to systems analysts will inevitably result in more serious appraisals of systems under study. There is no end of technical problems that a systems analyst can study; he can avoid making critical appraisals as long as he likes.

One instance of this limitation was seen earlier in the failure of the researchers to consider the possibility of eliminating the grand-jury step from the criminal-justice system. It can also be seen in the following analysis by the task force of a prisoner-rehabilitation plan.

The task force proposed the use of programmed instruction for incarcerated youths to reduce recidivism.[14] The researchers describe the typical career of the youthful offender as follows: academic failure→school dropout→idleness and unemployment→criminal activities→apprehension→incarceration in prison→release from prison→idleness and unemployment→ criminal activities→apprehension→incarceration in prison, and so forth. According to the task force, educating youthful offenders in prison through programmed instruction would change this progression to the following, more desirable career: . . . incarceration in prison→programmed instruction→release from prison→steady employment→noncriminal activities.

A number of difficulties occur here that make the recommendation less sound than it appears. To begin with, it is supported by just one study. This study found a much lower rate of recidivism among offenders who had completed a course of programmed instruction while in prison than is usual among persons released from prison. I find that study unconvincing by itself.[15] It is not clear how the offenders were selected for the program, and the number of persons (78) who graduated from it was small. The researchers are careful to point these problems out and to advise caution until further experimentation is carried out. Nevertheless, they believe that programmed instruction is worth trying, even though they have little scientific basis on which to make that recommendation.

Two assumptions about programmed instruction are questionable. First, improving skills through education may help in general to get steady employment, but not necessarily this special population of youthful offenders. As is well known, employ-

---

[14]Ibid., pp. 46–48.

[15]My comments are based only on the task force's report of the study by John McKee, Donna M. Seay, and Anne Adams.

ers shun persons with criminal records. Secondly, I do not believe that lack of steady employment is the cause of crime. The career step from "idleness and unemployment" to "criminal activities" should be regarded more cautiously as a description of successive events for *some* persons and not as a causal relation.

Finally, penal authorities have instituted programs of education endlessly in prisons without having found them an antidote for recidivism. I don't believe that the new wrinkle, programmed instruction, can by itself turn a largely ineffective strategy into an effective one.

The difference in success between the court-system analysis and the programmed-instruction analysis rests essentially on our relative understanding of the two systems involved. In the court-system analysis, methods were proposed to reduce the amount of time spent by persons in a system whose "steps" and pathways are well understood. In the programmed-instruction analysis, however, a method was proposed for reducing the number of persons in a given category (repeating offender) when we simply do not understand the "system" that produces such alternative "steps" as "going straight" or continuing a life of crime.

Systems analysis was not effective in the latter instance because the real system—that is, the world entered by the released offender—was not well enough known to permit adequate simulation of it. If any innovation in prison procedure is to be assessed for its impact outside the prison, the "civilian" life of the offender would have to be known in a form sufficient for systems analysis, and that knowledge is not presently available.[16] Basically, the researchers moved too far into the substantive issues in corrections for the amount of expertise that they had in that field. I think they accepted uncritically the point of view of the task force on corrections that programmed in-

[16]In defense of the researchers, it should be said that they never tried to make a systems analysis of the reintegration process of youthful offenders upon release from prison. Their systems analysis was limited to estimating how much it would cost to establish programmed instruction courses in correctional institutions.

struction in prison would reduce recidivism; they should have examined the hypothesis carefully.[17]

To repeat, then, the major limitation of systems analysis is that general features of the real system are too readily accepted, that proponents of systems analysis are too unwilling to challenge basic assumptions.

A second limitation is the "test of fit" problem. As noted earlier, the researchers in the court example departed from the actual operation of the court in various ways, leaving uncertainty about the closeness of fit between simulation and actual court.

There are several ways to attack the fit problem. First, assumptions made by the systems analyst in attempting to produce a concrete simulation should be studied. These assumptions, often implicit, should be made explicit and evaluated. The researcher is responsible for their theoretical worth, even if he makes them for practical reasons. For example, the researchers in the court analysis invented defendants for their simulation instead of using the actual defendants. They should explain why they made this choice. Secondly, the researchers must show that their assumptions will not distort the values of the dependent variables under study. These assumptions can be studied independently either through study of the existing literature or through new research. The important point is that

---

[17]The central recommendation of the task force on corrections was this: "Correction institutions should upgrade educational and vocational training programs, extending them to all inmates who can profit from them. They should experiment with special techniques such as programmed instruction." The task force on corrections admits that traditional education programs in correctional institutions have not worked. It points out that the major difficulty has been the lack of incentive for achievement among inmates, leading to low motivation to do well in educational programs, and it believes that "the way to help [inmates] is to make learning a rewarding experience and thus overcome the sense of failure and humiliation they have come to feel as a result of past performances in school." I find this view too Pollyannaish. Even if the inmate's "sense of failure and humiliation"—if that is his fundamental problem—could be overcome by programmed instruction, there is no strong evidence as yet that he would not just become better than ever at criminal activities. See President's Commission, *The Challenge of Crime*, pp. 174–175, for the discussion by the task force on corrections of its position.

the systems analyst cannot be excused from his theoretical responsibilities. If he chooses to be a theorist, he must pay the price; he must conduct research to test his theoretical inventions. The fewer the changes and the more the remaining changes are theoretically scrutinized, the more one can rely on the findings.

Thirdly, more thorough statistical tests of fit should be carried out on simulations. A simple, though expensive, test of the court simulation would be to rerun the "base line" simulation many times and compare the sampling distribution of generated delays between steps with the actual delays. If the mean of the sampling distribution is close (compared with its standard error) to the actual delay, the simulation fits well at that point; if it is not, the simulation should be studied for correction.

Another way, as noted in my "Comments" section, is to generate "values" of many statistics from the simulation and compare them with the actual values derived from the real system. The more actual values the simulation "matches" closely, the more confidence one has in the results of the simulation.

One further troublesome point in tests of fit is that simulations are based on official accounts of how real systems operate, and these accounts may or may not be accurate descriptions of the way in which systems do indeed operate. The systems analyst rather uncritically assumes that the system runs as it is supposed to run. But there are always deviations from what is supposed to happen, for all kinds of reasons. The nature and number of these deviations indicate how the system personnel go about following the rules to make the official system work. But official rules determine only part of the behavior of system members, not all of it. The rules are vague in detail, and system members are forced to implement them on their own initiative, at least in part. Thus, the official rules imply a set of implementation practices that are not completely specified in the rules themselves. In addition, the system member must be prepared to deal with unexpected events that may temporarily force him to alter his implementing procedures. Finally, "exceptions" to the official rules are often permitted—for example, when favors are done. The member of the real system, therefore, finds himself in a more complicated system than the "official" one simulated by

the systems analyst. He has to deal with implementation practices and exceptions as well as with formal regulations.

For many questions, such as the undue-delay question,
these unofficial aspects of the behavior of real-system members
may be ignored. Where members of the real system can be
counted on or forced to make it work, the results of systems
analysis will be useful. Where deviations in the behavior of real-
system members become so widespread that they can be called
"institutionalized evasions," the results of systems analysis will
be useless. Merton describes institutionalized evasions as follows:

> In . . . cases of gross discrepancy between legal norms and
> mores, all manner of procedures for evading the full force of the
> legal norms are instituted: circumvention, subterfuge, nullifica-
> tion, connivance, and legal fictions. Not infrequently, the social
> functionaries charged with carrying out and administering the
> norm are often the best situated to evade its literal force, and they
> do precisely that.[18]

Thus, systems analysis can produce specific answers to
questions of efficiency, but it is often unclear how much re-
liance can be put on those answers because of uncertainty
about "closeness of fit." The more attention paid to tests of fit
and the more experience the researchers have with the real
system under study, the more their findings can be relied upon.

My two limitations refer more to systems analysts than to
the method of systems analysis itself. I think it is much too early
to tell whether or not there are inherent limitations in the
method, and if so, of what kinds.

But what exactly is the force of my criticism? The systems
analyst would readily agree, I am sure, that there are weak-
nesses in systems analysis. But he would counter that his
method keeps him from making gross errors. All statistical
values produced from the simulation can be checked against

[18]Robert K. Merton, "Social Problems and Sociological Theory," in *Contemporary Social Problems,* ed. Robert K. Merton and Robert A. Nisbet (New
York: Harcourt, Brace & World, 1961), p. 730.

the corresponding values produced from the actual operation of the real system. If large enough discrepancies occur, they "notify" the analyst that his simulation needs to be corrected (see Point 1 under advantages). He can then ask why the discrepancy occurred, discover the error, and correct his simulation.

If no discrepancy occurs, the system analyst doesn't worry. It does not concern him that he may be right for the wrong reasons. In practical terms, unwarranted assumptions or the existence of "informal" practices are of no concern to him until they affect his results. At the worst, he worries a little about whether his recommendations, if put into practice, will lead to the predicted increase in efficiency.

This position is unassailable. The systems analyst can retreat behind it as long as he wishes. What I worry about is that he can also use it to be theoretically irresponsible. Since all mistakes will show up eventually, he need not worry about starting with a good simulation. Any simulation will lead him to a good simulation. Ultimately, that is true. In the meantime there may be much wastage in time, money, and effort. The only antidote I know is to keep putting simulation prediction to the test as often as possible. The more tests, the more mistakes and distortions will be eliminated from simulations, and the faster systems analysis will progress as a method.

SUMMARY

The decision by the President's crime commission to use science and technology to improve the efficiency of existing procedures in our criminal-justice system was a sound one, and I am impressed with the achievements of this task force. Systems analysis was its major tool, and the researchers demonstrated that it can be used effectively to answer questions about the efficiency of ongoing real systems. To be sure, I have concentrated almost entirely on problems of creating a simulation, and little on the use of it to answer questions of efficiency. I have taken this tack deliberately, because the most difficult problems for systems analysis lie in the "creation" part, not in the "costs versus benefits" part. And I do not mean to convey the impression that the task force researchers were unable to answer questions about efficiency; they did so in analyses that I did not discuss.

I am not impressed, however, with the initial decision to work within the existing system. I don't believe that the problems of crime in America will be solved by increasing the efficiency of the current criminal-justice procedures. I would have preferred that the task force use its powerful systems-analysis techniques to try to answer some of the formidable questions about the causes of crime.

Is that possible? My answer is that it would be difficult to apply systems analysis to the study of crime, but we must try. From the point of view of the analyst who must construct a model of the real system, the criminal-justice system was relatively easy to simulate because it is a complete system whose operation is known. Unfortunately, the system that would help us understand the causes of crime is not yet known, though fragments of it exist.

The difficulty of using systems analysis on the causes of crime, therefore, is fairly apparent. The real system that the analyst must simulate may be nothing less than everyday life itself. For the analyst would have to know the "processing system" that leads some persons to commit a crime but not others. And that processing system is obviously extremely complicated because it contains the set of lifetime paths that lead to committing a crime, step by step. From what we know now, such "steps" toward the commission of a crime consist of a frustration here, a neglect there, a "bad" companion, a broken home, and so forth. In other words, there are not just a few decisive steps, and that is why the system analyst's job of studying the causes of crime would be so troublesome.

Yet I see a ray of hope here. The analyst may not be able to deal satisfactorily with the causes of crime, but he knows what he would need to make a good simulation. If he will keep hounding social scientists like myself to give him an accurate, detailed description and theory of a system that "makes" criminals, he may encourage us to progress much more rapidly than we have in the past toward pinpointing the causes of crime. That alone would make systems analysis worthwhile.